A THOMAS WOLFE
COMPANION

A THOMAS WOLFE COMPANION

John Lane Idol, Jr.

GREENWOOD PRESS

NEW YORK • WESTPORT, CONNECTICUT • LONDON

Library of Congress Cataloging-in-Publication Data

Idol, John L.
  A Thomas Wolfe companion.

  Bibliography: p.
  Includes index.
  1. Wolfe, Thomas, 1900-1938—Handbooks, manuals, etc.
2. Wolfe, Thomas, 1900-1938—Bibliography,   I. Title.
PS3545.0337Z736   1987   813'.52   87-268
ISBN 0-313-23829-4 (lib. bdg. : alk. paper)

British Library Cataloguing in Publication Data is available.

Library of Congress Catalog Card Number: 87-268
ISBN: 0-313-23829-4

First published in 1987

Greenwood Press, Inc.
88 Post Road West, Westport, Connecticut 06881

Printed in the United States of America

The paper used in this book complies with the
Permanent Paper Standard issued by the National
Information Standards Organization (Z39.48-1984).

10 9 8 7 6 5 4 3 2 1

Copyright Acknowledgments

1929; London: Heinemann, 1930. Reprinted by permission of Charles Scribner's Sons; Reprinted by permission of William Heinemann Limited.

OF TIME AND THE RIVER by Thomas Wolfe. New York: Charles Scribner's Sons, 1935; London: Heinemann, 1935. Reprinted by permission of Charles Scribner's Sons; Reprinted by permission of William Heinemann Limited.

THE STORY OF A NOVEL by Thomas Wolfe. New York: Charles Scribner's Sons, 1936; London: Heinemann, 1936. Reprinted by permission of Charles Scribner's Sons; Reprinted by permission of William Heinemann Limited.

In memory of Annie Watson Idol
and in appreciation of Marjorie South Idol

Contents

Preface

Despite the huffing and puffing of Thomas Wolfe's detractors, most of them in academe, Wolfe's house of fiction has not been blown down. His drama pretty much toppled of its own accord, but even in that mode many signs of the artist Wolfe would come to be are visible. For Wolfe cultists, and their number is large, Wolfe's house represents one of the noblest structures in American letters. More objective students of American literature see Wolfe's house as a grandly conceived mansion that somehow came to be stuffed with mounds of trash thrown helter-skelter beside some of the best pieces of work on display in the nation. A third group has learned to step around the junk in order to enjoy the treasures. On the strength of this third group's forbearance and enthusiastic enjoyment of Wolfe, his work is now returning to standard anthologies of American literature, and his novels are once more being added to lists of required reading. A collection of his complete short fiction and two of his plays have recently been published, and two volumes of new letters have appeared within the past three years. A new biography, written by David Herbert Donald, the winner of a Pulitzer Prize for his work in history, has just been published. The Thomas Wolfe Society published a major new piece by Wolfe in 1986 when it brought out *The Hound of Darkness*. All of this activity, and more already in progress on Wolfe and his circle, means that more readers will be coming to Wolfe's life and writings.

The purpose of this reference book is to provide basic information about Wolfe's life, thought, and art. It is aimed more at beginning than-experienced readers of Wolfe's writing, but the latter group should find a few fresh insights and a handy means of getting at names, themes, ideas, and publication facts. The heart of the book is a descriptive and analytic bibliography of primary works and a glossary of character and place names. Additional features include a biography of Wolfe, essays on his ideas and attitudes and on major themes in his works, and chapters on Wolfe and his editors and Wolfe and his critics. Reference aids include a chronology of important events in Wolfe's life, information sources on collections and institutions, and an annotated reference list or bibliography of secondary works to which other sections of the book are keyed. I have included David Herbert Donald's new biography of Wolfe in the annotated reference list even though it had not been published at the time I was writing this book.

The major section on Wolfe's works provides, for each, publication facts, discussions of structure, themes, symbols, remarks on characterization, a concise survey of the critical reception where pertinent, and a statement about availability. Numbers following the entries refer to relevant items in the enumerated reference at the back of the book. Occasionally, I have referred to studies in addition to the ones listed by number, in these instances using customary documentation.

Coverage of characters in the glossary is not exhaustive. Unlike other major American novelists, Wolfe had scores of named characters in his novels, over two hundred, for example in *Look Homeward, Angel* (LHA). Many of his named characters appear only once, most of them students in classes attended or taught by Eugene Gant and George Webber. Another large group of named but ultimately insignificant characters is found lodging at Dixieland, the boarding house operated by Eugene's mother. If any of these named persons, or others like them, enters into the action or exchanges remarks with a major character, I have entered his (or her) name. For characters based on members of Wolfe's family, I have supplied the actual name along with other information. Actual names also appear for characters outside Wolfe's immediate family if the person upon whom Wolfe drew became a significant character, for example, Kenneth Raisbeck, an assistant at Harvard University to George Pierce Baker, or if the person upon whom the character is based had claim to notice because of personal fame or notoriety. As with names of characters, place names are selective. Since Wolfe's settings are usually well-known cities like New York, Paris, and London, I included only fictional place names or little-known actual place names.

For major characters I provide succinct literary analysis together with other identifying remarks. Besides my own analysis, I refer readers to critical studies noted in the backmatter reference list in which additional analytic remarks may be found. Similar numerical references are given for a few important place names. Alternate names of characters and places are cross-referenced within the glossary.

The arrangement of the glossary, the analytic bibliography of primary works, and the annotated bibliography of secondary materials is alphabetical. In addition, a selective classified primary bibliography, located at the beginning of the volume just after the chronology, groups Wolfe's work by genre, and, within genre, chronologically. Included are periodical pieces not separately described in the main bibliography of Wolfe's works.

Following the glossary are family charts of the Gants, Pentlands, Joyners, and Webbers. These observe customary genealogical practice and reveal the relationships of these fictional characters to Wolfe's kinfolk, whose names are given in brackets. Readers desiring more information about Wolfe's family should consult the genealogical studies of Richard Walser on the Pennsylvania Wolfs and the North Carolina Westalls (*Thomas Wolfe's Pennsylvania*, Athens, OH: Croissant & Company, 1978; *The Wolfe Family in North Carolina*. Raleigh, NC: Wolf's Head Press, 1976; "Thomas Westall and His Son William," in *The Thomas Wolfe Review* 8, no. 1 [Spring 1984]: 8–18; "Major Thomas Casey Westall," in *The Thomas Wolfe Review* 8, no. 2 [Fall 1984]: 1–10; and the recollections of Julia Westall Wolfe in *The Marble Man's Wife* (52), and Mabel Wolfe Wheaton in *Thomas Wolfe and His Family* (88).

Descriptive and evaluative remarks in the annotated bibliography of secondary sources are brief, largely because the judicious and ample annotations of John S. Phillipson in *Thomas Wolfe: A Reference Guide* (Boston: G. K. Hall & Co., 1977), and its continuation in the Spring 1981 issue of *Resources for American Literary Study* and in the semiannual issues of *The Thomas Wolfe Review* offer easily available descriptions and evaluations of critical and scholarly activity about Wolfe and his times. Professor Phillipson and Aldo P. Magi have in progress a bibliography of secondary works, which will bring Phillipson's bibliographic work conveniently together and correct the numerous errors of Edgar Johnson's *Thomas Wolfe: A Checklist* (Kent, OH: The Kent State University Press, 1970).

I offer the essays in this volume as general introductions to the topics they treat. My hope is that in some small measure they conform to the standards the late C. Hugh Holman set for Wolfe scholars, and reveal "judicious tolerance, good humor, critical acumen, and scholarly seriousness." If I have not hit the mark with them, perhaps they will call forth the work of those who can. Provided at the conclusion of each essay are numbers referring to critical or scholarly pieces listed in the secondary bibliography. The cited articles or books often treat in depth what I handled tersely, my intent being not to explore every topic thoroughly, especially if, in my judgment at least, a topic has received outstanding treatment by another hand.

Since my expectation is that most readers will consult specific items in the book rather than read it straight through, out of necessity I have repeated a few points. For example, in my discussion of individual works in the analytic bibliography of primary works, I have routinely included remarks on themes. Similar remarks occur in my separate chapter on Wolfe's thematic concerns. I assume that some readers will not want to examine that chapter if all they are looking for is a succinct overview of a particular work. From those readers who go from cover to cover, I ask indulgence for the occasional repetition along the way. I consider the chapter on Wolfe's thematic concerns a kind of window to his philosophic notions, and hope that it will help readers see how thought and art merge as Wolfe developed as a writer.

Appendix A contains information useful to students, scholars, and general readers alike. It describes the important collections of Wolfe materials, gives a short history of The Thomas Wolfe Society and its official organ, *The Thomas Wolfe Review*, and offers helpful facts about two Wolfe memorials: The Old Kentucky Home (Dixieland) and the Thomas Wolfe Memorial Angel, both located in Asheville. Appendix B is the annotated reference list of secondary sources mentioned above. Each entry bears a number, and where appropriate, these numbers appear as references singly or in clusters in other sections of this book.

Throughout the book I have used abbreviations for *The Thomas Wolfe Review* and its forerunner *The Thomas Wolfe Newsletter*. These abbreviations appear without italics and are listed in the table immediately following this preface.

With few exceptions, I have treated only those works by Wolfe published in book form, chiefly because most readers lack easy access to the magazines in which Wolfe's writings appeared. Some characters in the periodical versions of Wolfe's writings do bear names different from the same characters in versions published in book form. For example, the character called Piggy Logan in *You Can't Go Home Again* (YC) is called Piggy Hartwell in the version published in *Scribner's Magazine* in May 1939. Anyone coming upon these different names can readily make the transference of names to the names given in books and thus use the glossary without difficulty.

Above everything else, I have tried to place information before readers in a readily accessible format. Instead of having to dig out remarks on *Of Time and the River* (OT), for example, in a lengthy discussion of Wolfe's major works, the reader need only turn to the OT entry in the bibliography of primary works to find the core of my commentary on that novel. My commentary draws heavily on a formalistic approach to literature and leaves to readers and other critics a variety of other critical approaches. As a result, I have stuck closely to an analysis based on a study of structure, symbols, themes, and characterization. I chose the formalistic because I believe that approach to be the starting point for all other considerations of a literary artifact.

Acknowledgments

I am grateful for the help of Thomas Noonan and other members of the staff of the Houghton Library, Harvard University; to H. G. Jones and Frances Weaver of the North Carolina Collection in the Wilson Library, University of North Carolina; to Marian Withington of the Cooper Library, Clemson University; and to Philip Banks of the Pack Memorial Library in Asheville, North Carolina.

I am grateful to Paul Gitlin, administrator of the Thomas Wolfe Estate, for permission to examine Wolfe materials in a variety of projects over the years, an experience which made innumerable contributions to my knowledge about Wolfe and his writings.

I gratefully acknowledge the help and encouragement of M. Thomas Inge, the person most responsible for my launching this project. I am grateful to Dean Robert A. Waller, College of Liberal Arts, and to George W. Koon, head of the English Department, Clemson University, for helping to arrange a sabbatical leave. I happily acknowledge the advice and encouragement of my colleague Carol Johnston, whose bibliography of Wolfe's writings was in progress while this book was being written.

I also thank Richard S. Kennedy, Aldo P. Magi, Richard Walser, Morton Teicher, Elizabeth Evans, Leslie Field, Suzanne Stutman, Sue Fields Ross, John S. Phillipson, Carole Klein, Louis D. Rubin, Jr., Duane Schneider, and James Lister Skinner, III, for insights and information shared both in print and in conversation over the years. Regretfully, I must inscribe posthumous thanks to David Reid Hodgin, H. Blair Rouse, and C. Hugh Holman for all they taught me about Wolfe.

Finally, I thank my editor, Marilyn Brownstein, for her wise and patient help.

Abbreviations

All abbreviations refer to titles of Wolfe's works and appear without italics.

AAN   *The Autobiography of an American Novelist*, edited by Leslie Field and combining *The Story of a Novel* and Wolfe's address at Purdue University

BLL   *Beyond Love and Loyalty: The Letters of Thomas Wolfe and Elizabeth Nowell*

CSS   *The Complete Short Stories of Thomas Wolfe*

FDTM   *From Death to Morning*

HB   *The Hills Beyond*

JB   "Justice Is Blind." In *The Enigma of Thomas Wolfe*, edited by Richard Walser.

LHA   *Look Homeward, Angel*

LTM   *The Letters of Thomas Wolfe to His Mother*

LTW   *The Letters of Thomas Wolfe*

MH   *Mannerhouse*

MOL   *My Other Loneliness: The Letters of Thomas and Aline Bernstein*

MTS   *The Mountains*

NB   *The Notebooks of Thomas Wolfe*

NE   *A Note on Experts: Dexter Vespasian Joyner*

OMR   "Old Man Rivers." In *Atlantic Monthly*, December 1947

OT   *Of Time and the River*
RBG   *The Return of Buck Gavin. In Carolina Folk-Plays*
SN   *The Story of a Novel*
TWR   *The Thomas Wolfe Review*
WR   *The Web and the Rock*
WTOC   *Welcome to Our City*
YC   *You Can't Go Home Again*

A Chronology of Thomas Wolfe's Life

1900 October 3, Thomas Clayton Wolfe born in Asheville, NC

1904 Brother Grover Cleveland Wolfe dies in St. Louis

1905 Began schooling at Orange Street Elementary School in Asheville

1912 Enrolled in North State Fitting School and developed a lively interest in poetry under the influence of Margaret Roberts, whom he later called "the mother of his spirit"

1916 Entered the University of North Carolina at Chapel Hill

1919 Wrote a folk play entitled "The Return of Buck Gavin"; became editor of *The Tar Heel*, the student newspaper; won the Worth Prize in philosophy for an essay, "The Crisis in Industry"

1920 Was graduated from the University of North Carolina and began studies at Harvard for an M. A. degree in English; enrolled in playwriting course taught by George Pierce Baker

1922 Fulfilled requirements for the M. A. degree; his father died on June 20

1923 A ten-scene play called *Welcome to Our City* staged May 11, and rejected as too long for New York production by December

1924 Accepted teaching position at Washington Square College of New York University; made the first of seven trips to Europe

1925 Met Aline Bernstein, stage designer, who became his mistress

1926 Began writing the book that became LHA

1928 Completed the manuscript of LHA; made fourth trip to Europe; injured in a beer hall brawl in Munich; received letter (dated October 22) from Maxwell Perkins, an editor at Scribner's, expressing interest in manuscript

1929 LHA accepted by Scribner's; "An Angel on the Porch" appeared in *Scribner's Magazine*; LHA published October 18

1930 Won Guggenheim Fellowship and returned to Europe for the fifth time; Sinclair Lewis praised LHA during Nobel Prize speech

1931 Met Sinclair Lewis in London; began living in Brooklyn

1932 Broke off with Aline Bernstein; tied for $5000 prize in Scribner's short novel contest with "The Portrait of Bascom Hawke"; published "The Web of Earth"; visited father's childhood home in Pennsylvania

1933 Delivered a manuscript called *The October Fair* to Perkins

1934 Attended the World's Fair in Chicago; published several short stories

1935 Published OT, fifteen short stories, and FDTM; attended Writers' Conference in Boulder, CO

1936 SN published; quarrels with Perkins start with the publication of that work; libel suit against Wolfe filed

1937 Published "I Have a Thing to Tell You" and "The Child by Tiger," his first and only appearance in *The Saturday Evening Post*; broke with Scribner's and signed with Harper and Brothers; returned to Asheville for the first time since 1929

1938 Made speech at Purdue University; toured the West; became ill in Seattle; died at Johns Hopkins University Hospital on September 15

1939 WR assembled by Edward C. Aswell and published

1940 YC assembled by Edward C. Aswell and published

1941 HB published with essay by Aswell on editing Wolfe

A THOMAS WOLFE
COMPANION

Classified Primary Bibliography: A Selected List (Arranged Chronologically)

DRAMA

The Return of Buck Gavin: The Tragedy of a Mountain Outlaw. In Frederick H. Koch, ed. *Carolina Folk-Plays*, Second Series. New York: Holt, 1924.

The Third Night. In Frederick H. Koch, ed. *Carolina Folk-Plays*. New York, 1941.

The Mountains: A Play in One Act and *The Mountains: A Drama in Three Acts and a Prologue*. Edited by Pat M. Ryan. Chapel Hill: University of North Carolina Press, 1970.

Welcome to Our City: A Play in Ten Scenes. Edited by Richard S. Kennedy. Baton Rouge: Louisiana State University Press, 1983.

Mannerhouse. Edited by Louis D. Rubin, Jr. and John L. Idol, Jr. Baton Rouge: Louisiana State University Press, 1985.

NOVELS

Look Homeward, Angel. New York: Charles Scribner's Sons, 1929; London: Heinemann, 1930, with textual differences.

Of Time and the River. New York: Charles Scribner's Sons, 1935; London: Heinemann, 1935, with textual differences.

The Web and the Rock. New York: Harper and Brothers, 1939.

You Can't Go Home Again. New York: Harper and Brothers, 1940.

STORIES, ADDRESSES, AND ESSAYS

The Crisis in Industry. 1919. Reprint. Winston-Salem, NC: Palaemon Press, 1978.
From Death to Morning. New York: Charles Scribner's Sons, 1935.
> [Contains previously published stories, all in periodicals: "No Door," "Death the Proud Brother," "The Face of the War," "Only the Dead Know Brooklyn," "Dark in the Forest, Strange as Time," "The Four Lost Men," "Gulliver," "The Bums at Sunset," "One of the Girls in Our Party," "The Far and the Near," "In the Park," "The Men of Old Catawba," "Circus at Dawn," "The Web of Earth."]

The Story of a Novel. New York: Charles Scribner's Sons, 1936.
A Note on Experts: Dexter Vespasian Joyner. New York: The House of Books, 1939.
The Hills Beyond. New York: Harper and Brothers, 1941.
> [Contains some previously published materials: "The Lost Boy," "A Kinsman of His Blood" (published earlier as "Arnold Pentland"), "Chickamauga," "Portrait of a Literary Critic," "The Lion at Morning," "God's Lonely Man," and the following heretofore unpublished pieces: "No Cure for It," "Gentlemen of the Press," "The Return of the Prodigal," "On Leprechauns," and ten chapters of an unfinished novel, "The Hills Beyond."]

The Complete Short Stories of Thomas Wolfe. Edited by Francis Skipp. New York: Charles Scribner's Sons, 1987.
> [The titles of the pieces included in CSS are listed in the entry in The Works: A Descriptive and Analytic Bibliography, contained in this volume.]

LETTERS, NOTEBOOKS, JOURNALS

A Western Journal. Pittsburgh: University of Pittsburgh Press, 1951.
The Correspondence of Thomas Wolfe and Homer Andrew Watt. Ed. Oscar Cargill and Thomas Clark Pollock. New York: New York University Press, 1954.
The Letters of Thomas Wolfe. Ed. Elizabeth Nowell. New York: Charles Scribner's Sons, 1956.
The Letters of Thomas Wolfe to His Mother. Ed. C. Hugh Holman and Sue Fields Ross. Chapel Hill: University of North Carolina Press, 1968.
> Replaces the 1943 edition by John Skally Terry.

The Notebooks of Thomas Wolfe. Ed. Richard S. Kennedy and Paschal Reeves. Chapel Hill: University of North Carolina Press, 1970.
Beyond Love and Loyalty: The Letters of Thomas Wolfe and Elizabeth Nowell. Ed. Richard S. Kennedy. Chapel Hill: University of North Carolina Press, 1983.
My Other Loneliness: Letters of Thomas Wolfe and Aline Bernstein. Ed. Suzanne Stutman. Chapel Hill: University of North Carolina Press, 1983.

PERIODICAL PIECES

[Since Wolfe or his agent or editors often reworked pieces ultimately intended for his novels before incorporating them in their destined places, many periodical pieces demand separate study.]

"An Angel on the Porch." *Scribner's Magazine* (August 1929): 205–10.
"A Portrait of Bascom Hawke." *Scribner's Magazine* (April 1932): 193 + .
"The Web of Earth." *Scribner's Magazine* (July 1932): 1 + .
"The Train and the City." *Scribner's Magazine* (May 1933): 285–94.
"Death the Proud Brother." *Scribner's Magazine* (June 1933): 333 + .
"No Door." *Scribner's Magazine* (July 1933): 7 + .
"The Four Lost Men." *Scribner's Magazine* (February 1934): 101–8.
"Boom Town." *American Mercury* (May 1934): 21–39.
"The Sun and the Rain." *Scribner's Magazine* (May 1934): 358–60.
"The House of the Far and Lost." *Scribner's Magazine* (August 1934): 71–81.
"Dark in the Forest, Strange as Time." *Scribner's Magazine*. (November 1934):
    273–78.
"The Names of the Nation." *Modern Monthly* (December 1934): 598–605.
"For Professional Appearance." *Modern Monthly* (January 1935): 660–66.
"One of the Girls of Our Party." *Scribner's Magazine* (January 1935): 6–8.
"His Father's Earth." *Modern Monthly* (April 1935): 99–104.
"Old Catawba." *Virginia Quarterly Review* (April 1935): 226–38.
"Arnold Pentland." *Esquire* (June 1935): 26 + .
"Gulliver." *Scribner's Magazine* (June 1935): 328–33.
"The Face of the War." *Modern Monthly* (June 1935): 223 + .
"In the Park." *Harper's Bazaar* (June 1935): 54 + .
"Only the Dead Know Brooklyn." *The New Yorker* (15 June 1935): 13–14.
"Polyphemus." *North American Review* (June 1935): 20–26.
"Cottage by the Tracks." *Cosmopolitan* (July 1935): 48 + .
"The Bums at Sunset." *Vanity Fair* (October 1935): 30 + .
"The Story of a Novel." *The Saturday Review of Literature* (14 December 1935):
    3 + ; (21 December): 3 + ; (28 December): 3 + .
"The Bell Remembered." *American Mercury* (August 1936): 457–66.
"Fame and the Poet." *American Mercury* (October 1936): 149–54.
"I Have a Thing to Tell You." *The New Republic* (10 March 1937): 132–36; (17
    March): 159–64; (24 March): 202–7.
"The Far and the Near." *Short Short Story Magazine* (April 1937): 3–6.
"Return." *The Asheville Citizen-Times*, (16 May 1937): sec. B, p. 1.
"Mr. Malone." *The New Yorker* (29 May 1937): 22–27.
"Oktoberfest." *Scribner's Magazine* (June 1937): 27–31.
" 'E. A Recollection." *The New Yorker* (17 July 1937): 22–26.
"April, Late April." *American Mercury* (September 1937): 87–97.
"The Child by Tiger." *The Saturday Evening Post* (11 September 1937): 10 + .
"Katamoto." *Harper's Bazaar* (October 1937): 74 + .
"The Lost Boy." *Redbook* (November 1937): 25 + .
"Chickamauga." *The Yale Review* (Winter 1938): 274–98.
"The Company." *New Masses* (11 January 1938): 33–38.
"A Prologue to America." *Vogue* (1 February 1938): 63 + .
"Portrait of a Literary Critic." *American Mercury* (April 1939): 429–37.
"The Party at Jack's." *Scribner's Magazine* (May 1939): 14 + .
"The Birthday." *Harper's Magazine* (June 1939): 19–26.
"The Golden City." *Harper's Bazaar* (June 1939): 42 + .
"The Winter of Our Discontent." *The Atlantic* (June 1939): 817–23.

"Three O'Clock." *North American Review* (Summer 1939): 219–24.
"Nebraska Crane." *Harper's Magazine* (August 1940): 279–85.
"The Dark Messiah." *Current History and Forum* (August 1940): 29–32.
"The Hollyhock Sowers." *American Mercury* (August 1940): 401–5.
"So This Is Man." *Town and Country* (August 1940): 28+.
"The Promise of America." *Coronet* (September 1940): 9–12.
"The Hollow Men." *Esquire* (October 1940): 27+.
"The Anatomy of Loneliness." *American Mercury* (October 1941): 467–75.
"The Lion at Morning." *Harper's Bazaar* (October 1941): 66+.
"The Plumed Knight." *Town and Country* (October 1941): 74+.
"Old Man Rivers." *The Atlantic* (December 1947): 92–104.
"Something of My Life." *The Saturday Review of Literature* (7 February 1948): 6–8.
"Welcome to Our City." *Esquire* (October 1957): [58–83].

THOMAS WOLFE SOCIETY PUBLICATIONS

London Tower. Ed. Aldo P. Magi.
The Proem to "O Lost". Ed. John L. Idol, Jr.
The Streets of Durham. Ed. Richard Walser.
K–19: Salvaged Pieces. Ed. John L. Idol, Jr.
The Train and the City. Ed. Richard S. Kennedy.
Holding on for Heaven. Ed. Suzanne Stutman.
The Hound of Darkness. Ed. John L. Idol, Jr.

SELECTIONS FROM WOLFE'S WORKS

The Face of a Nation: Poetical Passages from the Writings of Thomas Wolfe. Selected and edited with an Introduction by John Hall Wheelock. New York: Charles Scribner's Sons, 1939.
A Stone, A Leaf, A Door: Poems by Thomas Wolfe. Selected and arranged in verse by John S. Barnes, with a Foreword by Louis Untermeyer. New York: Charles Scribner's Sons, 1945.
The Portable Thomas Wolfe. Ed. Maxwell Geismar. New York: Viking, 1946.
The Short Novels of Thomas Wolfe. Ed. C. Hugh Holman. New York: Charles Scribner's Sons, 1961.
The Thomas Wolfe Reader. Ed. C. Hugh Holman. New York: Charles Scribner's Sons, 1962.
Thomas Wolfe: The Autobiography of an American Novelist. Ed. Leslie Field. Cambridge: Harvard University Press, 1983.

The Life of Thomas Wolfe

Thomas Clayton Wolfe, the eighth and last child of William Oliver and Julia Elizabeth Westall Wolfe, was born in Asheville, North Carolina, October 3, 1900. A stonecutter and tombstone dealer, W. O. Wolfe was reared in Pennsylvania among people of German descent before moving to North Carolina, first to Raleigh, where he was twice married, and then to Asheville, to which he and his second wife, Cynthia, came in search of a better climate for her tuberculosis. Following her death, he married Julia Westall, a part-time book seller and schoolteacher, and brought her to his home at 92 Woodfin Street, the house he had built for the tubercular Cynthia. Julia's family, of Scotch and English origin and pioneer settlers in the North Carolina mountains, had begun to leave their small farms or cottage industries to take up jobs as builders and lumber dealers in Asheville, which was fast developing into one of the South's most popular summer resorts. Many kinsmen, however, remained on the farms and held to the traditional beliefs and values of isolated mountain folk. When Thomas Wolfe first looked back on his mountain kin, he tended to see their rigidity, narrowness, superstitious-ness, fanaticism, and an obsession with financial insecurity, which stemmed in large measure from the devastating effects of Reconstruction politics on the mountain folk. In later years, he recognized that many of his kin had lived heroically, almost Homerically, in their mountain fastnesses, and he was proud to acknowledge a family tie to the fabulous Davy Crockett.

One of the strongest convictions of his Presbyterian forebears was that a good education formed the basis of all of life's pursuits. Evidently, this belief was a determining factor behind Wolfe's mother's decision to remove her last-born son, named for her bookish father, from the public schools of Asheville and to enroll him in the North State Fitting School, founded and operated by Mr. and Mrs. J. M. Roberts. Margaret Roberts became a vital force in Thomas Wolfe's life, opening to him the beauty and power of poetry, becoming "the mother of his spirit," and receiving from him some of his clearest statements of what his creative efforts were designed to do. This preparatory background gave Wolfe a wider view of his educational options than many of his public school peers had, and led him to think of the University of Virginia or Princeton instead of the State University at Chapel Hill. His father, for all his love of drama and poetry, considered law as the surest means of success and the University of North Carolina as the college best suited to prepare his son for the kind of life he envisioned for him. Hence, in the bluntest terms possible, he said that Tom would attend Chapel Hill if he wanted his backing. That dictum settled the issue, and, after his sophomore year at Chapel Hill, Tom dropped all thought of going elsewhere. He had hardly arrived on campus, however, before declaring to the members of the Dialectic Literary Society upon induction into their body that he "hoped they would have the pleasure some day of seeing [his] picture hang beside Zeb Vance's" (LTW 4). That pleasure was realized October 27, 1979, when Frank Mason's portrait of Wolfe was added to the row of paintings of distinguished alumni of the Society, including the portrait of Zebulon B. Vance, the foremost politician to come from the mountains of North Carolina until the appearance on the national scene of Wolfe's Chapel Hill contemporary, Sam Ervin. (When Wolfe turned his attention to tracing the Joyner ancestry of George Webber, he was to draw upon the life and deeds of Zeb Vance to help him create the character of Zack Joyner.)

Unhappy because he had been "forced" to come to Chapel Hill, Wolfe made few friends his first year there in 1916. He looked to one of his teachers, famed Miltonist James Holly Hansford, to recommend him to Princeton, but, when Wolfe's parents held firm, he returned to Carolina, as everyone called it, to thrust himself forward in the social and literary life of the campus. He began to write poetry for a literary magazine, articles for the weekly school newspaper, and humorous skits for college smokers. During the fall of 1918, he enrolled in the playwriting course of Frederick H. Koch, a leader in folk drama whose ideas inspired the work of Paul Green and lesser dramatists. Wolfe was soon writing and acting in one-act folk plays, the earliest of which was *The Return of Buck Gavin*, performed March 14–15, 1919, by the Carolina Playmakers, and featuring Wolfe in the title role. Later that same year, December 12 and 13, he performed in his second one-act folk play, *The Third Night, A*

Mountain Play of the Supernatural. Meanwhile, he became editor of *The Tar Heel*, the student newspaper, and won the Worth Prize for an essay in philosophy entitled "The Crisis in Industry." He also contributed to the humor magazine, *The Tar Baby*, and continued to write humorous or satiric skits. Besides finding (and making) a niche for himself as a promising literary talent, Wolfe was gaining the respect of a few of Carolina's most revered teachers, among them Horace Williams, who joined Hegelian views to some down-to-earth notions to become one of Chapel Hill's celebrated personalities, and Edwin Greenlaw, whose ideas on the relation of life to literature and whose high and rigorous standards as an editor of Spenser's works made him a scholar of national prominence. Having grown up in a family constantly tugging and bickering over the relative merits of life in Pennsylvania and the North Carolina hill country, the wisdom of investing in land and buildings or salting extra money away in banks, and Julia's decision to buy and operate a boarding house, Wolfe knew all about polarities in day-to-day existence. Williams taught him to identify more and advised him and his classmates to strive for a synthesis. That Wolfe could follow his advice on the abstract level is clear from his efforts to resolve some of the differences between workers and management in "The Crisis in Industry." Whether Williams's teachings were good for a lifetime would have to be proved, and he continued to weigh them and the example of Greenlaw's professional dedication when he moved on to Harvard and began to draft a play in which the views of the two men were dramatized. This lingering evaluation of the two men suggests that their influence exceeded that of any other Carolina teacher, a point given much attention in Richard S. Kennedy's *The Window of Memory: The Literary Career of Thomas Wolfe*.

Wolfe spent two of his summer breaks in Asheville and one in the area of Norfolk, Virginia, doing civilian war work, but there is a connection. On his first break in the summer of 1917, Wolfe met Clara Paul at his mother's boarding house, The Old Kentucky Home, and fancied himself her suitor. Already engaged to be married soon, a fact she withheld from Wolfe, she obviously felt that a skillfully handled summer romance would be harmlessly enjoyable. She did not reckon on the depth of feeling she would stir in Wolfe. He was hurt when the truth came out, but he could not forget her. He went to the Norfolk area the following summer to find work near where she had settled, hoping to be able to see her.

A far deeper loss came that fall when, on October 19, Tom's brother Benjamin Harrison died. Of all his siblings, Ben was dearest to Tom, the two of them sharing a grander, nobler view of human potential than their parents or brothers and sisters ever envisioned. Ben's untimely death stunned Wolfe, causing him to ponder human mutability and to

appetite for the visual arts, thanks to his friendship with Baker's assistant, Kenneth Raisbeck, and repeated visits to the Boston Museum of Fine Arts, one room of which in the Egyptian section Wolfe had used as a setting for an unfinished play.

Well-prepared though he was, and conscientious as he proved to be about his teaching duties, his heart was not fully in his work. Fame and fortune might await the well-written play, but neither would be the reward of the overburdened grader of freshman composition themes. When he accepted a job at NYU, he wanted Homer Watt, his department head, to know that he still intended to pursue a career as a dramatist. He met his first class on February 6, 1924, at the Washington Square College of NYU and continued to accept appointments on an irregular basis from an understanding Watt until January 1930, when the success of LHA and the hopeful prospect of being awarded a Guggenheim Fellowship led him to resign his post. He never again returned to the classroom except to give invited lectures. While in class, he read poems with passionate energy and involvement. His written responses to themes sometimes ran to fairly full paragraphs, but the tales about his remarks being longer than his students' themes seem legendary. His grade books and the testimony of his students prove that he was a tough grader. He left teaching not because he came to dislike it but because it took from him the energy he wanted to pour into creation (LTW 103).

While teaching, he tried to place WTOC with a producer and pushed ahead with MH, shifting ideas for it as he went along. His hopes for both continued high for a time, but eventually were dashed when every company rejected his plays outright or dawdled so long over making a decision that Wolfe demanded their return. Also while teaching he decided that his modest income would stretch further and thus allow more time for writing if he went to Europe. Accordingly, he left New York October 25, 1924, and spent over nine months touring England, France, Italy, and Switzerland, and working, first on a potpourri of essays, reflections on his education, stories, and journal entries entitled "Passage to England," then on MH, starting afresh, with outrage, after the version he had carried with him from New York was stolen in Paris. For a few weeks in early 1925, he explored Paris with his old friend Kenneth Raisbeck and two of Raisbeck's friends from Boston, Marjorie Fairbanks and Helen Harding, the latter of whom aroused Wolfe's romantic interests.

Little but frustration was to come from the relationship, but just ahead was the liaison that Wolfe would one day turn into one of the most idyllic but troubled and tormented love affairs in the annals of American literature, his affair with Aline Bernstein. She became the Esther Jack of his fiction, and was a talented stage designer, gifted writer, and superb cook. Wolfe met her on his return voyage from Europe in August 1925, and found in her autumnal beauty and wisdom (she was about nineteen years older than he) one of the great joys of his life. Even as he entered the Edenic phase of their relationship, Wolfe warned Aline: "Whoever touches me is damned to burning" (MOL 44). He would demand more than she wanted to give up: her marriage, her circle of friends in the theater, and her objections to his promiscuity. She would cling too tightly, wear her heart too openly on her sleeve, and weary him with her resolute solicitousness until he no longer enjoyed her company. Despite their problems, both considered the affair the richest, most satisfying, and happiest event in their lives. Her belief in his talent and her generous financial and emotional support proved to be the bridge he needed to cross from his unpromising start as a playwright to his celebrated beginning as a novelist.

It was during his vacation with her in England's Lake District in 1926 that Wolfe began the work he eventually called *Look Homeward, Angel*; it was in an apartment he shared with her in New York that he completed it. Her friend Madeleine Boyd, a literary agent, placed the novel with Charles Scribner's Sons, and Aline's telegram to him was Wolfe's first notice of the interest Scribner's had shown in the work. Thus it was with both love and appreciation that Wolfe dedicated the novel to her, drawing upon another admirer of autumnal beauty, John Donne, to help him express the depth of affection he had for her.

If Wolfe here thanked a lover/mother for her part in getting him launched as a novelist, he was just beginning a relationship with an editor/father, Maxwell Perkins, that would both enrich and frustrate his life as a writer. Now regarded as the greatest American editor of his era, Perkins, who in part found in Wolfe the son he never had, entered into Wolfe's literary life in ways Aline could not, or would not. Perkins steered him away from some works, such as "The River People," a story about artists and rich families along the Hudson and in Europe, and "K–19," a novel about a train trip from New York to the South. He argued against Wolfe's plan to make fictional use of his (Wolfe's) association with Scribner's, suggested a major theme to Wolfe, a man's search for his father, and sent a work (OT) to press before Wolfe, away on a holiday, was ready to see it go. Perkins helped to see that Wolfe's stories (or excerpts from his novels or works in progress) saw print in magazines that would boost Wolfe's standing as a writer, entered one of Wolfe's pieces ("A Portrait of Bascom Hawke") in *Scribner's Magazine* Short Novel Contest, for which Wolfe shared the first-place prize of $5,000 in 1932, and rescued Wolfe from the maze he had built for himself in trying to deal fictionally with the materials he had accumulated since the publication of LHA.

The way out, as Perkins came to see matters, was to pick up the story of Eugene Gant once more, something Wolfe felt uncomfortable with, since he was still smarting from Asheville's angry reception of his novel and still worrying about the critics who asked whether he had more in him than the autobiographical first novel. Once Wolfe saw that the maze could be solved, he and Perkins laid out a grand plan in a Publisher's Note in the front matter of OT for a hexology of novels:

Look Homeward, Angel (1884–1920)

Of Time and the River (1920–1925)

The October Fair (1925–1928)

The Hills Beyond Pentland (1838–1926)

The Death of the Enemy (1928–1933)

Pacific End (1791–1884)

How all of this came about is the substance of one of the most remarkable books in American literature, *The Story of a Novel* (1936), Wolfe's frank account of his entrapment in this labyrinthian maze and a gracious and candid acknowledgment of the extent of Perkins' role in leading him out.

Long before Perkins and Wolfe became something of the modern-day counterparts of Daedalus and Icarus, Wolfe had moved from Manhattan to Brooklyn (March 11, 1931), where housing was cheaper and social demands on his time far easier to control. His affair with Aline was no longer idyllic, though he was happily drawing upon her willingness to serve as a self-described Scheherazade. She continued to tell him stories of her childhood in New York and to relate anecdotes about her father's life as an actor. Wolfe put much of her material into "The Good Child's River," much of which later became part of WR and an episode in FDTM. Even after his break with her in early January of 1932, an ugly event in which his mother helped him angrily berate Aline and her friends in Wolfe's Brooklyn apartment, Mrs. Bernstein held firm to her role as muse and instructor, encouraging Wolfe to fulfill his promise as a writer and answering questions about the life of the city at an earlier time.

Amidst all the poverty and suffering of Brooklyn in the depths of the Great Depression, Wolfe saw that his earlier goals of fame and love were too egocentric, that his role as an author should embrace social as well as personal problems, that the downtrodden and unlettered masses of humanity around him needed a strong voice if their needs were to be heard, and that a change in political and economic thought must occur if America was to avoid the loss of cherished democratic institutions. He began to question his political allegiances, asking himself if he were communist, socialist, or revolutionary. His discussions with Perkins, a conservative, revealed a Marxist tendency, something Perkins fought to keep out of OT, largely, so he wrote Hemingway, on the grounds that such views were anachronistic in relation to Eugene Gant's development. Wolfe, however, refused any label save that of social democrat. He looked to Franklin Delano Roosevelt and his reform measures for social changes needed to preserve essential American ideals and worked as a writer to lead Americans to loathe that part of America that had betrayed itself out of greed, toleration of the beginning of a privileged class, and resignation in the face of serious economic problems. As a partial result of his political self-examination, Wolfe looked closely at the economic circle in which Aline had moved and thoughtfully weighed his sometimes heated conversations with Perkins on political issues. Out of these self-probings and attempts to understand the background and views of Aline and her class and Perkins and his, Wolfe would create "The World That Jack Built" and George Webber's long letter to Foxhall Edwards, both finally placed in YC by Edward Aswell, with some changes. Thus the move to Brooklyn and Wolfe's discovery there that his allegiance as a man and artist was with the working class had a profound effect on his life and fiction.

His four-year stay in Brooklyn, first at 40 Verandah Place and then at 101 Columbia Heights and 5 Montague Terrace, was a highly productive period, even though marked by much confusion about what work should follow LHA. With some pressure from Perkins, he pushed far enough along with "K–19" for Scribner's to announce its publication in the fall of 1932, completed "The Web of Earth" early that year, and worked on the literary party that a fictional surrogate attended at the home of Rebecca Feitlebaum or Esther Jacobs, early names for Aline Bernstein, in the fall and winter of 1932. By February of the following year, he completed *No Door*, a short novel. That same year saw the publication, in *Scribner's Magazine*, of "The Train and the City," in May, "Death the Proud Brother," in June, and *No Door*, in July. Earlier that year he had taken a huge stack of material to Perkins to ask his advice about whether the long-awaited second novel lurked somewhere among the thousands of pages Wolfe had written since his auspicious beginning as a novelist. Though many parts obviously remained to be written and transitional and connecting passages would have to be done, Wolfe had, so Perkins thought, a promising sequel to LHA if he would consent to return to Eugene Gant's story. Instead of something called "The October Fair," which moved on beyond Wolfe's surrogate's years at Harvard and first European sojourn to the love affair with Rebecca Feitlebaum, Perkins argued that Wolfe should concentrate on Eugene Gant and leave the love story until later. Perkins gave Wolfe a deadline to push him along. Despite steady work, Wolfe shaped nothing as satisfying to his own esthetic standards as LHA. That was a distinct disappointment as he thought of his reputation, for it was important to show growth as an artist, especially after the long delay between novels. The novel was, accordingly, postponed, and Wolfe and Perkins started early in January 1934, to put together the sequel to the first book.

Characteristically, when Wolfe knew what direction the book would take, he drew up lists of what time periods, characters, and episodes should be included. The book as he now conceived it should trace Eugene Gant's experiences from the time he departed for graduate studies at Harvard until his return from his *Wanderjahr* in Europe. So conceived, the book would be long, for, as Wolfe was later to tell Scott Fitzgerald, his was the method of the putter-inner and not the taker-outer. One thing he wanted to put in was the death of W. O. Gant, despite Perkins' objection that Eugene, through whose point of view the story is told, was not a witness to that event. Here Wolfe won, but Perkins held his ground on other fronts, insisting that Wolfe write necessary episodes and transitional passages, and refrain from his practice of fleshing out revised sections until they were much longer than the original draft. The revisions and new material required months of work, much of it done after Perkins had put in a full day at the office. Finally, in September, Wolfe had talked, written, and sweated as much as he could stand and decided to spend a few days at the World's Fair in Chicago. To his chagrin, Perkins placed the remaining portion of the novel in the hands of the printer during Wolfe's absence. Practically speaking, Wolfe began to withdraw from the novel at that point, though he did give a few new touches to the concluding part. His withdrawal can best be seen in the fact that Wolfe, uncharacteristically, became sullen about reading and correcting proof and ultimately left the job to John Hall Wheelock, an editor at Scribner's, and Perkins, complaining bitterly when the novel appeared about its numerous misreadings of his hand and printers' errors. He felt that the work had been taken from him, that he had not been given the chance to make it as good as he was capable of doing, and that his rights as an artist had been compromised. When he later broke with Scribner's, he pointed to this experience as one of his reasons for leaving.

While steady progress was visibly occurring on OT, Wolfe now enjoyed the expert help of someone who could see not only the merit of his work but its potential in the marketplace beyond *Scribner's Magazine*. Elizabeth Nowell, a literary agent associated with the Maxim Lieber Agency who later founded her own firm, provided that expert assistance by going through Wolfe's mounting stacks of manuscripts and suggesting what could be culled for use in magazines. She knew what editors liked, what length to aim for, what stylistic pitfalls to avoid. She began working with Wolfe's materials in December, 1933, and celebrated her first breakthrough on his behalf when *American Mercury* took a much revised version of "Boom Town," published in May 1934. For the remainder of Wolfe's life, she found outlets for his stories and sketches and reduced to acceptable length for *The Saturday Review of Literature* his lecture at the Writers' Conference at Boulder, Colorado, a talk Wolfe entitled "The Story of a Novel." Her success reduced his worries over money and taught him how to shape his material for magazine readers. (She also became his biographer and the editor of his selected letters.)

While she brought stability and security to Wolfe's life during the time he was wrestling with OT, she effectively prepared the way for a double success when the novel finally appeared in 1935, for in that year, besides enjoying the triumph of having a critically acclaimed bestseller in the form of a novel to celebrate, Wolfe could point to thirteen pieces in magazines and a collection of sketches, stories, and short novels called *From Death to Morning*.

Wolfe's misgivings about OT had their roots in his fear that critics and readers would quickly see that he had fallen below the marks set by LHA and some of the pieces, one a prize-winner, recently appearing in *Scribner's Magazine*, and his need to rest from his many months of steady work led him to make his sixth trip to Europe, sailing on the *Ile de France* on March 2, 1935, and going first to Paris. Feeling certain that OT would be deemed a failure, he roamed the streets of Paris, drank much too heavily, and wearied himself sick with "damnable incertitude" (LTW 434). When Perkins cabled him on March 14 that the novel had fared well indeed with the critics, Wolfe's spirits began to brighten, but he still felt distraught over the scores of errors in the text and heartsick over the fact that he had not been granted more time to finish. He wrote Perkins that "the book, like Caesar, was from its mother's womb untimely ripped" (LTW 446). Just how successful the book was, despite its errors and Wolfe's belief that he could have done a better job, began to sink in during the following six or seven weeks, most of which he spent in London. By the time he reached Berlin on May 7, he was greeted as a literary giant, enjoying the experience immensely, since he had always felt a special kinship with the people of his father's ancestral homeland. In conversations with America's ambassador to Germany, William E. Dodd, Jr., and Dodd's daughter, Martha, Wolfe learned that all was not well; that something ugly and evil in the German spirit was finding expression in the rise of Hitler and his faction. He relished the role of the literary lion so much, and reveled so happily in the thought that he came from a culture that produced Beethoven and Goethe, that the talk he heard about the dark side of Nazi Germany gave him only momentary pause, but it did prepare him to keep his eyes and ears open.

He returned from his European sojourn on July 4, immediately joining Perkins for drinks, lunch, and shop talk, some of it involving Aline Bernstein, who had come to Perkins' office to tell him that she would try to block the publication of "The October Fair" if she were to appear as a character in it. They ended their reunion by going to the roof of the Prince George Hotel in Brooklyn and gazing at New York. Wolfe was later to recall this day as one of the happiest in his life, for he was convinced now that he was indeed a famous literary figure who had the respect of a great editor and the majority of America's leading literary critics. His happiness was shortcircuited, however, a few days later when, on July 12, Aline apparently attempted suicide at Scribner's. The reconciliation that followed endured just a few months because Wolfe wanted no tie stronger than friendship.

As Wolfe went through the stack of mail awaiting his return from Europe, he spotted one invitation he wanted to accept, a talk at the Writers' Conference sponsored by the University of Colorado at Boulder. Not ready to settle down to writing, and wanting to see the American West, Wolfe agreed to participate and set off, by train, to take part in the conference from July 22 to August 7. He decided against a formal lecture, choosing instead to talk informally on how he had written OT, which was still much in the news because of its critical and commercial success. His frank talk won the hearts of his audience, who encouraged him to continue with his tale after he has used his alloted time. The talk formed the core of SN, published in abbreviated form in *The Saturday Review*, and in an expanded form by Scribner's. The candor of the talk and the articles and book opened Wolfe to criticism, which came in spirited, even vicious, form from Bernard DeVoto, who assailed Wolfe and Scribner's for an assembly-line method of producing novels. All this carping was in the future, however. Meanwhile, Wolfe was discovering new projects for himself. One was a better job of recording and celebrating America. He told Perkins after reaching Colorado, "The journey across the country was overwhelming—I've never begun to say what I ought to say about it" (LTW 483). Another was a book about America at night, something he started talking about at Boulder and became more certain about as he pushed farther westward. That ideas was to take shape as "The Hound of Darkness," a series of vignettes done in lyrical and dramatic modes over the remainder of Wolfe's life. The work would be "a great tone-symphony of night—railway yards, engines, freights, dynamos, bridges, men and women, the wilderness, plains, rivers, deserts, a clopping hoof . . . " (LTW 489). He gathered impressions and materials for the new book as he continued his trek toward the Pacific, coming eventually to Hollywood, where he entertained and rejected an offer to write filmscripts and met some movie celebrities, including Jean Harlow. But he carried something away from Hollywood even if he did refuse a handsome salary, a renewed appreciation of cinematic techniques, which he adopted for use in "The Hound of Darkness" when he came back to New York in September.

Much work awaited him. First, he had proofs for FDTM to correct and revise. This time he did not want anyone to charge him with shirking his proofreading duties. The book had some of his finest writing in it, and he wanted it to be arranged both for the best possible impression upon the reader and for thematic agreement with the progression implicit in the title. Second, he wanted to push ahead with "The Hound of Darkness," which he believed could become "a great and original book" (LTW 489). Accordingly, he pulled out yet another ledger, his favorite place to record first drafts of his work since Aline had presented ledgers to him before he undertook LHA. Even as he energetically turned to this new project, he knew he should be making headway with "The October Fair," but his interests in this work were waning. Scattered throughout the new ledger were signs of a new character, Paul Spangler, and a fresh theme, the differences between what one expects of life and what one actually experiences. This shift away from Eugene Gant marked a turn from the heavy influence of James Joyce, the most potent force behind LHA and its sequel. Although Wolfe was not to evoke their names until later, other authors seemed to offer him a better example of how to handle his new character and theme, among them Swift, Tolstoy, Dickens, Voltaire, Goethe, and Cervantes. In "The Vision of Spangler's Paul," as he now began to call this new work, he would leave behind much of the aestheticism and rebellion of Eugene Gant and try to show how an artist, as one of the working class speaking for his unlettered brothers and sisters, could probe into the troubles besetting the nation and celebrate, at the same time, the promises and potentials of the country. These jottings in the ledger proved so full of a more mature, more objective vision of the role of the artist and the growth and destiny of the nation that Wolfe announced to Perkins on March 17, 1936, the start of "The Vision of Spangler's Paul": "Wrote book beginning, Goes wonderfully. Full of hope" (LTW 496). But troubled times lay just ahead.

One problem involved Wolfe's disagreement with Scribner's over the price of the book version of SN and his percentage of the royalty. If, as Wolfe hoped, the book could be sold for a dollar or less, he would be content with 10 percent. When it finally appeared with the price pegged at $1.50, he argued that his royalty should rise to 15 percent. When Perkins directed the business department to disregard the contracted 10 percent, Wolfe wrote Perkins that he intended to hold to the terms of the contract, adding that he valued Perkins' friendship above all else.

The second problem resulted from the publication of SN, a review of which in the April 25 issue of *The Saturday Review of Literature* by Bernard DeVoto tore vigorously and sometimes viciously into Wolfe's failings as a writer. Building his case on Wolfe's candid statement of indebtedness to Perkins as friend and editor for helping to get OT to print, DeVoto blasted Wolfe and Scribner's, denouncing them for jumbling the roles of author and editor. The charge stung deeply and became a significant factor in Wolfe's eventual decision to break with Scribner's.

The third problem touched Wolfe even more deeply, since it involved his freedom as a creative artist. He began to draw upon his experiences at Scribner's for the novel in progress, turning his attention to such people as Robert Bridges and Charles Scribner II, and using anecdotes about them passed on to him by Perkins. When Elizabeth Nowell carried one of the finished portions to Perkins to get his reaction, she quickly learned that Wolfe's satiric treatment of the firm and its employees jarred Perkins, leading him to say that he would resign his post if Wolfe published stories and sketches based on information shared in confidence with Wolfe. Wolfe was absolutely within his rights, Perkins said, to write about Scribner's, but inasmuch as he had told Wolfe things about people whose lives, he thought, would be ruined if the material came out, he felt honor bound to leave the firm. Wolfe no doubt appreciated the pinch that Perkins would experience upon publication, but he was outraged to think that satire was acceptable if aimed at Asheville and his own family and unwanted if pointed at Scribner's. Wolfe staunchly asserted his determination to write as he pleased when Nowell reported how Perkins had reacted. Here was another of the factors behind Wolfe's eventual break with Scribner's.

The fourth problem stole time from Wolfe's writing schedule, but fueled a fire against lawyers and lawsuits that had been flaming high ever since he had been sued by Madeleine Boyd for agent's commissions on LHA and OT the previous year. This matter involved the sale of Wolfe's manuscripts by a young and eager agent, Murdoch Dooher, whose services and scruples Wolfe called in question. He wanted to dismiss the agent, just then starting out, and reclaim the manuscripts Dooher was holding. In response, Dooher threatened legal action. Wolfe's recourse was to hire a lawyer to protect his interests. This encounter with the legal system, and the one he was soon to have when his former landlady in Brooklyn, Marjorie Dorman, sued him for libelling her and her family in "No Door" put Wolfe to thinking about a satiric book on lawyers and their ways, but he lived to complete only one brief episode.

When the hot days of summer arrived, he fell victim to wanderlust again, leaving on July 23 on the *Europa* for his seventh and last trip to Europe, where he spent most of his time in Berlin and Paris. He attended the Olympic Games in Berlin and cheered lustily when Jesse Owens raced to victory after victory to the chagrin of Hitler and his henchmen. He continued to see the Dodds family and his German publisher, Ernst Rowohlt, but a brief romance with the talented artist Thea Voelcker added an unexpected pleasure to his German outing. Yet something was obviously rotten in Germany now. A "Dark Messiah" had come among the Germans and was working his corrupt will upon them. Wolfe saw that he must speak the truth about Hitler's Germany, even if speaking out meant that he could never return to the beloved country. That decision was confirmed by an incident that occurred as he left Germany. He witnessed a grimly callous episode of Anti-Semitism on board a German train. Before he left Paris, he was already at work on a piece based on the episode, "I Have a Thing to Tell You," one of his most powerful stories. He came back to New York resolved to expose Naziism for the real menace it was. His social consciousness was no longer an echo of Sinclair Lewis or H. L. Mencken, as it had been when he was revolting against the village or flailing the booboisie in earlier works; it was the strong voice of a man convinced that humanity's securest hope for protecting human rights was the alliance of the democratic nations against Hitler and likeminded leaders. He refused to join committees or protest groups, preferring instead to write letters, publish in liberal magazines, and examine his own political views in his notebooks or on odd scraps of paper. The upshot of these activities and musings was, inevitably, a firmer conviction that the artist must thrust himself more fully into the affairs of the nation and help to lead by uttering the timely word.

His role as a Shelleyan legislator could not be fully assumed, however, because he found himself the defendant in a libel suit brought by Marjorie Dorman. Although the legal staff at Scribner's advised Wolfe to settle out of court, he first insisted on having the case go before a jury, but finally agreed to split the settlement fee by paying $2,745.05, a piddling sum in view of the $125,000 demanded in the suit. Wolfe felt betrayed by Perkins and Scribner's and decided to sever his seven-year relationship.

But the separation was not going to be easy, for Wolfe had such a depth of affection and respect for Perkins that he found breaking off with him the most wrenching experience in his life since the death of his brother, Ben. Typically, Wolfe sat down to count the ways Perkins had disappointed or failed him and scrawled letters he never mailed, in which he closely examined all his grievances. Even more typical was the letter he finally mailed from New Orleans, a rambling but often eloquent *apologia pro vita sua*. Besides revealing why Wolfe felt unhappy with his situation at Scribner's—the charge that his works rolled off the assembly line there; the advice of the legal department to settle suits out of court; Perkins' willingness to side with the legal staff, his promise to resign if Wolfe used tales about Scribner's personnel, and his decision to send OT on to the printer before Wolfe was ready to turn it loose— the letter traced Wolfe's development as an artist and stated many of his basic aesthetic principles. It revealed the depth of the rupture but clearly indicated Wolfe's desire to retain the friendship of Perkins. He stopped short of declaring himself free of Scribner's.

As Wolfe resumed his travels in the South, going to Atlanta and then to Chapel Hill but not to Asheville (owing to his misunderstanding about how he would be received there), he agonized over the step he felt he must take. Still he delayed, waiting until March, 1937, to draft a letter to other publishers announcing his desire to open talks about future books. He held onto this letter, handing it to Edward Aswell only after he signed a contract with Harper and Brothers.

Meanwhile, he took advantage of a fresh burst of creative energy, for after his journey to the South he was ready for work. The source of the new impetus was his hope of writing a kind of American *Gulliver's Travels*, a work to be called "The Ordeal of the Bondsman Doaks," and featuring a protagonist who discovered the differences between the world as he envisioned it and how it actually turned out to be. The protagonist would be named Paul, a holdover from "The Vision of Spangler's Paul," or Joseph Doaks. Where to do the exciting work ahead of him now became a question, for Wolfe had grown tired of the frequent interruptions he endured in New York. His search for a place to write led him to a cabin at Oteen, North Carolina, just a short distance from Asheville, which he had not visited since the outcry there over LHA. After he left New York, he came to Asheville and Oteen in a roundabout way, stopping off in Burnsville in Yancey County, the seat of his maternal ancestors, to visit with cousins there. One of them, John B. Westall, told him about his experiences as a soldier in the Confederate army, out of which Wolfe drew material for "Chickamauga." Wolfe also witnessed a shooting in Burnsville and was later called to testify for the prosecution. This taste of mountain life behind him, he ventured on to Asheville, discovering that few remained so angry that they wanted to drag his "overgrown carcass" out of town. Instead, most Ashevillians warmly welcomed him, some complaining because they had been left out of his books. For most, he was not an enemy of the people, as he had feared, but the toast of the town, the conquering prodigal son. Wolfe was gratified, of course, but nonetheless surprised. He had expected a far different homecoming.

The warmth of the welcome proved a hindrance to his hope of reaping a full harvest from the fresh sprouting of creative energy. He did find time to write a draft of "The Party at Jack's" and to give further thought to what he wanted to do with the Doaks material. Within less than two months of mixing partying and writing at the Oteen cabin, he was ready to resume his old pattern of life in New York.

A tough decision lay ahead of him, however. He had to resolve his differences with Scribner's or find a new publisher. He returned to New

York to discover that his intended break with Scribner's was already public knowledge, and that fact made it easier for him to open his search. He quickly learned of the interest of Houghton Mifflin, Doubleday, and Harper and Brothers. He liked Robert Linscott at Houghton but obviously preferred Harper's offer of an advance of $10,000, a royalty of 15 percent, and no demand to see a manuscript before signing a contract. His decision to sign with Harper's brought a young southerner and Harvard graduate, Edward C. Aswell, into his life, for Aswell would become the editor assigned to Wolfe.

Now that his much-delayed decision was behind him, he could settle down to his work again, feeding off the creative juices that had been flowing strongly for about a full year despite the interruptions and the break with Scribner's. There were magazine pieces to finish, fictionalized accounts of how Asheville had fared in the aftermath of the stock market crash to write, and an outline of the Doaks material to do for Aswell. As all this was going forward, Wolfe found himself less and less happy with the name of Joe Doaks and more and more enthralled with the words of an acquaintance: "You can't go home again." Somehow the words captured the essence of what his experience had taught him, that no one can hope to return to one's home, family, dreams, old forms or systems, or conceptions of beauty and love. The seriousness of the thought seemed inappropriate for the comic figure of Joe Doaks, though Wolfe was far from giving up on the notion that he wanted a protagonist whose discoveries about life's discrepancies would constitute the narrative pattern of the work in progress. The narrative would reach back beyond the birth of the protagonist and forward to the protagonist's attempt to deal with the sorrows and joys of being an artist in a troubled but hopeful America. Along the way, material from "The October Fair," "The Vision of Spangler's Paul," "The Hound of Darkness," and "The Ordeal of the Bondsman Doaks" could be woven together with the new episodes he was doing, or planned to write, to tell the story of the rise of the artistic spirit and to weigh the place of the artist in American society. He chose to call his new protagonist George Webber. Although the narrative scheme matched the one Wolfe had used for Eugene Gant, the treatment of material would be more objective and the hero less egocentric. To help Aswell see the design of the story and the role of the characters, Wolfe put together a statement of purpose and a long catalog of characters. He wanted Aswell to have a chance to study his heaps of manuscripts while he took a break and traveled to Purdue University to give a lecture and relax a bit. As late as the day he was to board his train, Wolfe was sifting through his material to see how much of his outlined task was done. On May 17, he placed the manuscript in Aswell's hands and departed for Indiana.

At Purdue, he looked back over his writing career and traced his development as an artist, calling his lecture "Writing and Living." Later, Aswell was to use a major portion of the address to help round out George Webber's story. A well-received talk behind him, Wolfe went on to Chicago and then headed for the American Northwest, the only portion of the nation he had not seen. His route carried him through Colorado, Wyoming, Idaho, and Washington, where he called upon some cousins. A stopover in Portland and an interview with a Portland newspaperman led to a proposition Wolfe could not resist: a car tour of the western national parks in thirteen days, covering almost 5,000 miles. He set out with Edward M. Miller, the journalist, and Roy Conway, manager of the Oregon State Motor Association, on June 20 and left them on July 2 at Olympia, Washington, with the adventure and the images gleaned along the way recorded in a journal crowded with over 11,000 hastily scrawled words.

He arrived the next day in Seattle, and received a telegram from Aswell expressing his belief that the manuscripts he had been reading would yield Wolfe's greatest novel. Not yet ready to cease his wanderings, Wolfe quickly answered a few letters and booked passage for a boat trip to Vancouver. Aboard the ship, he drank from a whiskey bottle shared with him by "a poor, shivering wretch" (LTW 776). Perhaps he contracted a respiratory infection from this drinking companion, or perhaps he was simply physically exhausted after his rapid odyssey with Miller and Conway. He returned to Seattle ill and failed to shake the cough and fever by taking to his hotel bed. Friends in Seattle arranged for him to be examined by Dr. E. C. Ruge, whose diagnosis was pneumonia. Dr. Ruge advised Wolfe to enter Firlawns Sanitorium in Bothell, Washington. At first Wolfe's response to the treatment seemed encouraging, but when his fever returned and his coughing persisted, Dr. Ruge agreed with a consultant, Dr. Charles Watts, to do X-rays of his lungs. The spot found on the upper lobe of the right lung was thought to be an old tubercular lesion. Wolfe remained in Providence Hospital from the first week of August until September 4. On August 12, he found the energy to write a letter, his last, to Perkins. "I'm sneaking this against orders, but 'I've got a hunch'—and I wanted to write these words to you. . . . Whatever happens—I had this 'hunch' and wanted to write you and tell you, no matter what happens or has happened, I shall always think of you and feel about you the way it was that Fourth of July day three years ago when you met me at the boat, and we went out to the cafe on the river and had a drink and later went on top of the tall building, and all the strangeness and the glory and the power of life and of the city was below" (LTW 778).

Meanwhile, Fred Wolfe and Mabel Wolfe Wheaton had rushed to Seattle to be at Tom's side. His worsening condition became more obvious every day, for he now suffered tormenting headaches and occasional irrationality. Mabel and Fred sought another medical opinion and concluded, upon weighing their options, that the man best qualified to · attend to Wolfe was Dr. Walter Dandy at Johns Hopkins Hospital in Baltimore. That meant a long train ride across the breadth of the nation, one that Mabel, Tom, and a nurse would undertake together as far as Chicago, where they were joined by Wolfe's mother, strong and talkative as ever. Tom withstood the demands of the trip surprisingly well, but he was desperately ill. Dandy therefore wasted no time in probing the cause of his illness.

His preliminary examination left only a slight hope, perhaps a five percent chance, if the source of the problem was an abscess or a tumor lodged at the back of the head. The family decided that Wolfe deserved that chance, however small. Meanwhile, Dr. Dandy suggested that he could be spared the pain of those violent headaches if he underwent immediate trephining. The procedure revealed that Wolfe suffered from tuberculosis of the brain. The best the family and Tom could hope for now was a tuberculoma. When he was operated on, on September 12, his brain was found to be covered with tubercles. Nothing remained for Dandy to do but to put aside his scapel and bear the horrid news to the family and Aswell, who had come down from New York to be with Tom. Dandy said that Wolfe might linger a few weeks but that it would be better if he could die soon. Wolfe was lucky enough to have the better way, for he died in three days, having remained in a semi-coma for most of that time. He died on September 15, eighteen days short of his thirty-eighth birthday.

Baltimore could not supply a coffin big enough to hold his body, and one had to be sent in from New York to carry it to Asheville. His funeral was held at the First Presbyterian Church, where Tom had attended Sunday school, and he was buried in the family plot in Riverside Cemetery, also the resting place of Zebulon B. Vance and O. Henry. One of the mourners making the trip to that spot was his friend Max Perkins.

On Wolfe's headstone, these words were engraved:

TOM

Son of
W. O. and Julia E. Wolfe
A Beloved American Author
Oct. 3, 1900—Sept. 15, 1938
"The Last Voyage, The Longest, The Best"
—Look Homeward, Angel

"Death Bent To Touch His Chosen Son With Mercy, Love And
Pity, And Put The Seal of Honor on Him When He Died."
                                        —The Web And The Rock

References: 2, 4, 6, 11, 13, 14, 22, 28, 38, 40, 43, 45, 46, 51, 53, 54, 56,
58, 65, 68, 69, 76, 83, 88, 89.

Wolfe's Ideas and Attitudes

Wolfe shied away from any Ben Franklinish system of ethical or social philosophy. His undergraduate course in philosophy at the University of North Carolina introduced him to some of the great philosophical notions of the Western world, notions filtered through the mind of Horace Williams, a southern disciple of Hegel more noted for his personal magnetism and teaching techniques than his strength of intellect. Wolfe enjoyed Williams's classes, kept in touch with him for a few years after leaving Chapel Hill, and spent some time trying to write a play in which a character based on Williams would figure prominently in a clash over the issue of research versus teaching, an ageless academic question. Hegelian ideas cropped up again at Harvard when Wolfe studied the works of Coleridge under John Livingston Lowes, who was writing *The Road to Xanadu* at the time Wolfe took his course. In Philosophy 102 under Professor Herbert Langfeld, he heard lectures on the aesthetics of Hegel and his followers.

The philosophical and aesthetical dialectics encountered in his formal studies had a familiar ring when Wolfe thought of the conflicts, some of them in the spirit of fun and others deadly serious, between the northern outlook of his Pennsylvania-bred father and the southern Appalachia values of his mother and her large clan of mountain kinfolk; between his father's loyal and stout allegiance to the Republican Party and his mother's fidelity to the Democratic; between the aristocratic pretensions of eastern North Carolina and the egalitarian principles of the western section of his native state. He had grown used to polarities by the time he packed his bags for college, and he was to pick up the jargon of Hegelian philosophy very quickly, *thesis, antithesis, synthesis*. Once on campus, he found a split between advocates of the New South and champions of the Old. That he listened to the debates and took part in them can be seen in his stand for the working class in "The Crisis in Industry," an essay that brought him the Worth Prize in Philosophy, and in his dramatization of parts of the doctrines of the New South and the Old in WTOC, where one character, a political adviser named Professor Hutchings, represents Progressivist ideas, and another, Will Rutledge, represents the aristocratic planter society. That Wolfe had reached something of a synthesis himself by the time he wrote the play (1922–1923) appears in his ability to treat both men satirically. Also, the barbs tossed into the camp of the Agrarians show his refusal to take a stand beside those spokesmen who scoffed at the social, agricultural, and economic ideas being taught at the University of North Carolina during Wolfe's time there by the intellectual heirs of Henry Grady.

Although reared in a household and in a region where an ideational tug of war occurred repeatedly, Wolfe hesitated to throw his weight on one side or the other, preferring to sort things out for himself and, like Emerson, balking when someone wanted him to shoulder a placard or join a parade. He could see, for example, that the "austere decency" of the Presbyterian Church in which he had been brought up did not capture the "pain, mystery, and sensuous beauty of religion" (LHA 140), and he therefore chose not to carry on the Scotch-Irish tradition of his mother's family by remaining a Presbyterian. Even as he was withdrawing from that church, he was taking with him the Calvinistic doctrine that man is afflicted by something dark and corrupt within, Wolfe's most terrifying example being Judge Rumford Bland of YC. Before he came to that conviction, however, he confessed that he had been driven from his church by those who saw church attendance as a boost to better economic and social standing (NB 10), a point he raised in WTOC and LHA. But the concept of Original Sin must be seen as an idea running parallel to a pagan and Christian notion that Wolfe was to use as a means of suggesting those chthonic and celestial forces playing roles in the destiny of mankind; the notion coming down from Plato and some Platonic Christians that a good or a bad daemon helped to shape or control the mind and conduct of mankind. Wolfe, of course, did not adopt this discredited pneumatology as an act of asserting his return to some primitive form of religion. Rather, he was able to reap considerable metaphorical benefits from turning to the lexicon of a culture that had meditated on the subject of humanity's good and evil traits long before St. Augustine or Calvin pondered the mystery, for the Greeks had asked why men had such dual natures, and had broadened Plato's description of the function of daemons to cover both benign and malign influences on man, the chthonic and the celestial. That classical lexicon seemed all the more relevant because such admired authors as Burton, Goethe, Coleridge, and Keats had drawn upon it. One of Wolfe's earliest uses of the word *daemon* appears in a note that he probably meant to hand George Pierce Baker when he asked him to read a draft of MH. Referring to Eugene Ramsay, Wolfe wrote: "It would perhaps be much better for Ramsay if he could limit himself thus. His own common-sense tells him that a sane limitation is the only solution in this present frame of things. But the daemon goads him on" (William Wisdom Collection, bMs AM 1883 [1274]). The word turns up in LHA in Wolfe's description of Luke: "There was in him demonic exuberance, a wild intelligence that did not come from the brain" (253). The concept of the demonic underlies Wolfe's explanation of Eugene's occasional outbursts: "At times his devouring, unsated brain seemed beyond his governance. . . . And this demon [assigned the shape of a bird] wheeled, plunged, revolved about an object, returning suddenly, after it had flown away, with victorious malice, leaving stripped, mean, and common all that he had clothed in wonder" (224). Something malign must be associated with the demonic as presented in connection with Luke and Eugene in these two passages, but the most potent use of it is benign. That use is strictly Platonic in that Ben assumes the classical role of the guardian angel, but Wolfe also capitalized on a Shakespearean adaptation of Graeco-Christian pneumatology by evoking thoughts of *Hamlet* in the final scene in LHA. Yet here, as in the passages relating Luke and Eugene to the demonic, Wolfe is careful to keep within the bounds of the demonic as used metaphorically by Burton, Goethe, Coleridge, and Keats to explain those human activities and notions that spring from the unconscious mind. To put it another way, Wolfe did not literally believe in daemons, but he found the concept of the demonic a helpful means of figuring forth both the power of goodness and the power of blackness in human existence. Once a reader catches Wolfe's intent to use the demonic metaphorically, his frequent allusions to chthonic and celestial gods and goddesses and to the Faustian legend become more readily understandable, as do, also, his titles for his most famous novel, one of which was drawn from *The Rime of the Ancient Mariner*: "O Lost"; the other, from Milton's "Lycidas." His friend Desmond Powell, whom he had known from their teaching days at NYU, concluded that a daemonic spirit touched not only Wolfe's work but his life as well. "[Wolfe] *was* possessed, possessed by that daemonic spirit that Goethe so admired in Byron, which worked on him more powerfully than upon any other American writer of his period. For the working of that spirit he had paid his bond in blood. At the command to that spirit he lived his life over a thousand times, and he tried to live in the imagination the lives of a thousand men, that he might write the book of all their days. Being possessed by the spirit he wandered lonely through worlds long lost, finding no place to assuage his weariness" ("Of Thomas Wolfe." *Arizona Quarterly* 1,1 [Spring 1945], 36).

Another of the classical notions as transmitted and transmuted by Renaissance and Romantic poets strongly appealed to Wolfe, the idea of preexistence, first hinted at in WTOC, picked up for further development in MH, and used as a recurrent theme in LHA. His favorite way of suggesting an earlier life is to ask who can tell who is alive, who the ghost, and to utter the words: *Et ego in Arcadia.*

The aesthetic ideas that Wolfe followed owed something to the classical tradition, but a Renaissance professor at Chapel Hill, the Romantics, and James Joyce offered Wolfe a good deal more. The Homeric epic taught Wolfe to value concrete detail, colorful language, and the potency of allusion, and the epic tradition emboldened him to assume the role of a nation's spokesman, a role that the Romantics also stressed. From Edwin Greenlaw, the leading authority on Edmund Spenser, Wolfe heard the notion that literature should be a transcript of life, a guiding principle also given considerable emphasis in the folk drama course and folk plays being done under Frederick Koch at Chapel Hill. These two Chapel Hill teachers helped to sharpen Wolfe's interest in the techniques of naturalistic writers. He would say soon after reaching Harvard and having heard the devotees of beauty argue that the proper function of the artist was to acquire a sense of the beautiful and to create beauty, that "We don't need a 'sense of the beautiful' any more than we need a 'sense of the ugly,' for the world is full of ugly things . . . and we've got to face them with our heads up. I have no use for the kind of 'culture' that could discern the hand of the great artist in painting but would cringe from the dirty, ugly, sweating crowd" (LTW 28). From the Romantics, English as well as American, Wolfe seized upon the idea that the artist was a kind of bard: "He is the tongue of his unlettered brothers, he is the language of man's buried heart, he is man's music and life's great discoverer, the eye that sees, the key that can unlock, the tongue that will express the buried treasure in the hearts of men . . . and he has all, knows all, sees all that any man on earth can see and hear and know" (OT 551). Behind all of these claims are the arguments and practices of Wordsworth, Coleridge, Shelley, and Whitman. Some of the stances taken by these writers had been converted and condensed into a kind of aesthetic code by the time Wolfe reached Harvard, a code owing something to the portrait of the artist as drawn by Joyce: "This artist that we talked about so much, instead of being in union with life, was in disunion with it. . . . The total result of [our talk] was inevitable: it was to develop a kind of philosophy, an aesthetic, of escapism. It tended to create in the person of the artist not only a special but a privileged character, who was not governed by the human laws that govern other men, who are not subject to the same desires, the same feelings, the same passions—who was, in short, a kind of beautiful disease in nature, like a pearl in an oyster" (AAN 113). The Joycean "wounded faun" lost its staunchly guarded preserve in Wolfe's artistic habitat when he began to see how important the writer's function was in calling attention to social ills. Even as that insight came to him, he was glad that Joyce had shown him how to explore both the buried life of a would-be artist and the infinitely varied life of a town and its people.

Having considered the creeds and practices of the Harvard aesthetes and Joyce's Stephen Dedalus, Wolfe apologized for leaning too far in their direction. The social problems of the 1930s brought him back to his roots: "By instinct, by inheritance, by every natural sympathy and affection of my life, my whole spirit and feeling is irresistibly on the side of the working class, against the cruelty, the injustice, the corrupt and infamous privilege of great wealth, against the shocking excess and the wrong of the present system. . . . I think the whole thing has got to be changed, and I'll do everything within the province of my energy or talent to change it for the better" (LTW 519–20). He did not rush forward to become a part of any radical movement, although he weighed the social programs of various political factions. Among his many introspective notes are the following: "If it is necessary for me here to define my own political position, I should say it was definitely socialistic veering to the left. . . . If I had to state my politics I'd call myself a social democrat. And by social democrat I would understand a man who believes in socialism but not in communized socialism, and in democracy but not in individualized democracy" (NB 915). This look at the political programs of the day led Wolfe to make up and then respond to his own political questionnaire:

Q: Are you a Republican?

A: No.

Q: Democrat?

A: No.

Q: Socialist?

A: No.

Q: Communist?

A: No.

Q: What are your political affiliations?

A: None; save to vote at present for that party in America which at the present time best embodies ideas of social revision in which I believe. At the present moment that party is the Democratic Party. (NB 957)

The upshot of these questions was his decision to cast his vote for Franklin D. Roosevelt. That vote came as a result of his belief that Roosevelt was serious about curing the worst faults of the capitalistic system by introducing reforms drawn from socialist teachings. Even as he voted for a reformer he clung to the hope that certain of the cherished positions of southern conservatives would not be swept aside, the most important ones being the rights that Jefferson had argued so hard to secure: "I do not believe in the abolition of private property, in the class warfare, or in the so-called dictatorship of the proletariat. I do not believe also in the abolition of free inquiry, or that the ideas represented by 'freedom of thought,' 'freedom of speech,' 'freedom of press,' and 'free assembly' are just rhetorical myths. I believe rather that they are among the most valuable realities that men have gained, and that if they are destroyed men will fight to have them" (NB 916). It was Wolfe's belief that Americans had betrayed their political heritage, that they had allowed greed and selfishness and the growth of a privileged class to destroy the promise of America. He assumed the mantle of a seer to speak of these ills.

The political woes of his own country awakened in him a keen desire to warn against the dangers of the kind of social reform that Hitler had brought to the country he loved best after his own, Germany. Not only had Hitler denied some of the basic human freedoms, but he had also destroyed human trust and dignity. This was what Wolfe felt he had to tell his countrymen about Germany, even though he knew he could not return to that beloved land again as long as Hitler and his followers remained in power. Fascism, he believed, was the worst solution any nation could endorse.

That he could say this in the face of an idea that he seems to have in some measure shared with Hitler, the belief in the philosophical principle known as vitalism, shows how deeply Wolfe was committed to democratic values. As defined by Bella Kussy, vitalism is an "emphasis on life as an all-pervasive force and especially as the supreme value" ("The Vitalist Trend in Thomas Wolfe," *Sewanee Review* 50 [July–September, 1942], 307). She links this notion to Nietzsche, Whitman, and Hitler, showing that their belief in an elemental and driving force governing all life corresponds to Wolfe's notion that primitive or atavistic urges stand behind the conduct of men. Wolfe, Whitman, and Nietzsche differ from Hitler in refusing to accept the notion that the primitive Teutons represented man at his best. Hitler, in short, saw in vitalism a way of supporting his anti-intellectual ploy to squash truth while gaining backing for a myth built upon primitive emotionalism. Rather than the complex explanations and distinctions that the term *vitalism* forces upon both trained philosopher and common reader, a simpler way to suggest Wolfe's adherence to a belief that celebrates life on an elementary or primitive level is to say that he stood with George Bernard Shaw in subscribing to the notion of a life force or *elan vital*, the Bergsonian term for the creative force inside an organism that brings about physical form and enables it to grow and achieve the adaptations necessary to promulgate itself.

Wolfe had something else from Bergson to weigh, as he sought a way to define time. Attempting to discover an extended definition of time, Wolfe turned to articles on that subject in both the *Encyclopedia Americana* and the *Encyclopaedia Britannica* in the summer of 1931. Here he found a survey of various theories, including those of the Greeks, Bergson, William James, and Einstein. He entered direct quotations and paraphrases in his pocket notebook, and later he ripped out the pages on which he made his notes, redated them December 23, 1924, and placed them in OT (670–671). He obviously wanted the notes to help him underscore a major thematic concern of that novel. When he told how he wrote OT, he explained that he divided time three ways: (1) present time, (2) past time, (3) time immutable, which he defined as eternal and unchanging, the time of rivers, mountains, the earth. As Margaret Church found when she compared Wolfe's ideas on time with those of Bergson and others, Wolfe's views are fairly simple. He was not so much involved in stating a theory as trying to resolve an old, nagging question: can there ever be fixity amidst all the change everywhere evident? Neither present time nor past time offers any hope of fixity or permanence, since present time rushes headlong into the immediate future and past time retreats in the opposite direction just as rapidly. In time immutable, Wolfe thought he found something to stand fixed, something against which the "bitter briefness" (SN 52) of man's transient life could be played. Wolfe's comments on time suggest that he may have wanted to do something akin to what Proust had done in his fiction. Church says that Wolfe's desire to capture bygone time, to get at the realm of essence, resembles Proust's efforts; and Muller, stressing the difference between the two novelists, points out that Wolfe wanted "to render permanence and change as they are felt in immediate experience, in which both are very real; whereas Proust, like the mystics, aspired to the realm of pure time, the realm of Essence or Being, where change is mere appearance" (75). Although Wolfe developed no elaborate theory about time, he firmly believed that he could become its victim if he didn't use it well to get his work done.

Few things mattered more to Wolfe than work: "Living and working," he wrote Sherwood Anderson, "are so close together with me that they are damned near the same thing. I do carry my work too much with me—when I'm doing it, I take it to bars, restaurants, railroad trains, parties, upon the streets, everywhere" (LTW 655). From his working-class parents, from one of his earliest literary heroes, Thomas Carlyle, and especially from Aline Bernstein, he heard about the nobility of labor.

Work is a recurring theme in his correspondence with his mother and Aline. As he said in his talk at Purdue University, his mother had little understanding of the nature of a writer's work, thinking that it required no sweat and not much time, and paid handsomely. She was not easily disabused of this notion, believing that if she put her hand to the job, she could write something that would turn a quick buck. Her insistence that everyone find a job and do it, to pay his way, to do his part, proved to be a sore point in her relationship with her family. She committed herself wholly to the ethics of success, seeing no value at all in loafing. That much as least she shared with Aline, to whom Wolfe felt compelled to defend loafing after repeated urgings from her to settle down to a routine of work: "In America we very properly abominate 'loafing,' but we are not always sure what loafing is. I am sure that a good deal of the cultivation in the world may come from the appearance of loafing, and that most creation comes that way—that is to say when a man's body is indolent and lazy but his mind fiercely and mercilessly at work" (MOL 282–283). When Aline could no longer share Wolfe's life as his mistress, she held firm to her role as muse, pleading with him to keep to his work. Wolfe's tribute to Esther Jack's dedication to work must certainly express how much he admired Aline's commitment to her job as a stage designer:

It was as a worker and as doer that this woman was supreme. The true religion of her soul, the thing that saved her and restored her from the degradation of the wasteful idleness, the insane excess of self-adornment, the vanity of self-love, and the empty ruin of hollowness that most women of her class had come to know, was the religion of her work. It saved her, took her out of herself, united her life to a nobler image, which was external to her and superior to the vanities of self. There was no labor too great, no expenditure of time and care and patient effort too arduous and too exacting, if, through it, she could only achieve 'a good piece of work.' (WR 403)

That exalted notion of work came, in part, to be Wolfe's too, but, unlike Aline, he lacked the discipline to make efficient use of his time and ended by not achieving a really "good piece of work" as often as he wanted to, the most obvious instance being OT.

No doubt his background and loyalties had much to do with his belief that certain kinds of work were better than others. No one earning his living by dealing in stocks, bonds, or loans stood very high in Wolfe's ranking of a worker's worth. Such a person earned his keep by the sweat of another man's brow, and too often, Wolfe thought, brokers and money managers came to see themselves, and came to be seen, as a privileged class, a point made in YC. This attitude is provincial, of course, but Wolfe, in moments of charity and insight, asserted that the "best thing that a man can do is . . . the work he is able to do, and for which he is best fitted . . . " (LTW 738).

Wolfe was too much the humanist not to appreciate or accept a career or profession capable of bringing out a person's greatest worth. This humanistic attitude colored the rest of his thinking as well. It is true that, like Mencken and Lewis, he delighted in berating boobs and lacerating philistines, missed no chance to sneer at the preachers of the gospel of progress, and poked fun at business and civic boosters. He did this out of no adherence to a religious doctrine opposed to materialism, but rather from his belief, shared with Emerson, that things had climbed into the saddle and were riding rough-shod over the human spirit. The way of the greatest religious leaders, even Jesus himself, could not be Wolfe's way, as he confessed in "God's Lonely Man" (HB 196). Wolfe's manner of helping mankind would therefore be secular and compassionately humanistic. What he saw happening around him in Brooklyn as the Great Depression gripped the nation more fiercely each day stirred and deepened that concern: "The staggering impact of this black picture of man's inhumanity to his fellow men, the unending repercussions of these scenes of suffering, violence, oppression, hunger, cold, and filth and poverty going on unheeded in a world in which the rich were still rotten with their wealth left a scar upon my life, a conviction in my soul which I shall never lose" (SN 60). The jungles of Brooklyn, where he saw most of the downtrodden Helots and rejects of the crippled economic system, compelled him to turn from his "self-centered vision" and "to learn humility" (YC 725). The humanistically motivated desire to do something to alleviate the problems befalling the poor led to long discussions and then arguments with Maxwell Perkins, whose willingness to subscribe to the "hopeful fatalism" of the Preacher in the book of Ecclesiasticus upset Wolfe. Perkins took the view that the problem would in time work itself out, that it was man's lot to suffer at times and to prosper at others, that the condition of man is ultimately tragic. Wolfe could not gainsay any of this, but not to strike against present ills seemed to him a betrayal of humanistic traditions: "The evils that we hate, you no less than I, cannot be overthrown with shrugs and sighs and shakings of the head however wise. It seems to me that they but mock at us and only become more bold when we retreat before them and take refuge in the affirmation of man's tragic average" (YC 738). Having come to this position, Wolfe had moved a large step further in his break with Perkins. Words taken from Wolfe's letter explaining his reasons for breaking with Scribner's, and given by Aswell to George Webber, affirm his belief in proceeding quickly to find human cures for the nation's ailments.

You and the Preacher may be right for all eternity, but we Men-Alive, dear Fox, are right for Now. And it is for Now, and for us the living, that we must speak, and speak the truth, as much as we can see and know. With the courage of the truth within us, we shall meet the enemy as they come to us, and they *shall* be ours. And if, once having conquered them, new enemies approach, we shall meet them from that point, from there proceed. In the affirmation of that fact, the continuance of that unceasing war, is man's religion and his living faith. (YC 738)

Here, clearly, is no preachment meant to lead readers to endure pain and deprivation now and to expect a reward or a more just system in the hereafter. These words thus provide the ideational base for Wolfe's decision to put his pen to use in behalf of humanity. Underlying this affirmation is a sort of battered and bruised meliorism. Perhaps, Pamela Hansford Johnson put the case best in *Hungry Gulliver*: Wolfe's "saving force was his natural optimism and his belief in the grandeur of mankind, but this was an optimism in conflict with an instinct to despair, a belief in conflict with an instinct to condemn" (121). This insight helps to explain Wolfe's celebratory chants about America and his satiric assaults on American ills. Wolfe became America's bard as well as its secular Isaiah.

A corollary to his optimism and meliorism was something he shared with John Dewey. As Herbert J. Muller observes, Wolfe's philosophy is like Dewey's, with Wolfe's "emphasis upon Becoming instead of Being, constant inquiry instead of absolute knowledge, truths instead of Truth. It is in line with the current scientific conception of a creative, evolving universe in which reality is on the make, and there are new things under the sun" (151). Using George Webber as his mouthpiece, Wolfe expressed his position this way: "My life, more than that of anyone I know, has taken on the form of growth" (YC 739). He considered himself "Time's plant" (YC 739). "Time's plant" as individual man could grow toward a fullfillment of personal potential and "Time's plant" as a nation could one day expect that the highest and best promises of its system would be realized.

"Time's plant" is subject to forces within and outside itself, a point given close attention by Richard S. Kennedy in *The Window of Memory*: "Wolfe looks about him to see a disordered world of chance [but] disputes the reality of this world. . . . In the chronicle of time man's course moves along guided by Necessity. But the "fatality of things" does not totally determine his life. Man's choices, both good and bad, can in some measure control his life within the areas of Necessity. . . . But within Necessity and beyond the control of Will are accidents that further alter man's course. With this last addition we see that the scheme is similar to Melville's warp of Necessity, shuttle of Free Will, and sword of Chance" (101). Another way of expressing Wolfe's ideas on human destiny is to say that he found Fate an older and more potent god than

Jove, Zeus, or Yahweh. But Fate itself seemed sometimes to tremble when challenged by the Life Force. Here, however, man enters the realm of the inscrutable, and must try to be content to contemplate "the dark miracle of chance which makes new magic in a dusty world. . . . The seed of our destruction will blossom in the desert, the alexin of our cure grows by a mountain rock, and our lives are haunted by a Georgia slattern, because a London cutpurse went unhung. Each moment is the fruit of forty thousand years" (LHA 3). Somehow, the flower of life and the seed of destruction flourish together.

That realization gave Wolfe, for all his optimism, a tragic sense of life, as he explained in an early letter (12 March 1924) from New York, after beginning his job at New York University: "Life is brutal and has a tragic underscheme: we mean nothing in [the] Great plan, and the breath may be crushed from us at any moment, by the same careless, unseeing fingers which have flung billions of men before us into the earth to rot. . . . We are as the men of former time—no different, and in the end we, too, shall turn our faces to the wall, and the light will go out; and we shall go into a place where there is darkness,—nothing but darkness" (LTM 60). Before sinking back into darkness—and it is uncertain whether Wolfe held to this nihilistic notion throughout—man must wage his best fight to give his life dignity, beauty, integrity, courage, purpose, meaning, and nobility.

He must do all this with the certain knowledge that the struggle will be a lonely one, an idea most succinctly expressed in a letter to his mother in defense of his purpose in LHA: "We are born alone—all of us who have ever lived or will live . . . " (LTM 155). Try as he may, man cannot really know other people, cannot escape that "incommunicable prison" of self. Yet man, especially the artist, as Hawthorne stated, desires more than anything else perhaps, a chance, a means, of opening channels of intercourse with his fellows. Herein lies the greatest challenge for the artist, and here rests his highest potential for triumph, for fame, for enduring respect and love.

References: 8, 11, 13, 14, 16, 17, 20, 22, 24, 28, 40, 42, 46, 47, 51, 57, 61, 65, 66, 68, 69, 72, 73, 75, 79, 82, 87.

Major Themes in Wolfe's Works

Wolfe's words to Margaret Roberts, his early teacher and "the mother of his spirit," state his thematic concerns in the broadest terms: "I go so far as to say that an artist's interest, first and always, has got to be in life itself" (LTW 520). A putter-inner, as he liked to call himself, Wolfe reached out in all directions to record his external world and looked inward to examine his reactions to that world. Let writers who chose to be selective focus on a single theme, or a major theme with clearly subordinated minor themes, go their way, and with his blessing. His was the way of Dickens, Dostoevsky, Sterne, Cervantes, and Shakespeare in literature, or Bosch, Breughel, or Hogarth in painting. His scenes would burst with the images of bustling life, and his themes would follow the ebb and flow of human existence. Of course, he could never hope to get everything down that he wanted to capture, and, expectedly, he ran into problems trying to design ways to share his impressions. Just one book could not hold them. At least the kind of book that novelists were expected to write in the post-James and post-Flaubert age would not do. What to call his big books has been a critical problem, since Wolfe settled upon nothing for a label and no other writer has done exactly the kind of thing he did. Suffice it to say here that Wolfe struggled tirelessly to find a form to allow ample scope for all the themes he wanted to treat. Like Boccaccio or Chaucer, Wolfe sought a framework to contain his many impressions and stories. That framework came to be the encompassing theme of the development of the artistic spirit in America, and an artist's attempt to record the face, heart, and soul of America as one artist came to know them, paying heed to the problems and promises of the nation as he wrote. The following discussion considers theme in both its older meaning as topics or subjects of discourse and as the controlling idea of a story or novel.

One of Wolfe's favorite topics is food, whether he is writing of the tables laden with all the vegetables and fruits of W. O. Gant's bountiful garden, the sumptuous fare of the Pierce family on the Hudson, or the succulent dishes prepared by Esther Jack. A justly celebrated passage from LHA shows Wolfe at the top of his form:

In the morning they [the Gants] rose in a house pungent with breakfast cookery, and they sat at a smoking table loaded with brains and eggs, ham, hot biscuit, fried apples seething in their gummed syrups, honey, golden butter, fried steak, scalding coffee. Or there were stacked batter-cakes, rum-colored molasses, fragrant brown sausages, a bowl of wet cherries, plums, fat juicy bacon, jam. At the mid-day meal, they ate heavily: a huge hot roast of beef, fat buttered lima-beans, tender corn smoking on the cob, thick red slabs of sliced tomatoes, rough savory spinach, hot yellow corn-bread, flaky biscuits, a deep-dish peach and apple cobbler spiced with cinnamon, tender cabbage, deep glass dishes piled with preserved fruits—cherries, pears, peaches. At night they might eat fried steak, hot squares of grits fried in egg and butter, pork-chops, fish, young fried chicken (68).

What was good to the palate of Eugene Gant was a treat also to George Webber, whose appetite was just as ravenous as Eugene's. But George has an advantage, a beautiful and superb cook, Esther Jack, whom he wants to devour along with her exquisite meals. "You are my food!" [George] cried, seizing her again with singing in his heart. "You are meat, drink, butter and bread and wine to me! . . . You are my cake, my caviar, you are my onion soup!" he cried (WR 451).

Wherever Eugene and George travel, they are sure to sample and comment on the food and drink of the places they visit, England, France, Germany, and in part judge a country's character on the basis of its fare and eating and drinking habits. Food is an index to a nation's ability to enjoy the finer things of life, to cherish nature's bounty, to show hospitality.

Although Wolfe apparently never bothered to learn any culinary arts well, he ate with gusto, and his increasing bulk over the years testified to his appetite and lack of exercise. Not that he did not like sports. From Eugene Gant's fantasies about football heroics at Yale, to Jim Randolph's electrifying touchdown run against Madison and Monroe, to Jack Dempsey's fight with Firpo, and on to the gold medal dashes of Jesse Owens at the 1936 Olympics in Berlin, Wolfe had an abiding interest in sports. He described how Americans followed baseball games in small-town America by waiting outside newspaper offices for reports from the wire services, how local wrestlers took on the latest visiting Masked Marvel, how college students celebrated football victories and revered sports heroes, how a college star, Jim Randolph, outlived his fame and drifted into membership in the Lost Generation, and how a part Cherokee boy, Nebraska Crane, made it to the big time and won fame as a New York Yankee. He also used these two sportsmen to help him comment on a theme central to the aspirations and discoveries of George Webber. The victories of Jesse Owens in Berlin helped him to show the absurdities of Hitler's racial theories and to expose Hitler's dark and evil nature.

Sports also gave him a chance to write a spoof of sports journalism in *A Note on Experts*, and the opportunity to pay a tribute to Ring Lardner by echoing something of his style in the pages devoted to Nebraska Crane.

Wolfe even caught sports entering college life off the playing field, and becoming one of the metaphors for education. In an episode presaging the formation of the Fellowship of Christian Athletes and its methods of trying to advocate its cause on American college campuses, Wolfe presents Preacher Reed, whose ministry to the undergraduates of Pine Rock College is couched in the language of sports. Yet that is only a minor indication of Wolfe's interest in education.

Education figures prominently in both the Gant and Webb cycles. Eugene's special grooming at the North State Fitting School, where he learns about the magic and potency of poetry from Margaret Leonard, has much to do with his yearning to become a writer and the jealousy of his siblings, all of whom had been educated in the public schools. More so than any other major American novelist, Wolfe dwells on education, showing students and teachers at work in the classroom, and placing a protagonist in front of and behind a desk, as he does for both of his fictional surrogates. He draws a portrait of a famous scholar, Edwin Greenlaw, who appears as Randolph Ware in WR; he explains how a philosophy teacher, a backwoods Hegelian in WR and Horace Williams in real life, helped to shape the lives of George Webber and his classmates, and he presents the nation's most honored drama teacher, George Pierce Baker (James Graves Hatcher), tutoring his hopeful playwrights at Harvard. But the teacher receiving most attention is himself, or rather his surrogates, who attempt to carry on the tradition of humanistic arts and letters in New York City. This experience allows Wolfe to explore a problem now at the core of much of the nation's creative life: how to flourish, or exist, as an artist while putting bread on the table by teaching, which is the lot of scores of the country's writers nowadays, but was something just beginning to happen when Wolfe took up the theme. Yet Wolfe's surrogates had concerns other than the conflicts resulting from the demands of teaching on energy and time and the need to create, for the classroom often brings teacher and student into an awareness that their relationship cannot stop when the bell rings or the term ends. Such is the circumstance when Abe Jones and Eugene Gant discover that their demands on each other's talents and time could be met only by lowering the barriers that keep pupil and mentor in separate spheres. Teaching also involves colleagues, who delight in riding hobbyhorses, and engage in departmental politics as a matter of advancement or survival. All this Wolfe catches up in his treatment of George Webber's experience as a member of the faculty of The School for Utility Cultures, Inc. His tone is usually satiric, implying that the idea of a true university does not exist among such people, who could no more feed someone with a Faustian hunger for knowledge than they could inspire someone to excell creatively. The model educator is someone like Margaret Leonard, whose respect for her student's mind and heart matches her understanding of and love for the subject she teaches. Such teachers truly help shape and mold lives.

Of course, education goes on outside the classroom, and Wolfe deals meaningfully with the theme of how people acquire codes of conduct and traits of character. More so with Eugene Ramsay and Eugene Gant than with George Webber, he examines how an aristocracy of spirit sets the well-educated person off from the philistine. Nobility of mind means not only refinement of one's sensitivities but also the acquisition of such traits as generosity, valiance, loyalty, a respect for order and justice, hospitality, empathy, and compassion. The last two traits mentioned apply particularly to George's development, since his narcissism almost evaporates when he sees the suffering and deprivation caused by the Great Depression. Playing the wounded faun, going on to become the well-wrought aesthete that Eugene Gant aspired to be, simply wouldn't do. Other things, like friendship and finding a father, meant a great deal more.

Friendship touches the lives of both George and Eugene, George's more significantly than Eugene's. Eugene rarely associated with anyone closely enough in his childhood or at school or college to call someone friend. Not until he meets Francis Starwick at Harvard does he form such an association. Its fruits at first bring much pleasure, for the two of them enjoy walking, talking, and dining together. Its end is bitter when, in Paris, Eugene discovers Starwick's homosexuality and sees that his friend will never use his creative talents. Eugene's relationship with Abe Jones comes close to being a friendship as Jew and Gentile, city boy and provincial southerner, student and mentor learn to understand and appreciate each other, but some unbridgeable depths created by the difference in their heritage keep them from a true friendship. A gulf in wealth does not, however, prevent Eugene from becoming a valued friend of Joel Pierce, whose belief in Eugene's talents is matched by his genuine esteem for him as a person, and Eugene is able to admire

Joel's humanity without the toadyism that sometimes occurs when the person admired also has great riches.

Unlike Eugene, George has a close childhood friend, and the friendship endures into adulthood, though there are gaps in it. That friendship is the one between George and Nebraska Crane. The warmth of their reunion in New York and the confidence they share as they ride together back to Libya Hill prove that a strong bond still exists between them. Also unlike Eugene, George develops a bond with an older man, in this case his editor, Foxhall Edwards. Here is someone to whom George can wholly unbosom himself, as he does in the long letter to Foxhall at the end of YC. Here, too, George learns to accept the fact that friendship can endure, and even flourish, despite sharply differing outlooks on life. Perhaps that acceptance is based in part on a new factor in this relationship, Foxhall's role as a surrogate father. In any case, Wolfe was pursuing a theme that finds expression in OT, WR, and YC when Eugene and George search for a source of wisdom, strength, and solace; in short, a father.

Family relationships indeed loom large in Wolfe's canon, being a major focus in *The Mountains*, and running throughout his work from that early play onward. His concern for the family takes him into such subjects as feuds (MTS), clannishness (MTS, LHA, OT, WR, YC, HB), relationships between father and son (MTS, MH, LHA, OT, WR, YC, HB, and FDTM), relationships between mother and son (MH, LHA, OT, FDTM, and HB), relationships between husband and wife (MTS, WTOC, MH, LHA, OT, WR, YC, and HB), the clashes among siblings (MTS, MH, LHA, OT, and HB), the conflicts between youth and age (MTS, MH, LHA, OT, WR, and HB), the problem of establishing a self-identity amidst the demands and needs of the family (MTS, MH, LHA, OT, FDTM, WR, YC, and HB), and the gathering of families for weddings and funerals (LHA, OT, FDTM, YC, HB).

Whether looking back on his family ties in Asheville, recalling his visits to his uncle in Boston, or reporting his stay in a British lodging house or a train ride through the French countryside, Wolfe is sure to notice families and certain to attempt to discover the dynamics of their relationships. He had a similar interest in tracing the dynamics of a small town. That interest surely resulted in part from his hope of doing for Asheville something closely akin to what Joyce had done for Dublin. But Joyce yielded some ground to Sinclair Lewis, H. L. Mencken, and Mark Twain, whose piercing observations about life in small-town America helped Wolfe see Asheville more sharply and more satirically, and of course, there was Sherwood Anderson to offer a few lessons on how to get at the buried lives of the townsfolk. By his own admission, LHA was Wolfe's Joyce book, and his notebooks and letters reveal a working knowledge of the writings of his aforenamed countrymen.

However he came about equipping himself to portray a small town, Wolfe proved himself an astute analyst, exploring in detail such facets as boosterism (WTOC, LHA, and YC), land speculation and development (WTOC, LHA, OT, FDTM, YC, and HB), cultural and artistic projects (WTOC, LHA, and YC), denominational loyalties and the belief that church attendance is good for politics and business (WTOC, LHA, WR, and YC), the relationship with neighbors (LHA, OT, WR, YC, and HB), professional associations among groups such as doctors, nurses, journalists, shopkeepers, and boardinghouse owners (LHA, OT, WR, and YC), overreaching bankers and businessmen (LHA, OT, WR, and YC), the trouble resulting from teaching some controversial theory or holding some unpopular belief (WTOC, LHA, OT, WR, and YC), and the practice of usury (YC). Related to his treatment of small-town America is his depiction of protagonists from a small town in the metropolitan areas of Boston and New York. Both Eugene and George carry with them the values and prejudices acquired during their years in Altamont and Libya Hill and the small towns in which they attend college, respectively, Pulpit Hill and Pine Rock.

Altamont and Libya Hill are not just small American towns, and not just small Southern towns, but small towns in southern Appalachia that had begun to prosper in the form of a summer resort and center for the cure of lung diseases. Like Hannibal, Missouri, through which a variety of Americans passed on their way to the Middle West or like the Mississippi River, which gave Mark Twain a chance to meet every kind of American and many foreigners, Asheville offered a cross section of America, bringing together hill-bred folk with their clannish and Calvinistic ways, merchants from the Piedmont crescent of the Carolinas and Georgia, tourists from much of eastern America but especially from the Deep South, and plutocrats from the North seeking to build baronies or hotels. As citizens of a southern Appalachian town, Altamontians and Libya Hillians were an independent sort, slow to accept outsiders, and fierce in their loyalty to the Baptist, Methodist, or Presbyterian church; quick to defend the family's good name and willing to condone killings done among themselves in the name of revenge, but instantly ready to hang a stranger who killed or harmed one of them; understanding of superstitiousness and even fanaticism, suffering from the split among themselves during the Civil War, but more from the deprivation occasioned by both national and state policies during Reconstruction; given to a love of tall tales, broad humor, folk ballads, long sermons, and opposed to divorce, public or private drunkenness, and rapid changes in their way of living.

All this is simply to say that Wolfe had a much different South to write about than did Glasgow, Faulkner, and Caldwell, though many similarities linked Richmond, Oxford, and Augusta, Georgia, to Asheville. The hold of the South on Wolfe and his surrogates was tenacious. He visualized the South as a possessive woman, a dark, clinging Helen who refused to free her sons. The golden cities of the North and West seemed to offer liberation, but ties to the South were too strong to be broken. Out of the tug between the pull of the heart (the South) and the desires of the head (the North) grew a creative tension that gave Wolfe a theme closer to that of European writers like Stendahl, Flaubert, and Joyce than to Faulkner, Glasgow, or Caldwell. All of these points receive excellent attention in Rubin's *Thomas Wolfe: The Weather of His Youth* and Floyd C. Watkins' *Thomas Wolfe's Characters*. As always, Kennedy's *The Window of Memory* is helpful on this topic as well. All of them deal sensibly and insightfully with the subject of the provincial southerner in the city.

Wolfe's protagonists see many of Europe's finest cities, London, Paris, Berlin, Munich, but their visions of the golden cities of the American North, Boston and New York in particular, provide a kind of dream landscape, a place of freedom, fame, and fulfillment, for Eugene and George in their boyhood. The paradigmatic catalogue of George's reasons for loathing South Carolina shows how fervently Wolfe's surrogates longed to sever their ties to the South. Since reality rarely matches visions, Eugene and George undergo disillusioning experiences when their great expectations cannot be achieved in the city. On closer inspection, neither Boston nor New York looks so golden, although there is gold enough to turn one's head if he doesn't watch himself. For George, the gold comes through his liaison with Esther Jack, whose wealth and talents place her in the best circles of New York society. The son and kinsman of artisans and farmers, George admires the tastes, culture, and possessions of Esther and her friends, but he comes to think of their wealth and power as ill-begotten, inasmuch as they created no wealth of their own and made money by brokering the hard-won earnings of the working class or playing the stock market. The city also reveals a definite class structure, the have-nots suffering while the haves pursue their pleasures heedless of the pain and loss of self-worth around them. The privileged class can buy and discard talent, moving from artist to artist as their whims and the fads of fashion lead them. The privileged class winks at the petty crimes of its servants and excuses the moral corruption of its peers. Although they might talk of relieving the hunger and sorrow of some distant coal miner or Southern field hand, they underpay the servants in their own employ. All of this comes to the fore in "The World That Jack Built," Wolfe's most thorough look at the forces capable of making a city glitter and a provincial's head spin.

But the city has dross as well, much of it appearing as a faceless manswarm, to use one of Wolfe's favorite neologisms, during Eugene's rambles about Boston and New York. The dross became more and more abundant as the nation sank deeper and deeper into the Great Depression, but Wolfe was not content to leave its victims faceless and nameless, hence his vivid descriptions of Brooklyn in the early 1930s and his narration of the death of C. Green, a man down on his luck, but not without his pride and a will to assert his identity in a world where men, women, and children could be thrown away.

The political problems of the city fueled Wolfe's thoughts about the nation's economic and moral history, and that became one of the weightiest themes of the final years of his life, leading him to pinpoint "compulsive greed" and "single selfishness" as prime factors in the country's troubles, and convincing him that the good will of a basically democratic nation would assert itself and that "the true fulfillment of our spirit, of our people, of our mighty and immortal land, is yet to come" (YC 741).

The foregoing list of themes shows Wolfe's alertness to social institutions, practices, needs, demands, and problems, incidentally giving the lie to the still-lingering critical assertion that he had little or no social consciousness until he came to the Webber cycle. Wolfe's autobiographical approach deceives some readers, causing them to follow the development of his surrogates so closely that his wide-ranging social concerns have garnered less attention than they deserve. To be sure, however, those social concerns are reflected through the process of discovery and initiation revealed in the comings, goings, and musings of Eugene and George. Thus, what happens to them tends to become the focal point. They demand attention because they are interesting in and of themselves and because knowing them well no doubt helps us understand Wolfe better, also.

The theme most readily associated with Eugene Gant is loneliness, a concern caught up in the Proem to LHA, "Which of us is not forever a stranger and alone?" The theme branches out to include practically every member of the Gant family, but perhaps is most keenly felt by W. O. in his wanderings, by Eliza in her lack of family support in her effort to run Dixieland, by Helen in her failure to become an established professional singer, by Ben in his memories of his dead twin, Grover, by Eugene in his inchoate feeling that nature or God has singled him out to be the voice of his unlettered brethren. As artisans, the Gants romanticize the writer's craft and isolate Eugene by thinking he belongs in the rank of the Shelleys and Lord Byrons and not in their group.

Loneliness hits George, too, especially after his family breaks up and he must live with his spinsterish Aunt Maw. His grotesque appearance further isolates him, and his life's work forces him to endure extraordinary periods of solitude, an outcome surely akin to the opening words of Wolfe's powerful essay on loneliness, "God's Lonely Man": "My life, more than that of anyone I know, has been spent in solitude and wandering. Why this is so, or how it happened, I cannot say; yet it is so.

From my fifteenth year—save for a single interval—I have lived as solitary a life as a modern man can have" (HB 186).

Forced to turn inward, Wolfe's protagonists explore their buried lives, finding them overflowing with fantasies, burdened with anxieties, thwarted by the inability to turn the right stone, to open the right door, to speak the magical word. But they don't become students of their own navels, both struggling to realize their ambitions as writers, both wrestling with a kind of demon or daemon within, as Wolfe says of Eugene, but could also have written of George: "Unknowingly, he had begun to build up in himself a vast mythology for which he cared all the more deeply because he realized its untruth. Brokenly, obscurely, he was beginning to feel that it was not the truth that men must live for—the creative men—but for falsehood. At times his devouring, unsated brain seemed beyond his governance: it was a frightful bird whose beak was in his heart, whose talons tore unceasingly at his bowels. And this unsleeping demon wheeled, plunged, revolved about an object, returning suddenly, after it had flown away, with victorious malice, leaving stripped, mean, and common all that he had clothed with wonder" (LHA 224). Within these words lies much of the explanation of how poetic rhapsody gives way to lacerating satire in Wolfe, how fantasy and myth are yoked together with some of the most brutally frank naturalistic writing in American fiction. Here Harpies dwell in the same body as a kind of Apollo or Prometheus, the creative force eager to be mankind's loving benefactor. Here are Coleridgean opposites to be resolved if readers hope to grasp the essential Wolfe.

Another set of Coleridgean opposites appears in the themes of imprisonment and liberation. On its simplest level, the level Ketti Frings stressed in her dramatization of LHA, the first of these themes treats Eugene's attempt to escape from his materialistic, bickering, insensitive family, or George's efforts to stop his ears to the mundane concerns of Aunt Maw and her Joyner kin. On a higher level, one highlighted by its appearance in the Proem to LHA, the theme of imprisonment is tied to Wolfe's attempt to deal with man's inability to communicate with his fellows: "Naked and alone we came into exile. In her dark womb we did not know our mother's face; from the prison of her flesh have we come into the unspeakable and incommunicable prison of this earth" (2). Until man finds the language to unlock his prison door, he is "prison-pent." These words in the Proem are thus foreshadowings of Wolfe's intent to explore the themes of imprisonment and liberation.

Here too are foreshadowings of words describing Eugene's state of mind when he went off to college. Eugene "was a child when he went away: he was a child who had looked much on pain and evil, and remained a fantasist of the Ideal. Walled up in his great city of visions, his tongue had learned to mock, his lip to sneer, but the harsh rasp of the world had worn no groving in the secret life. . . . He was not a child when he reflected, but when he dreamt, he was; and it was the child and dreamer that governed his belief. He belonged, perhaps, to an older and simpler race of men: he belonged with the Mythmakers. For him, the sun was a lordly lamp to light him on his grand adventuring" (LHA 391). In a confessional mood, George could well have spoken the same words.

A mocking tongue and sneering lip, a loving heart, a man of doubt, a child of faith, a scorner of Jews, a lover of Esther Jack, quintessentially Jewish in all ways but wholeness of blood: these are but a few of the paradoxes Wolfe explores as he delves into the deeds and thoughts of Eugene and George. Wolfe sought to learn why mankind behaved so much like a Janus, hoping to shed light on an ancient riddle: why is it that reality seldom equals appearance? Writing to Perkins about his development as an artist, Wolfe said, "I was a child of faith. I grew up in the most conservative section of America, and as a child I put an almost unquestioning belief and confidence in the things that were told me, the precepts that were taught me. As I grew older I began to see the terrible and shocking differences between appearance and reality all around me" (LTW 581). Exposing the hypocrisy could be fun at times when the satiric wag dislodged the poet or the objective journalist, but peeling away what was rotten to get to the remaining good, if any, left Wolfe asking himself whether he should wield the knife and what such an act cost him emotionally and socially. One justifying response argued that "this business about the artist hurting people is for the most part nonsense. The artist is not here in life to hurt it but to illuminate it. He is not here to teach men hatred but to show them beauty. No one in the end ever got hurt by a great book, or if he did, the hurt was paltry and temporary in comparison to the immense good that was conferred" (LTW 593). But this is self-deluding because it is still too self-serving, too much the voice of a defender of aestheticism. More honest is George's admission to Randy Shepperton that the "wounded faun business . . . gets in and it twists the vision" (YC 385). If the artist is truly to speak for his unlettered fellows and to portray himself as a representative American, he must paint himself as he is, "The bad along with the good, the shoddy alongside of the true" (YC 385). Thus will the artist learn to deal with humanity honestly, stripped of illusions and able to face reality.

Ridding oneself of illusions and gaining the strength to face reality come through loss of innocence and the metamorphosis that that loss necessitates. The processes of growth and change are thus major thematic concerns in Wolfe's drama and fiction, receiving close scrutiny first in MH and continuing with great emphasis in both the Gant and the Webber cycle. In MH Wolfe implies that a life robbed of its illusions leads to bitterness and nihilism. If change comes about on terms unacceptable to the hero, the honorable course is to tear down the offending society even if it means that he destroys himself in the act of razing it. Resistance to change is not so radical in the works that followed. A conservative impulse indeed remains throughout Wolfe's career, the kind of impulse one associates with great satirists like Swift and Pope, and with lesser satirists like Mencken and Sinclair Lewis. But Wolfe knew that change was inevitable, that Samson-like acts might win momentary glory but leave the world to be ruled by evil men like Judge Rumford Bland and Hitler. Battling such men with ideas picked up from the cult of aestheticism would not do. Hurling a lily at a rumbling tank might be symbolically appealing, but stronger measures would be required if the tank were to be stopped. Eugene Gant would be transformed into George Webber, a protagonist willing to do battle with the forces threatening to undermine the nation and to destroy the values it had been built upon. That transformation proceeded through Wolfe's work after he turned from drama to fiction. He faithfully, if somewhat fitfully and incoherently from time to time, traced the initiation of Eugene and George into the circles of home, school, community, and professional life. He watched them as they accepted or, more often, rejected the ideas and manners of the people they encountered. He was as interested in their egocentrism and provincialism as he was in their idealism and dreams. As an artist, he was committed to writing something that might be called a cross between a *Künstlerroman* and a *Bildungsroman*. That meant that he would portray them as artists learning through experience how to respond to the full range of human experience, from the innocent joys of childhood to the stern realities of adult life.

One of the hardest realities to confront is death, a theme revealing Wolfe's greatest powers as an artist. He pauses to describe death in the city in "Death the Proud Brother"; he inspects the aftermath of C. Green's suicide (YC); he records the shooting spree of Dick Prosser and displays Prosser's bullet-ridden body for public viewing (WR); he examines the impact of Grover Gant's death on various members of the Gant family ("The Lost Boy" in HB); he reports the quiet and bloody end of W. O. Gant's heroic struggle to fend off death (OT); and he gives us one of the greatest scenes in American fiction in the powerful and passionate narration of Ben Gant's death:

We can believe in the nothingness of life, we can believe in the nothingness of death and of life after death—but who can believe in the nothingness of Ben? Like Apollo, who did his penance to the high god in the sad house of King Admetus, he came, a god with broken feet, into the gray hovel of this world. And he lived here a stranger, trying to recapture the music of the lost world, trying to recall the great forgotten language, the lost faces, the stone, the leaf, the door. (LHA 557)

This moving conclusion to Ben's death scene shifts to a language and belief found throughout Wolfe's work, words suggesting his shared conviction with Wordsworth that mankind "came trailing clouds of glory" from some previous life. That notion first appears in WTOC and MH, but becomes quite pronounced in LHA. It never wholly disappears in later works. Wolfe simply seems to believe, along with the Welsh metaphysical poet Henry Vaughan, that men one day would "travel back / And tread again that ancient track!" To look homeward was indeed to look back to that state of preexistence, in the philosophical consideration of his most famous title. Thus the themes of death and preexistence merit joint attention.

Even though Wolfe stands with Walt Whitman and Emily Dickinson in his ability to treat the theme of death, he, like them, had a multitude of other subjects to explore, one of which was the pangs and joys of love. The early plays have a "romantic interest," to use some Hollywood jargon, as elements of the plot. Should Dr. Weaver give up his medical practices among his native mountain folk so that his wife can live in safety and comfort away from the threat of feuds and certainty of inadequate income? Would Dr. Johnson have changed his mind about selling an old plantation house to Will Rutledge if he had not discovered that his daughter was having an illicit love affair with Will's son, Lee? These questions, of course, figure, respectively, in the plots of the MTS and WTOC. Wolfe doesn't pause to explore the nature of love (or lust) in these plays, but the same can't be said about MH. There he is much concerned about the nature of love, yet he has a difficult time deciding how Eugene Ramsay and Margaret Patton should express their love. Part of the problem is that he refuses to let them be themselves: at times they are Hamlet and Ophelia, at times Cyrano and Roxanne. A further complication involves the question of whether they are really alive, and war and the forced separation resulting from it together with the deprivation caused by Reconstruction add other factors that keep them from truly being themselves, for Eugene assumes a bravado as he marches off to battle and dons the mantle of a sardonic wiseacre when he returns in defeat, and Margaret must play both the role of the girl he left behind him and the confused friend who can't fully grasp how devastating an experience war is. The result of all this imitation and shifting of roles is an unconvincing, awkward treatment of love. As lovers, Margaret and Eugene sprang untimely from Wolfe's head; they have about as much feeling as a heart of lettuce.

The novels present none of the problems Wolfe created for himself in the plays: lust is lust, and is enjoyed or decried as such; love is the most complex of human relationships, a source of both sorrow and happiness, a measure of a person's character, a guerdon to be valued above all others. These, and other aspects of love, Wolfe attempts to fathom as he presents Eugene's poetic adoration of Laura James, as he traces Eugene's impassioned wooing of Ann, the "big, dumb, beautiful Boston bitch" (OT 757), as he sorts through the threads that held W. O. and Eliza together during the stormy years of their marriage; as he tries to account for the magic and misery of the exhilarating and crushing, tender and tormented, liberating and imprisoning, beautiful and ugly love of George Webber and Esther Jack. In George's case he once more has a question, not one of plot this time, but of character. Is love enough to give him the degree of happiness and fulfillment he wants from life? The answer comes in George's letter to Foxhall Edwards: "Even while I was most securely caught up and enclosed within the inner circle of Love's bondage, I began to discover a larger world outside. It did not dawn upon me in a sudden and explosive sense, the way the world of Chapman's *Homer* burst upon John Keats:

> 'Then felt I like some watcher of the skies
> When a new planet swims into his ken.'

It did not come like that at all. It came in on me little by little, almost without my knowing it" (YC 724). Romantic love gives way to a love for humanity, especially those who suffer. After years of confusion about the goals he should set as an artist, he realizes that Fame and Love, the twin hopes of his early years as a writer, though good in themselves, are not enough. To this broader, more demanding love George now dedicates himself. The most poignant expression of that broader love appears in a novella called "I Have A Thing To Tell You," a longer version of which was published in YC. The suffering and anguish he sees in the face of the little Jewish man, whom Wolfe calls "Fuss-and-Fidget," compels George to rethink his goals as an artist, a process eventually leading him to a role as an American seer, for American social conditions now call for more than a bard, something Wolfe had aspired to be ever since he came to set for himself the theme of tracing the development of the artistic spirit in America.

That spirit would rise among one of the artisans, manifesting itself first of all, perhaps, among the storytelling Joyners or Pentlands, whose rhetorical gifts would show the way to belles lettres even as they established a tradition of folk tales and ballads. The next stage occurs in the longing of W. O. Gant to carve an angel. The frustration stemming from his failure to carve the angel accounts for some of his personal problems, but his role as a failed artist is really paradigmatic, since the industrial and commercial demands of the country leave him inadequate time and resources to develop his talent. His is the lot of the artist in a country not yet ready to support its own artists. If the nation is to have artists, someone must be brave and strong enough to step forward without the support, encouragement, and understanding needed to realize his fullest potential as an artist. That brings us to Eugene Gant, John Hawke, Paul Spangler, Joe Doaks, George Webber, or any other name Wolfe might have chosen for the artist standing at the center of his fiction. The growth of that artist would lead from the special pleadings of Wolfe's early aestheticism to the soothsaying of his final years, from "Eugene Gant-i-ness" to a soberly reflective democrat wrapped in Whitman's mantle, still mindful of Whitman's great chants for the land, yet a man such as the times demanded if the nation were to overcome its problems; hopeful rather than fatalistic, compassionate rather than selfish, openhanded rather than greedy, willing to stand firmly behind those values that had brought the country greatness, and eager to expose and excise all moral corruption threatening to destroy the democratic system. The body of Wolfe's fiction, published and unpublished, can be organized around this theme, for, in choosing to write autobiographical fiction, Wolfe had the story of an emerging artist to tell. What remained to be done was the foreshadowing, which he achieved by revealing artistic longings in W. O. Gant and rhetorical brilliance in Zach Joyner.

For the American artist as writer there was much work to be done. That work would require Wolfe to handle scores of minor themes: the names of American towns and rivers; the pounding and whistling of trains as they thundered across the landscape of America; the thrill of seeing or performing in a circus; the song and sweat of working American men and women; the joy and anxiety of preparing for opening night at the theater; the anticipation of submitting a play or novel for publication and the depression that follows its rejection; the aroma of a holiday meal; the restlessness of American youth; scenes of bridges and building; the colors and odors of the seasons; drunkenness, dreams and fantasies, diseases and hospitals, doctors, and nurses, restaurants, newspaper boys, the coming of the automobile, preparations for war, tin soldiers and militarism, fashionable shops and clothing designers, dwellers in richly furnished apartments, bums and derelicts sleeping in the streets, and Americans wondering where to turn and what to do next, now that a bright past had given way to a dark present. This catalogue is, of course, incomplete, yet it suggests how absorbed Wolfe became in his native land after discovering in France how much he needed it to fulfill himself as an artist: "I found out during these years that the way to discover one's own country was to leave it; that the way to find America was to find it in one's heart, one's memory, and one's spirit, and in a foreign land" (SN 30). That discovery was the making of both the bard, the follower of Whitman in trying to create an American epic, and the

soothsayer, the southern conservative with populist leanings who decided that he had some scolding to do and some advice to give.

References: 2, 6, 9, 13, 14, 15, 18, 19, 22, 24, 28, 30, 36, 38, 39, 40, 46,
51, 54, 61, 65, 68, 69, 76, 82.

Wolfe and His Editors

By his own admission, Wolfe heavily depended on Scribner editor Maxwell Perkins during the time he pulled together the material that was eventually published as OT. His dedication of it to Perkins, much trimmed from the first version, almost fulsomely spells out Wolfe's sense of indebtedness to his patient, understanding, devoted friend and editor. Wolfe wanted to make the dedication longer to provide more information about how Perkins had helped him and to praise Perkins for rescuing him from the floundering state that bordered on despair. That tale of rescue appears in SN, where Wolfe heaped praise on Perkins. Wolfe's candid statement of appreciation and the details about how OT came into being ultimately did not serve him well, for critics and literary gossipmongers readily pounced upon his tribute to Perkins as evidence of his inability to perform the editing tasks thought to be incumbent upon all writers of the first water. Ever since the literary gossipers had learned of the bulk of LHA, stories about how much extra work Perkins and the editorial staff at Scribner's had to do to see the first novel into print had been making the rounds of New York's literary circles. A favorite anecdote was that the manuscript was so big that it was delivered in a truck, although in the accounts less given to hyperbole the vehicle was merely a cab.

The Story of a Novel expresses Wolfe's gratitude to his wise counselor and friend, describes some of the problems confronting them and steps taken to resolve them, points to their discovery that Wolfe's mounds of materials needed radical cuts, and states, with no hint of bitterness, that

Perkins sent the book to the printer while Wolfe was absent and then told him that the novel was finished. Although Wolfe gave specific examples of the kinds of cuts made to reduce the book to roughly 400,000 words, and reported that Perkins helped him see where he was going and worked closely with him in weaving the parts together, he did not fully explain the nature of Perkins' role in playing midwife to the book. The fervency of his gratitude and his lack of specificity left him open to the serious charge that he was an incomplete artist, incapable of seeing a work through from conception to publication. The charge came from Bernard DeVoto in a review of SN in *The Saturday Review of Literature*. There was enough truth in it to cause Wolfe real pain and to set him to thinking about how he could become a more complete writer.

From his days as a fledgling playwright under Professor Baker at Harvard, Wolfe had not taken kindly to suggestions for cuts. His unwillingness to trim characters and lines from WTOC for New York producers spoiled a good chance to see that play staged commercially. His impulse was to add, not subtract. But his playwriting background had taught him a useful lesson about handling his materials: how to use a synopsis. That device, transmuted into something he referred to as his "Autobiographical Outline," served to give direction, coherence, and continuity to "O Lost," his working title for what became LHA. It would help him structure his first novel and, happily for him, leave it subject almost exclusively to cuts when Perkins settled to the task of helping him edit the novel. By the estimate of Francis E. Skipp, whose Duke University dissertation examines the editorial help that Wolfe received from Scribner's, Wolfe eventually agreed to cuts amounting to "nearly thirty per cent" (91) of the original text. Many of the cuts resulted from artistic considerations (91–92):

1. material not central to the novel's theme or outside its scope (the largest chunk, 3267 lines)
2. redundant development
3. banal or mannered material
4. vulgarity
5. excessive development of a character of limited importance
6. intrusions by the author
7. non-dramatic characterization
8. material left dangling owing to prior cuts
9. repetition

But the practical consideration of publishing a huge novel by an unknown writer was by no means slight. If the work could be seen as the story of Eugene Gant's development and emerging artistic consciousness, then a long section treating the migration of Gilbert Gant from England could be pruned, and away it went. The integrity of Wolfe's synopsis, the Autobiographical Outline, was not seriously impaired by this cut or by the others he consented to make. Nothing of great import seems to have surfaced in the editing process to keep him from achieving a book faithful in its essentials to his creative conception of the story he had to tell, the themes he wished to pursue, the symbols he wanted to use, and the characters he sought to develop. Yet, he appears to have thought the typescript more amorphous than it was, and to have been too much impressed by the highly skillful editorial hand of Perkins. He quickly saw what others knew to be the case, that Perkins was the great editor in his generation. As a novice to commercial publishing and as an author whose habit was to rewrite a piece from start to finish rather than buckling down to the hard job of trimming and polishing, (though he could and did do those tasks), Wolfe found Perkins a marvel and, more importantly, a tireless mentor. Where he was weakest, Perkins was strongest, and for LHA Perkins had the good sense and detachment to give only as much as Wolfe needed to make the work publishable.

Wolfe, moreover, had the good sense to see what he should take. But ultimately, good sense did not prevail on either side. For his part, Wolfe, overreacting to the critics who wondered if he had more in him than an autobiographical first novel, spent most of his time on "The River People," "The Good Child's River," and mythic constructions of Perkins' notion that the search for a father would be a good theme to pursue. Although a few of his letters and some of his notebook entries show that Wolfe had not forgotten the importance of a synopsis to his working process, he failed to elaborate anything as fully as he had the Autobiographical Outline. The result was the piling up of many episodes relating to Wolfe's life and observations. He was creating a logjam for himself, something that he would continue to do until he once more turned to a synopsis to break it. For his part, Perkins kept thinking of how important it was to Wolfe and to Scribners to keep Wolfe's name before the public. One way to do that was to see that Wolfe's short pieces went to *Scribner's Magazine*. Another way was to encourage him to develop a story about a train ride from New York to Altamont into a novel and to announce its forthcoming publication in the house organ. That novel was to be *K–19*. Wolfe had been drawing up a passenger list and a rough chronology for the work for a couple of years before Perkins suggested that he focus his attention on this material, but once again Wolfe went to work without a detailed synopsis to guide him. The result should not have surprised either man: a rambling, disproportionate, brilliant, and insightful piece on the confused state of Americans in the period following the stock market crash in 1929. Unhappy with Wolfe's hastily written treatment of one passenger's rise and fall during the Roaring

Twenties in an episode called "The Man on the Wheel" (an account of a boyhood friend's tempestuous life that careened to a total of 180 pages in typescript), Perkins convinced Wolfe that "K–19" was not a suitable successor to LHA. No further steps to make something good out of all the material Wolfe had written or planned to write were taken. The project was dropped, but not before a publisher's dummy was printed. (A facsimile of the dummy was published by the Wolfe Society in 1983.) Having lost his hope for another novel, Wolfe spent many months writing sketches, essays, and the short novel "No Door." All this came in a period when his creative powers were at their highest, a period beginning with the work many critics rank as his best, "The Web of Earth." Perkins declared this piece nearly perfect, beyond the need of any of his editorial skills. Good or bad as these separate pieces were, Wolfe now began to flounder because he had no compelling force to hold everything together except his desire to serve as an American minstrel. He spent most of his time writing, being led more by whim than by any outline or grand scheme or framework, and most of what he did was autobiographically based. The discovery of that fact by Perkins, when Wolfe finally brought a stack of manuscript for him to peruse, led to a suggestion that Wolfe return to the story of Eugene Gant, despite Wolfe's repeated efforts to develop another center of consciousness for his stories or a more objective means of using the substance of his life. The seed for Perkins' suggestion lay in a long note, a kind of rough outline or synopsis, that Wolfe gave Perkins along with the heap of episodes and lyrical chants. The suggestion broke the logjam.

Wolfe could now resort to his proven technique for putting a work together, the synopsis, something made simpler in his case because it had the earmarks of an Autobiographical Outline. In late October of 1933, he was able to provide Perkins with a plan, and to indicate what had been written or remained to be. That plan carried Eugene from his departure to Harvard to his liaison with Esther and beyond. Perkins now had further suggestions: the work would be too long for one volume and could perhaps be best handled by tracing Eugene's further development in one volume and his love affair and its aftermath in a sequel. Wolfe agreed to focus on the first part and began almost a year's labor revising the material on hand, writing new episodes to fill in gaps, weaving old and new together, and hashing out everything, step by step, with Perkins. For Perkins, it was the highlight of an illustrious lifetime, for he was brought face-to-face with the creative process. While their joint labors were going on, Wolfe was grateful for Perkins' editorial expertise, and he seems never to have believed that Perkins overstepped his role as editor.

But that has not been the opinion of some scholars and critics. Loudest in his condemnation of the role that Wolfe permitted Perkins to play was DeVoto. More subdued objections came from many quarters, but the strength of these less clamorous denunciations of the symbiotic productions of Wolfe and Perkins is no less powerful. One of the most potent voices was that of the late C. Hugh Holman, who argued that Perkins enjoyed behaving as a kind of general among an army of writers. Holman's image of him as a dwarf on the shoulders of Wolfe is not malicious. Believing that Wolfe's forte was the novella, Holman thought that Perkins kept him from being the kind of artist he might have been if Perkins had been content to let his genius follow its own course after the publication of LHA. Marshalling Wolfe's energies and attention back into a novel was a mistaken act of editorial generalship, Holman insisted. (*Southern Review* 13, no. 2 [April 1977]: 240–49). To show what he considered could have been a wiser course of action, Holman edited an anthology entitled *The Short Novels of Thomas Wolfe*, a collection including "The Portrait of Bascom Hawke," "No Door," "The Web of Earth," "I Have a Thing to Tell You," and "The Party at Jacks," published by Scribner's in 1962.

The most thoroughgoing examination of Perkins' generalship in the making of OT was done by Francis Skipp, who meticulously traced the production of that novel from the time Wolfe brought materials for a work he was calling "The October Fair" to Perkins until only about a third of the original heap of manuscript emerged as Wolfe's second novel. Skipp patiently examined the nature of the cuts made by Perkins once the decision came to tell Eugene Gant's story up to the moment he sees Esther Jack. He found sixteen categories of cuts made by Perkins, several of them being exactly the kinds made in LHA: intrusion by the author, lack of dramatic characterization, repetition, shifts in point of view, cuts demanded by previously excised material, and banal, trite, dull, anticlimactic, false or ineffective writing. New to Perkins' list of cuts were libelous statements, something he watched for now since he had heard Asheville's outrage over Wolfe's use of real people in his first novel. New also were cuts of material deemed excessively violent or sordid and writing seen to be an unintentional expression of a "near-psychopathic attitude" on the author's part. The largest number of cuts, thirty-two altogether, resulted from Perkins' bluepenciling of 711 lines of lyrical prose. From an artistic viewpoint, Skipp concluded, only the pruning of the lyrical passages disserved Wolfe, for he appeared more of a novelist thereby and less of a minstrel (176–210).

Basing his argument on the artistic principle that Eugene Gant would not have espoused some Marxist-colored social and political views that Wolfe expressed in OT, Perkins finally led Wolfe to see that including such political notions, important as they were to Wolfe, would be an-

achronistic (Skipp 194–97). Although Wolfe consented to the suggested
cuts, he flung the matter of their political differences back in Perkins'
face when he listed his reasons for breaking with Scribner's.

Perkins' hand was far less visible in their next project, FDTM, although
he did apply pressure to Wolfe to get this collection of stories out while
the success of OT, a bestseller, was making him a hot item in the market
place. As Perkins worked to gather up material, Wolfe also turned his
thoughts to the contents of the new book and how he could arrange
them for best effect. He wrote Perkins from Hollywood, "I think you
may be a little inclined to underestimate the importance of arrangement
and presentation, and may feel that the stories can go in any way, and
that the order doesn't matter much. Perhaps you are right—my own
feeling, however, is that in a general way the stories do have a kind of
unity and should be presented with an eye to cumulative effect" (LTW
487). Then Wolfe added something that Perkins would not have particularly liked: "There are at least half a dozen big stories I should have
written and that should be included, and all kinds of minor things"
(487). The imploring note on which Wolfe ended the letter reveals that
he was still smarting from Perkins' decision to send OT to the printer
before Wolfe was ready to turn it loose: "Now, Max, please wait on
me—don't take the book away before I get back" (488). Instead of adding
the half dozen big stories and the minor things he was thinking of,
Wolfe apparently did only a conscientious job of proofreading and revising the galleys when he returned to New York.

Except in his eventual role as Wolfe's literary executor, Perkins from
this point ceased to be a significant editorial force, that function passing
in part to Elizabeth Nowell, whose knowledge of the likes and dislikes
of magazine publishers enabled her to show Wolfe how to mine his
cache for publishable pieces. She wielded a blue pencil expertly, and
one of her most successful exercises was reducing Wolfe's lecture at the
Writers' Conference in Boulder, Colorado, to a length acceptable to *The
Saturday Review of Literature*. She considered her work on this piece important enough to lay claim to her agent's fee when Scribner's later
published the lecture, as fleshed out by Wolfe, as a small book. Generally, she reinforced Wolfe's change to a leaner, more objective style,
seeing it as the manner most likely to please magazine editors. Although
she worked primarily on finding and shaping pieces suitable for periodicals, she came to know Wolfe's plans for his grander projects well
enough to help Perkins and Aswell see where Wolfe was heading in the
Webber cycle. Without her help, Aswell might never have found his
way through the "mess," as he came to call it, that Wolfe left him.

Aswell certainly stood in need of help, for he had known Wolfe for
just over six months before finding himself the guardian of something
Wolfe called "You Can't Go Home Again," when he turned his cache

over to Aswell. But Wolfe also left a key to the treasure horde, though it was not given to Aswell at the time Wolfe set out on his fatal journey. Among his papers was found a "Statement of Purpose," which evolved as it went along into a synopsis and portions of the Webber cycle. Besides these plans of arrangement, Aswell had access to a synopsis of the Bondsman Doaks material, and a rough outline of the story that Wolfe prepared to help himself sort through his completed typescripts and to indicate what remained to be written. Despite these aids, the task ahead of Aswell was formidable, owing largely to the existence of at least three recently created protagonists: Paul Spangler, Joe Doaks, and George Webber, and variant drafts of many episodes. Some parts reached all the way back to Eugene Gant, and the point of view jumped around from first person to third. Stylistically, the material reflected Wolfe's rhetorical shift from an overblown to a leaner mode. Relationships among some of the characters changed, many characters had not been fully developed, and, most crippling of all, Wolfe had done very little work on transitions needed to move from one stage of the work to another. Aswell's description of the pile of manuscripts stacked in three wooden crates as "chaotic" is not surprising. Yet, as he said in his note on Wolfe at the end of HB, he came to understand Wolfe's method of writing as he read and as he talked to Perkins and Nowell.

Wolfe's death cut short a stage of creativity that he had grown to depend upon during his association with Perkins, long conversations about the work in progress over lunch or drinks. From talks between them since Wolfe signed on at Harper's, Aswell had learned something of Wolfe's intentions. Still, he faced roughly a million words and a contractual obligation not to alter Wolfe's words without his consent, though he could make cuts. He had a taxing salvage job ahead of him to recoup something of the $10,000 advance Harper's had paid Wolfe, and to establish himself as a rising editor.

Most responsible Wolfe scholars and critics have agreed that Aswell did a satisfactory job of commercial editing, though John Halberstadt charged him with taking unwarranted liberties with Wolfe's materials and violating the terms of Wolfe's contract with Harper's. Nearly two decades before Halberstadt's charges, published in the autumn 1980 issue of *The Yale Review* (79–94), Richard S. Kennedy described Aswell's editorial challenge and explained how he met it, asserting that Aswell began to feel "free to play author with the manuscript" when he put together YC. Not only did Aswell continue his practice of writing links, printed in italics and unacknowledged as his until "A Note on Thomas Wolfe" in HB, he also tampered with Wolfe's style and added passages of his own (*The Window of Memory* 405–06). To Kennedy's brief illustration of Aswell's editorial intrusion, Halberstadt added other examples of liberties taken with Wolfe's text and ended by labelling Wolfe's posthumous novels hybrids, a concoction of collages representing the work of both Wolfe and Aswell. To Halberstadt, Aswell was guilty of both aesthetic and ethical sins.

In order to illustrate exactly what Aswell had done, Kennedy wrote a letter to the *New York Review of Books* in response to one by Halberstadt in that magazine on Aswell's role in editing Wolfe's materials. He also published articles in *Harvard Magazine* (September–October 1981, 48–53, 62) and in *Thomas Wolfe: A Harvard Perspective*, (Athens, OH: Croissant & Company, 1983, 87–108). These articles contain representative pages of manuscript as edited by Aswell, none of them resembling a collage and, taken in the aggregate, few giving substantial support to Halberstadt's claim that the posthumous works are hybrids.

One point of agreement between Kennedy and Halberstadt is that Perkins and Aswell, who discussed Wolfe's intentions for the Webber cycle and decided to adopt Wolfe's "A Statement of Purpose" as the "Author's Note" to set at the beginning of *The Web and the Rock*, created a critical problem for Wolfe, since the type of writing promised in that note applied more to YC than to its predecessor. Rightfully, critics were quick to point out that the second half of the novel does not mark a spiritual and artistic change from the Gant cycle, nor does it reflect the objectivity Wolfe was made to promise.

Since the publication of Kennedy's *The Window of Memory*, and his and Paschal Reeves' edition of *The Notebooks of Thomas Wolfe*, careful scholars and critics have often qualified their remarks on the posthumous works by some such statement as "as edited by Aswell." Such remarks have generally been made about Wolfe's fiction but rightfully apply to MH, as I found when I prepared a new edition of that play for publication. Without any acknowledgment of his editorial changes, Aswell reduced the play from four acts to three, cut out an expressionistic interlude before Act Four, removed characters and scenes, and added some stage directions. His changes tightened the play and improved its chances for professional production, something nearly accomplished when a group named "New Stages" agreed to produce the play in 1948. Plans for that production fell through, however, and the only performance of the play in this country occurred the following year at Yale University.

Although Aswell, perhaps more out of necessity than by design, engaged in what Kennedy called "creative editing" (*The Window of Memory* 390), he could have spared Wolfe's readers and critics some problems and a sensationalized airing of his role in the nation's press, which came to be known as "The Wolfegate Affair," by being more forthcoming about how he worked to prepare Wolfe's materials for commercial publication. Had he wanted to stoop to particulars, he could have shown that the bulk of his changes were either the kinds of textual adjustments

Wolfe himself would have had to make in weaving together old material to fit a new plan and a recently renamed protagonist, or the kinds of rewriting done to provide transitions and avoid banal or ineffective prose. That he had no intent to conceal his role from the eyes of scholars or critics is shown by his careful preservation of materials, both his and Wolfe's. His failure to be forthcoming did, however, create critical problems of many kinds: philosophic, aesthetic, textual, and moral, to list the most obvious. Wolfe's readers must now ask about the posthumously published works whether a particular segment is Wolfe pure and simple or Wolfe filtered through the mind of Aswell. Readers and critics must ask whether the Webber cycle should be edited by standards applied to such authors as Poe, Hawthorne, Melville, and Mark Twain, and how, once published according to those rigorous principles, Wolfe's standing as a novelist would be affected. (Those principles would, of course, force an editor to identify every alteration or addition by Aswell, or lead to the publication of the Webber cycle as handed over to Aswell by Wolfe.) Most importantly, Wolfe's admirers and scholars must ask what steps would have to be taken to reassess the place Wolfe now holds in the canon of American fiction. A corollary question is whether present-day critics and scholars want to spend time and energy correcting the canon of Wolfe criticism based on texts edited by Aswell. In any likely measures taken to accord Wolfe's work the status of a definitive edition, the name of Edward Aswell will be closely associated with everything linked to the Webber cycle unless the material were published just as Wolfe left it. (A definitive edition of the Gant cycle recognizing the contributions of Perkins and John Hall Wheelock is both possible and necessary if Wolfe's work is to be accorded the critical respect given the writings of other great American authors.)

Too slowly for the full realization of his reputation as a social critic, seer, and artist, Wolfe's editors came to perceive that Wolfe was actually writing one big book about a representative man who becomes an American artist, and that Wolfe looked to them for the practical help he needed in order to reach his countrymen. If critics and readers were willing to think of his plan of arrangement as a device in some ways similar to Chaucer's frame for *The Canterbury Tales*, each part could be judged not only on its own merits, but also on its contribution and relevance to the whole. Had Wolfe been less naive about the practical demands of the publishing business, he could have helped his own cause considerably. To his eventual regret, he leaned much too heavily on Perkins, whose benevolence as a friend sometimes hindered his role as an editor. In leaving Scribner's, Wolfe wanted to keep Perkins as a friend but to give him up as an editor without being so blunt about the matter. In turning to Harper's, Wolfe wanted to guard against editorial intrusions by contractual agreement. The synopsis and the "Statement of Purpose" which he drew up before showing anything to Aswell suggest that Wolfe had realized that, if he wanted future works to be as fully his as his first novel had been, he would have to be guaranteed the right to take as much time and do as much talking, rewriting, and revising as his un-economical methods required. The ironic twist to the quest for freedom from editorial intrusions and the return to a synopsis to lead the way through the process of assembling the Webber cycle is that Perkins interpreted Wolfe's contract with Harper's in such a way as to allow Aswell to cut away the family background of George Webber. This ed-itorial decision made it appear that Wolfe, by starting over with the boyhood of his new protagonist, had merely worked up materials over-looked when he created Eugene Gant, or had retold essentially the same story by using another center of consciousness. If the materials on the Joyners and Webbers are read in the sequence Wolfe meant them to be, readers can more quickly and fully understand George Webber's origins, his desire to be an artist, his mistakes as a provincial American in pursuit of fame, fortune, and love, and his gaining of self-respect and maturation as an artist once he realizes the importance of his roots.

By chance, choice, or both, Wolfe's editors had a larger hand in pre-paring his work than editors ordinarily have. That fact must always be considered by anyone who studies Wolfe's mind and art seriously. Wolfe's writing methods and untimely death left gaps in his work. His editors tried to fill the gaps because of desire to share in the creative effort that Wolfe had outlined for himself and out of (mistaken?) loyalty to Wolfe and to the publishing houses they represented. The enormity of their task would surely have daunted anyone interested simply in making money. Editors with less belief in Wolfe's greatness would surely not have worked so long on his behalf for love or money. For them, it was a rare treat to be a midwife to genius, but rarer yet to give, rather than to assist with, birth.

References: 2, 3, 6, 11, 12, 13, 14, 26, 27, 28, 31, 40, 48, 55, 57, 58, 64, 68, 70, 71.

Wolfe and His Critics

If stacks of scholarly and critical writings on Wolfe were tagged according to subject matter, perhaps the tallest heap would be labelled "The Life and Legend of Thomas Wolfe." Like Poe, Fitzgerald and Hemingway, Wolfe has inspired mounds of reminiscences, anecdotes, sketches, and full-length biographies. In many of these accounts, he stands as a kind of American giant, a tall man who wrote on top of a refrigerator, drank gallons of coffee or booze a day, ate steaks and chops like they were jelly beans, whored after hundreds of women at home and abroad, carried his manuscripts to his publishers in a truck and took the parts cut out of them home in large taxicabs, held the floor for hours when he talked with people at dinners or parties, engaged in emotional out-bursts like a lion roaring, and fell into fits of laughter, most often after telling one of his own adventures. The popular press, seeing in Wolfe something of a Paul Bunyan, has helped to mold and pass on this legendary material. Wolfe, of course, shaped some of the material him-self in such sketches as "Gulliver," a piece that inspired the title of Pamela Hansford Johnson's serious study of his art and thought, entitled in the British edition *Hungry Gulliver*. Other serious critics have explored the legendary traits of Wolfe's career by looking into Alexis de Tocque-ville's *Democracy in America*. Chief among such critics is Herbert J. Muller, whose early commentary on Wolfe suggested that Wolfe's fictional sur-rogates were fulfillments of Tocqueville's prediction that "The destinies of mankind, man himself . . . with his passions, his doubts, his rare pros-perities and inconceivable wretchedness, will become the chief, if not the sole, theme of poetry among these nations." Linking Wolfe to this forecast of what would happen in American letters meant that his name and his aspirations would be tied to the name and aims of Whitman, but that's a point to be examined later. Thus part of the legend is that Wolfe aspired to be another American bard, a writer who draped himself in Whitman's mantle and spoke in his "barbaric yawp."

Biographers not intent upon presenting a legendary Wolfe have usually tried to show that his life, thought, and character often differ from the lives, ideas, and traits of his fictional surrogates. A point repeatedly stressed, for example, is that Wolfe was a big man on campus, a champion of fun and frolic, an outgoing, suitably groomed, and socially and politically involved student at Chapel Hill, and anything but the lonely, put-upon, and unkempt Eugene Gant. The fullest, most accurate, and certainly the most readable biography of Wolfe's college years at the University of North Carolina, Richard Walser's *Thomas Wolfe: Undergraduate*, sets forth the roots of the legends while presenting a lively factual account of Wolfe's days at Chapel Hill. Richard S. Kennedy's examination of Wolfe's Harvard years likewise separates legend from fact.

Biographies covering all of Wolfe's career emphasize the New York phase of his life, spending much time on his relationship with Aline Bernstein and his association with Maxwell Perkins, the former being presented as substitute mother, mistress, and muse, the latter as surrogate father and loyal friend as well as an editor willing to give Wolfe the time and help he needed to shape his writing into publishable work. Less fully treated are Wolfe's European travels, his love affairs with women other than Aline Bernstein, and his southern Appalachia heritage. The best of these full-length biographies is Elizabeth Nowell's. It and Andrew Turnbull's less adequate account have been superceded by the recently published biography by David Herbert Donald.

Most of Wolfe's biographers have dealt with the dualities of his nature, his capacity to scoff or praise, his practice of spilling his guts or sitting quietly in a corner watching a party in full swing, his embodiment of traits of both the lamb and the tiger, his Byronic wanderlust and his willingness to put in months of steady writing in some steamy or cold room in Manhattan or Brooklyn, his tendency to turn on his friends or mistresses, and his wide swings in expressing himself emotionally. If he falls short of becoming an American version of Jekyll and Hyde, he could well stand in for Dorian Gray.

These dualities of personality, some of them given more stress than they merit because Wolfe's fictional surrogates are too closely identified with Wolfe himself, become Coleridgean opposites to reconcile for psychology-minded critics. But critics from the sociological camp found them germane to their ideas about such polarities as Wolfe's love and

hate for Jews, shame for and pride in his family, and his attitude toward
the South (a dark Helen of his blood) and the North (a land inspiring
golden visions). Philosophically oriented critics spotted more than a little
residue of the Hegelian teachings of Horace Williams, a Chapel Hill
professor whose thought was a countrified version of Hegel's notion of
thesis, antithesis, and synthesis, and those critics owing their viewpoints
to ethics or religion discovered a ready way of looking at the patterns
of rejection and acceptance in Wolfe's moral and religious life by examining these dualities.

However much scholars and critics explored Wolfe's personality, they
could not explain the man without seeing him in his time and place.
The effort to do just that engaged some of the best minds Wolfe's work
has attracted: Floyd Watkins, Ruel Foster, Louis D. Rubin, Jr., Paschal
Reeves, Richard Walser, and C. Hugh Holman. Watkins and Foster
showed how Wolfe drew upon his mountain culture, Rubin revealed
how the weather of Wolfe's youth touched his thought and artistry,
Reeves explained how Wolfe's background helped to shape his ethnic
and racial views and to inform his storytelling techniques, Walser focussed on his inheritance from and contribution to North Carolina letters, and Holman considered him and his work amidst both the tradition
of Southern letters, comparing his work to that of Glasgow and Faulkner
among others, and the tradition of American Transcendentalists. Lesser
known Wolfe critics have joined in their quest to reveal his Southernness
and his debt to southern Appalachian folkways. Leslie Field in "Wolfe's
Use of Folklore," (New York Folklore Quarterly 16 [Autumn 1960], 203–
15), Richard Gray in "Signs of Kinship: Thomas Wolfe and His Appalachian Background," (Appalachian Journal 1, no. 4 [Spring 1974], 309–
19), and John Miller MacLachlan, Hayden Norwood, and Mabel Wolfe
Wheaton (with the help of LeGette Blythe) have contributed importantly
to the body of materials treating Wolfe's mountain heritage and his
fictional and dramatic use of it.

Wolfe's region, with its blend of conservatism and populism, its primarily Calvinistic theology, its views on race, its attitudes toward women
and their role, and its debates between champions of New South ideas
and advocates of agrarian causes, helped to form Wolfe's thought. Much
as the South molded Wolfe's thought, he was to absorb notions far
different from the ones espoused in the Wolfe household or in North
Carolina schools. The fact that he did explains why some critics and
scholars have delved into his attacks on philistinism, his flirtation with
aestheticism, his political debates with Maxwell Perkins, and his eagerness to warn the world about the dangers of Nazi Germany. Other critics
turned to examining Wolfe's ideas on time, noting the weight he attached
to time in The Story of a Novel and elsewhere. Foremost among these
inquiries are those by W. P. Albrecht, Carl Bredahl, Jr. ("Look Homeward,

Angel: Individuation and Articulation," *Southern Literary Journal* 6, no. 1 [1973], 47–58), Margaret Church, Louis D. Rubin, Jr., and Karin Pfister, whose study in German (*Zeit und Wirklichkeit bei Thomas Wolfe* [Heidelberg: Carl Winter Universitatsverlag, 1954] is the fullest investigation of Wolfe's concept of time and his indebtedness to the thought of Bergson, Proust, and others. Other critics have seen indebtedness on Wolfe's part to the Neoplatonic thought of Wordsworth, to the metaphysics of Coleridge, to the teachings of Carlyle on the nobility of work and the role of masters and those they govern, to the vitalism of Nietzsche, Whitman, and George Bernard Shaw, and to the socialist thinkers associated with the New Deal. Few of these studies have been thoroughgoing, although the pieces by William F. Kennedy on Wolfe's economic ideas ("Economic Ideas in Contemporary Literature: The Novels of Thomas Wolfe," *Southern Economic Journal* 20, no. 1 [July 1953], 35–50), and by Bella Kussy on Wolfe's vitalist trend will scarcely need redoing soon.

For many critics, Wolfe's thought need not be taken seriously (one critic suggested that he had the mind of a five-year-old) because Wolfe lacked systematic approaches to ideas, perhaps excepting his notions on time, and revelled in giving his emotions free rein. To look for philosophical content in Wolfe's work was unwise. But an exploration of his psychic state could yield an understanding of his failures and triumphs as a man and a creative artist. Probings began early, the most notable one by Vardis Fisher, a teaching colleague at NYU and a minor novelist (*Thomas Wolfe as I Knew Him and Other Essays* [Denver: Allan Swallow, 1963], 24–41). These probings continued to appear, the most ambitious of them the work of professional psychologists, William Snyder, who wrote *Thomas Wolfe: Ulysses and Narcissus*, and Richard Steele, who added *Thomas Wolfe: A Study in Psychoanalytic Criticism* (Philadelphia: Dorrance, 1977) to the growing body of commentary on Wolfe's emotional life and how it manifested itself in his work. From Fisher on down to the professional analysts, probes into his psychic state have drawn directly on his writings, the result of an assumption that Wolfe's work is autobiographical and therefore a reliable indicator of his mental and emotional condition. Naturally, some hedging occurred as Wolfe's psychological profile was sketched, but such factors as his family relationships, dealings with women, dependence upon and breaks from friends, and his manic-depressive tendencies have been closely linked to his presentation of Eugene Gant and George Webber.

Autobiographical concerns have indeed been unavoidably an issue in Wolfe studies. Wolfe himself raised the issue in his prefatory note to LHA and it has hounded him ever since, becoming, in C. Hugh Holman's estimate, a stigma. Critics have sought to show the influences on Wolfe's mode of autobiographical fiction, and have suggested Joyce, Proust, Maugham, Lawrence, and the British Romantics as sources of inspiration. Most critics agree with Wolfe's claim that most good fiction has an autobiographical base, but they insist that Wolfe exercised too little imagination in shaping his experiences in ways to make them germane to the human condition and universally appealing. The most damning charge leveled against his manner of autobiographical writing came from Robert Penn Warren in a review of OT. He reminded Wolfe that he would do well to remember that Shakespeare was the author of *Hamlet*, not Hamlet himself.

Many critics argued that Wolfe's decision to use autobiographical fiction and to let Eugene and George stand as representative Americans contributed significantly to his alleged problems with form. For many critics Wolfe's novels were practically formless, the only structure perceivable in them a chronological scheme mirroring his own experiences and observations. Held up against the principles of the well-made novel as sired by Percy Lubbock on the musings and practices of Henry James and certain of his followers, Wolfe's novels looked amorphous, giant cubs in need of a mother's artful licking. He would be wise to follow the lead of Hemingway and Fitzgerald if he insisted on turning his own experiences to fiction. After all, they knew how to structure their novels, and they were not so self-indulgent. Wolfe's response to that advice, given in a famous reply to Fitzgerald when he joined the ranks of those critics telling Wolfe what to do to better his craftmanship, was that he was a "putter-inner" and meant to be as expansive as the occasion demanded. As Thomas Lyle Collins put the matter, Wolfe's novels were enough to give a critic a "nightmare" if they came to his fiction from the James-Lubbock camp. Collins and other defenders of Wolfe's method saw form in Wolfe's work, a form not realized in single works as published under the heading of novel. Wolfe, so his defenders claimed, was writing one book, a book about the discovery of America, the search for a father, the development of the artistic spirit in the nation, or one man's journey from innocence to experience, a book better compared to the movements of a great symphony like those of Mahler or to a cycle of operas like Wagner's. A few critics, mostly those mindful of the Melvillean practice of finding a form to fit the content of the novel, settled for no fanciful theories and asked readers to try to encounter the novels on their own terms, as they would *Moby-Dick*. The question of form also brought forward suggestions that Wolfe should be judged only on the basis of how he had designed LHA and his novellas and short stories and sketches. Of his major novels, only LHA had gone forward under his close supervision. Its form, though not Jamesian but rather Joycean if one had to have a taxonomy, was sound. Perkins, however noble and generous his intentions were, was largely responsible for the structure of OT, and Aswell ultimately shaped the Webber cycle, even though Wolfe left him a broad outline of his intentions. Thus discussions of form should be limited to those works in which Wolfe's stamp of approval was certain. Looked at in this light, Wolfe appeared a skillful, attentive craftsman, indeed a praiseworthy master of the novella form, as Holman so convincingly argued. Holman's case had to be built in the face of the doggedly persistent assertion by Bernard DeVoto that Wolfe and the Scribner assembly line spilled forth the placenta of art, not art itself.

If Wolfe's work seemed defective in form, it erred, for many critics, stylistically on the side of excess, being rife with serious rhetorical abuses ranging from the heaps of adjectives and adverbs piled into the sentences to the incoherence of his poetic chants. His prose was called "pretentious," "strained," "inflated," "torrential," "repetitive," "wearing," "inexact," "disgusting," "indiscriminate," "overblown," and laced with all the bad qualities of the southern tradition of political rhetoric. These are but representative descriptions from critics offended by Wolfe's style. Those readers not wholly put off by Wolfe's manner no doubt would have agreed with Robert Penn Warren that Wolfe's rhetoric, though at times grand in its sweep and power, was too often tedious and hysterical. His critical defenders rallied to his cause by proclaiming his manner Rabelaisian, Elizabethan in its energy, flow, and daringness, Miltonic in its grandeur, Whitmanesque in its rhapsodic response to the American scene, Melvillean in its willingness to bend language to meet artistic needs, Biblical in its ability to catch the directness and rhythm of everyday speech, and DeQuinceyean in its handling of the contrapuntal effects of phrasing. The battle lines were clear here: lovers of the opulent style had much to praise; devotees of the Attic style found much to damn. Had Wolfe not been writing in an age delighting in a parsimonious style, as exemplified by Hemingway, the battle would not have been so far-flung or so hotly contested. Critics removed far enough from the skirmishes largely agreed with Charles Angoff, an editor at the *American Mercury* who once prided himself on cutting a Wolfe story from 25,000 words down to 9,000, but later regretted not permitting Wolfe to appear in his opulent manner, that Wolfe's force as a writer can best be felt when his style is unchecked ("Thomas Wolfe and the Opulent Manner," *Southwest Review* 48, no. 1 [Winter 1963], 81–84). That means taking all the sound and fury with the glowing intensity and sharp directness. That Wolfe was not above the broil himself can be seen in his efforts to write leaner, cleaner prose in the Webber-Joyner materials. Trying to curb his spendthrift ways linguistically, he looked to the prose of Hemingway and left most of his adjectives and adverbs in his wordhoard while cutting his sentence length approximately in half. Readers who liked the Burtonian, Brownean, Sternean flavor of his style lamented his swing to the Attic school, pointing out that the cost of a brisker style was the loss of sonority and poetic prose. In style, matters of taste clearly

dictate responses to Wolfe's manner, a situation making objective analysis of his rhetoric quite rare, but essays by Floyd Watkins ("Rhetoric
in Southern Writing: Wolfe," *Georgia Review* 12 [Spring 1958], 79–82) and
Maurice Natanson remain the starting point for an informed discussion
of Wolfe's rhetorical strengths and weaknesses.

Any discussion of style must involve a close look at the writers Wolfe
read and admired. Critics concerned with placing him among writers in
the Anglo-American tradition have connected his themes, form, and
style to a virtual host of authors: Shakespeare, Jonson, Burton, Donne,
Nashe, Milton, Browne, Taylor, Swift, Fielding, Coleridge, Wordsworth,
Byron, DeQuincey, H. G. Wells, Samuel Butler, Lawrence, and
Maugham among English writers; Melville, Twain, Whitman, Dreiser,
and Sinclair Lewis among American. It's true, of course, that Wolfe was
widely read and lectured on many of these writers in his classes at NYU.
The names of most of them appear from time to time in his innumerable
lists of writers whose work was worth knowing. The extent of Wolfe's
indebtedness has been explored piecemeal (and most of the pieces deserve and repay attention), but a study pulling all the forenamed authors
together with James Joyce to determine how and why Wolfe drew upon
his Anglo-Irish-American forebears is sorely needed. Such a study could
also delve into his forays into French, German, and Russian literature,
especially the writing of Proust, Goethe, and Dostoevsky.

As an impressionable student in J. Livingston Lowes' class when *The
Road to Xanadu* was being written, Wolfe seems to have accepted his
professor's thesis that readings poured into the well of an attentive mind
bubbled back in refreshing ways. Tracing Wolfe's place in the tradition
of Western letters has thus been a favorite pastime of many Wolfe scholars, but work remains to be done on that subject. A close study of his
high regard for Coleridge is the most pressing need.

Another favorite pastime, ranking Wolfe among his contemporaries,
has had the glamorous result of involving no less a giant of American
letters than Faulkner, whose placing of Wolfe at the head of his list
caused the ever-jealous Hemingway to snarl a bit and raise his hackles.
Following up on Faulkner's answer to a query about how he ranked
Steinbeck (or Caldwell), Dos Passos, Hemingway, Wolfe, and himself
among contemporary authors, Richard Walser wrote Faulkner to ask for
a comment on his placing Wolfe first. Faulkner's letter confirmed his
ranking and offered fuller explanation of his decision to put Wolfe ahead
of himself and the others. Wolfe stood highest, he said, because he had
tried hardest, had dared to throw style to the dogs, and had willfully
broken rules in order to get the job of putting human experience in
words. As Faulkner was to say later in Japan on the same subject, Wolfe
deserved a place ahead of him because Wolfe's work represented the
"finest failure" among the efforts of the writers in question. This en-

dorsement, first offered sincerely by a gentleman in a class where notes were not to be taken, embarrassed Faulkner's admirers and had little force in keeping a works by Wolfe in standard anthologies of American literature. For a time, nothing of Wolfe's appeared in widely adopted texts, a situation no longer true. Inclusion in these standard textbooks along with the flurry of new books containing material by or about Wolfe, has led to the proclamation that the "kicking season" is finally over and that scholars and critics can get on with seeing what makes his work tick.

That concern has led Wolfe specialists to look for controlling themes in his canon. The search has proved interesting. Picking up on Perkins' suggestion that Wolfe's subject was the discovery and celebration of America in all its manifold appearances, one critic (Frederic Carpenter) asserted that "the idea which controlled Wolfe's life and writing was the American dream of freedom and democracy" ("Thomas Wolfe: The Autobiography of an Idea," *University of Kansas City Review* 12, no. 3 [Spring 1946], 179–87). Vardis Fisher, bringing personal acquaintance with Wolfe to bear upon Herbert Muller's thesis that Wolfe belonged with the mythmakers, said that Wolfe was indeed intent on creating an American myth. That idea also appealed powerfully to C. Hugh Holman, whose "The Epic Impulse," which is reprinted as the final essay in his collection of brilliant pieces on Wolfe entitled *The Loneliness at the Core*, is the fullest treatment of America as Wolfe's controlling theme.

Two other suggestions about Wolfe's controlling themes have appealed widely to scholars and critics. Joseph Warren Beach said the central idea was "the search for a spiritual essence or being . . . the source of wisdom and strength" (*American Fiction: 1920–1940* [London: Russell & Russell, 1960], 173–93). Perhaps an echo of Perkins' notion that a good theme for Wolfe was the search for a father, Beach's suggestion was extended by Cecil B. Williams, who found Wolfe's controlling theme to be "a quest for maturity and for a virility which would result in progeny, if not of the flesh then of living artistic creation" ("Thomas Wolfe Fifteen Years After," *South Atlantic Quarterly* 54, no. 4 [October 1955], 526). Williams' idea shades neatly into the second suggestion, that Wolfe's controlling framework was the story of the development of the artistic spirit in America. Louis D. Rubin, Jr., expresses this notion most succinctly: "In a sense, all of Wolfe's novels are about the feelings of a young man who wants to write, and it is to this that so many of his readers have responded" ("Thomas Wolfe Once Again," *North Carolina Historical Review* 50, no. 2 [Spring 1973], 170).

Rubin's statement takes into account another of the critics' concerns, Wolfe's audience. Foes of Wolfe like to dismiss him and his ilk by saying that his work is fit stuff for callow youth but dreadful going for adults. Youth, they argue, relish Wolfe's emphasis on feelings, sensory experiences, the struggle to find and establish a self-identity in the family, at school, and in the world at large, the discovery that appearances seldom match reality, and the process of maturation. They are caught up, too, in Wolfe's concern for fixity amidst change and his focus on youthful rebelliousness. Young readers will disregard the manner and engorge the message, but there comes a time to put away childish things, the argument continues. In some academic circles, Wolfe's works are childish things, something to be read, if anywhere, before a student comes to college but not taken up for discussion alongside Hemingway, Fitzgerald, and Faulkner. The counter-argument is that Wolfe's chronicle of his protagonists' development can be read and discussed as yet another example of an exceedingly popular form of American fiction, the initiation story. Seen as a work akin to *The Adventures of Huckleberry Finn* or *Winesburg, Ohio*, to name only two of its class, LHA provides a rich harvest.

Part of that harvest, one not limited to the pages of LHA, is Wolfe's remarkable array of characters. Praise for his ability to delineate character, while not universal, is generous and frequent. His detractors speak of his tendency toward caricature and dependence on verbal tags, and insist that he is guilty of some of the worst vices of Addison and Steele and Dickens when he portrays a character. Critics admiring his presentation of character write about his honesty in giving the worst sides of Eugene and George along with their good traits. Who but an honest artist would give us such a histrionically self-indulgent pseudo-Romantic as Eugene sometimes is, or such an insufferable cad as George proves to be in his quarrels with Esther? Besides the honesty and the accuracy, there is plenitude. Who among major American authors drew a greater number of sketches, many of them vividly memorable: W. O. and Eliza Gant and their numerous brood, Bascom Pentland (Hawke) and his Boston office mates, Francis Starwick and chuckling Professor Hatcher, Ann, Elinor, the Countess, Esther Jack, Mr. Katamoto, Dick Prosser, the Lampleys, Jerry Alsop, Nebraska Crane, Aunt Maw, and those lively and legendary hillfolk, the Joyners. Like Breughel or Hogarth, Wolfe crowded his scenes with characters who repay repeated study because they reveal so much about the human condition. Critics complaining that Wolfe merely flipped the pages of the family photography album and rendered back what he saw there have perhaps spent too little time learning how to appreciate artists whose work appears most brilliantly on crowded canvases. What death scene in American or British literature more fully and truthfully captures the torment, regrets, hopes, and devastation occasioned by losing a member of the family than that crowded scene in which Ben Gant dies in Dixieland? Here is something broad in scope yet deeply penetrating in detail, a masterful evocation of character.

If Wolfe's art is at its highest level here, and a good many critics agree that it is, his mastery of characterization has not been the aspect of his craft that most of the writers whom he influenced have imitated. Critical surveys of Wolfe's influence on James Agee, James Jones, Jack Kerouac, and Ross Lockridge, Jr., have correctly discovered that Wolfe's themes, poetic prose, and looseness of structure drew them to him and touched their own artistic practices. More work needs to be done on Wolfe's influence on American letters, including how Ray Bradbury, David Madden, and others have used him as a character or have placed characters of their own in his native haunts.

More work remains also to clear the air about how large a hand Wolfe's editors had in bringing his work to print. The efforts of Richard S. Kennedy alerted attentive readers to Aswell's intrusions, chiefly in YC. Francis Skipp's Duke University dissertation and the articles drawn from it established the nature and extent of Perkins' role in shaping LHA and OT. Wolfe scholars have long debated, more at symposia than in print, whether the Webb-Joyner materials should be reedited or merely presented as Wolfe left them. A sensationalized demonstration of Aswell's methods of editing created a brief tempest when John Halberstadt published the results of his Yale University dissertation in *The Yale Review* (October 1980). He charged Aswell with a violation of Wolfe's contract with Harper and Brothers, which contained a clause stipulating that no textual changes could be made without the author's approval. He also showed how Aswell wove episodes together, changed the names of characters or fused two or more characters into one, and wrote additional materials. Halberstadt both overstated and misrepresented his case, said Richard S. Kennedy in a rebuttal to Halberstadt's contentions published under the title "The Wolfegate Affair" in *Harvard Magazine* 84 (September–October 1981): 48–53, 62. The popular press took up the issue briefly, with articles appearing in the *Village Voice*, the *New York Times Book Review*, and other papers. When the clamor ceased, the problem remained. WR, YC, and HB have an identity and a body of criticism built on that identity. Should that identity and attendant criticism be cast aside, or should Aswell's best efforts to follow the intent of Wolfe, as he understood it from an outline Wolfe left him and from the counsel and help he received from Elizabeth Nowell and Maxwell Perkins, be allowed to stand with the carefully added statement that the Webber-Joyner material was being discussed as edited by Aswell? For years preceding Halberstadt's piece, such scholars as Kennedy, Holman, and Rubin were already making that additional statement. The entire question is under scrutiny again by Leslie Field, whose forthcoming book from the University of Oklahoma Press sets forth Aswell's practices. Inasmuch as some Wolfe scholars demand no editorial interference at all, being willing to take Wolfe's work as he left it, the Webber-Joyner material in an untouched state will likely remain unavailable except to readers willing to travel to the Houghton Library at Harvard University to peruse it. No commercial or university press could hope to recoup its investment from the sale of a scholarly edition.

Regardless of what edition some readers come upon, Wolfe will doubtless continue to be a kind of whipping boy. Attacks began early and now and then break out anew, as they did when Andrew Turnbull's biography appeared. Among the most direct assaults was Alfred Kazin's. His barbs proved Herbert J. Muller's early observation to be true: "To unsympathetic or satirically-minded critics, Wolfe offers . . . a target impossible to miss. The most random critical shot will find a bull's-eye, the bluntest shaff of irony or wit will stick in the soft stuff of some sections of his sprawling novel [OT]." This remark, appearing in 1937 in Muller's *Modern Fiction: A Study of Values* (New York: Funk & Wagnall's, 1937): 407, is indeed prophetic if one pauses to read the words of Alfred Kazin as he reviewed Turnbull's biography for the *Washington Post* (28 January 1968): "Under all those mountains of words, all that huffing and puffing, the mad days and nights . . . Wolfe remains a cipher, a cartoon of the great American Effort, his features as smoothly heroic as Li'l Abner's." Kazin's belittling remarks carry on a tradition of sarcasm dating back to Bernard DeVoto's caustic comments on Wolfe's working relationship with Maxwell Perkins. DeVoto seems to have granted Wolfe genius at least, Kazin would have his readers believe that Wolfe was beneath the notice of sensible readers. Readers and writers sympathetic to Wolfe, such as William Styron, Anne Tyler, and Barry Hannah, see him as working at his best in LHA and are willing to grant him his masterpiece. Cultists will no doubt continue to see few, if any, faults. Thus the critical battle over Wolfe's standing, energetically waged in the past, will likely rumble on noisily for years to come.

Readers desiring to survey Wolfe's standings among scholars and critics in greater depth than I could provide here, or explore points I failed to treat, will find the following list of reviews of Wolfe criticism helpful. The list is arranged chronologically.

1. Thompson, Betty. "Thomas Wolfe: Two Decades of Criticism." *South Atlantic Quarterly* 49 (July 1950): 378–92.

2. Holman, C. Hugh. "Thomas Wolfe: A Bibliographical Study." *Texas Studies in Literature and Language* 1, no. 3 (Autumn 1959): 427–45.

3. Field, Leslie. *Thomas Wolfe: Three Decades of Criticism.* New York: New York University Press, 1968.

4. Holman, C. Hugh. "Thomas Wolfe," in Jackson R. Bryer, ed. *Fifteen Modern American Authors: A Survey of Research and Criticism.* Durham, NC: Duke University Press, 1969. Pp. 587–618.

5. Field, Leslie. "Thomas Wolfe and the Kicking Season Again." *South Atlantic Quarterly* 69, no. 3 (Summer 1970): 364–72.

6. Wank, Martin. "Thomas Wolfe: Two More Decades of Criticism." *South Atlantic Quarterly* 69, no. 2 (Spring 1970): 244–56.

7. Holman, C. Hugh. "Thomas Wolfe," in Jackson R. Bryer, ed. *Sixteen Modern American Authors: A Survey of Research and Criticism*. Durham, NC: Duke University Press, 1974. Pp. 619–24.

8. Phillipson, John S. *Thomas Wolfe: A Reference Guide*. Boston, MA: G. K. Hall & Co., 1977.

9. Phillipson, John S. "Thomas Wolfe: A Reference Guide Updated." *Resources for American Literary Study* 11, no. 1 (Spring 1981): 37–80.

10. Under the heading "The Wolfe Pack: Bibliography" Phillipson updates his survey of Wolfe criticism and scholarship in the two semiannual issues of *The Thomas Wolfe Review*. Professor Phillipson and Aldo P. Magi are currently preparing a comprehensive bibliography of secondary Wolfe materials. Richard S. Kennedy has prepared an update for *Sixteen American Authors: A Survey of Research and Criticism*. The book is forthcoming.

References: 1, 9, 10, 17, 28, 44, 47, 51, 54, 65, 67, 68, 72, 76, 82, 83, 85, 87, 88, 89.

The Works: A Descriptive and Analytic Bibliography

THE AUTOBIOGRAPHY OF AN AMERICAN NOVELIST.
Edited by Leslie Field. Cambridge, MA: Harvard University Press, 1983.

Two addresses, one of them reworked for publication in magazine and then book form, appear together in this book. The first address was given at Boulder, Colorado, during a conference for writers, and revised for publication in *The Saturday Review of Literature* and, in expanded form, issued by Scribner's as *The Story of a Novel*. The second address, delivered May 19, 1938, at Purdue University, was edited by William Braswell and Field and issued under the title *Writing and Living* in 1964.

The title of this book is somewhat misleading in that it suggests that the whole of Wolfe's career as a novelist is treated. Such is not the case, even though the second address covers much of Wolfe's life. The first address, and its expanded variation, dealt largely with Wolfe's experience in writing OT. Wolfe covered his search for a theme, his manner of writing, his struggle to find a suitable form, his feelings of doubt, his enslavement to amount and number, and his rescue from despair by Maxwell Perkins, who helped him pull everything together. His description of how he and Perkins managed to find a way to make a novel out of all the torrents of words Wolfe had written since LHA led to Bernard DeVoto's notorious charge that Wolfe had to depend on Scribner's assembly line to shape his raw materials into fiction.

The second address provided Wolfe a chance to reflect on how he had developed as a novelist, to look at the attitudes of family members and friends toward writing as a profession, to consider the climate of aesthetic thought at Harvard when he tried to prepare himself as a playwright, and to note within himself a shift away from egocentric romanticism toward a desire to become the spokesman for his unlettered countrymen as they struggled through the Great Depression.

Wolfe indeed revealed much about himself and his goals and working habits in these two important pieces, but they have great interest as well for anyone wishing to study the process of creation. As honestly perhaps as any literary craftsman has ever done, Wolfe set forth the emotional and intellectual fermentation involved in the process of creating a work of fiction.

This edition is still available in hardback and paper.

BEYOND LOVE AND LOYALTY: THE LETTERS OF THOMAS WOLFE AND ELIZABETH NOWELL, TOGETHER WITH "NO MORE RIVERS".
> Edited by Richard S. Kennedy. Chapel Hill: University of North Carolina Press, 1983.

This exchange of letters, postal cards, and notes provides behind-the-scene glimpses of the workaday world of writers, literary agents, and publishers, revealing, most valuably, how Elizabeth Nowell helped Wolfe shape his material for magazines and reviews. Over the years, Wolfe and his agent grew to trust each other's judgment, realizing that what had to be trimmed for periodicals might come back in improved and polished form when worked into the longer stretches of fiction. Nowell's talent and strength of character appear best in the work she did to put Wolfe's speech at the Writers' Conference at Boulder, Colorado, in publishable shape. When the materials she had edited for *The Saturday Review of Literature* appeared, with revisions by Wolfe as SN under the Scribner imprint, she cogently and energetically argued for her right to a commission by detailing the work she had done. She won her case. These letters show why she was later to spend much of her life collecting and editing Wolfe's letters and writing his biography. Simply put, she admired Wolfe's genius and possibly came to know him much better than Max Perkins did.

Included with the letters is a story, previously unpublished, that she and Wolfe had sorted out of his series of sketches of characters based on persons he had come to know at Scribners. Using the name "James

Rodney & Company," Wolfe was now turning his experience at Scribner's, drawing upon both his own knowledge and out-of-school tales passed along by Perkins. The character drawn in "No More Rivers" is based on Otto Hauser, a reader at Scribner's. The fact that he appears as a piano player in this story is a sign of Perkins' wish that Wolfe refrain from making characters identifiable as members of the Scribner's staff, a sore point with Wolfe since he saw both a threat to his creative freedom and a double standard at work, arguing that no howls had been heard when he satirized people from Asheville, including members of his own family. Wolfe's attempt to portray a man whose capacity to live fully and well is held too much in check by his lack of trust in his ability to control his finely cultivated sensuousness never quite hit the mark. Although the sketch was accepted by *The Yale Review* for publication, Wolfe died before he could make the requested revisions, and Perkins, as his literary executor, refused to make the suggested changes, perhaps because he saw a chance to keep an old Scribner's friend, even in disguised form, out of print.

THE COMPLETE SHORT STORIES OF THOMAS WOLFE.
Edited by Francis E. Skipp. New York: Charles Scribner's Sons, 1987.

A gathering of Wolfe's short stories, essays, sketches, and lyrical chants, this collection contains fifty-eight pieces, all of them previously published except "The Spanish Letter." Thirty-five of these pieces had not been collected. Almost all of the material came from work being done for novels in progress or from episodes or sketches deleted when the novels were being trimmed. Several of them show only minor differences from the episodes or sketches subsequently used in the novels. A few of them have characters doing and saying the same things as the Gants, Webbers, and Joyners of the novels but bearing different names. In most cases, the new family names are Hawke and Doaks, the first a replacement for "Gant," the second a forerunner of "Webber." These families are surrogates for Wolfe's own family. In these pieces, non-family members sometimes bear names different from the ones Wolfe (or Edward Aswell) chose to use in the novels.

As published here, the stories, sketches, and essays come as close as possible to the texts prepared by Wolfe (or his editors) for magazine publication. Since several of these pieces appeared after Wolfe's death, the editorial hand most responsible for them is Edward Aswell's. A few of the posthumously published pieces do, however, reflect the editorial touches of Elizabeth Nowell or Maxwell Perkins.

In preparing these pieces for publication, Skipp compared the published versions with manuscript or typescript versions and noted any autograph correction or change. If the published versions revealed cuts or deletions that were not of Wolfe's making, Skipp took the longer version as his copy-text. For this reason, some of these sketches, essays, and stories differ substantially from the versions found in periodicals. When no manuscript or typescript version revealed autograph changes, Skipp chose as his copy-text the first published form.

Arranged in the order of their first publication, the fifty-seven previously published pieces precede "The Spanish Letter." The first of the stories, one of the best, "An Angel on the Porch," won praise from such contemporaries as Ernest Hemingway. The other pieces gathered here are "The Train and the City," which was republished by The Thomas Wolfe Society in 1984, "Death the Proud Brother," "No Door," which was included also in C. Hugh Holman's *The Short Novels of Thomas Wolfe*, "The Four Lost Men," "Boom Town," "The Sun and the Rain," "The House of the Far and Lost," "Dark in the Forest, Strange as Time," "For Professional Appearances," "The Names of the Nation," "One of the Girls of Our Party," "Circus at Dawn," "His Father's Earth," "Old Catawba," "Arnold Pentland," "The Face of the War," "Gulliver, The Story of a Tall Man," "In the Park," "Only the Dead Know Brooklyn," a favorite story among anthologists, "Polyphemus," "The Far and the Near," "The Bums at Sunset," "The Bell Remembered," "Fame and the Poet," "Return," "Mr. Malone," "Oktoberfest," " E, A. Recollection," "April, Late April," "The Child by Tiger," "Katamoto," "The Lost Boy," "Chickamauga," "The Company," "Prologue to America," "Portrait of a Literary Critic," "The Birthday," "A Note on Experts: Dexter Vespasian Joyner," which Perkins allowed to be published in book form in a limited edition, "Three O'Clock," "The Winter of Our Discontent," "The Dark Messiah," "The Hollyhock Sewers," "Nebraska Crane," "So This Is Man," "The Promise of America," "The Hollow Men," "The Anatomy of Loneliness," "The Lion at Morning," "The Plumed Knight," "The Newspaper," which appears also in *The Hills Beyond* and *The Hound of Darkness*, "No Cure for It," "On Leprechauns," "Return of the Prodigal," "Old Man Rivers," "Justice Is Blind," "No More Rivers."

As suggested by terms already used to describe this collection, the title of this volume is a slight misnomer if one comes to this book looking for short stories alone. Until near the end of his career, after Elizabeth Nowell became his agent, Wolfe seems to have made no conscious effort to write short stories. Practically everything he wrote was an episode in the Gant or Hawke chronicles, a part of the big book, a portion of his autobiographical fiction. Beginning with "An Angel on the Porch" self-contained units of Wolfe's work were pulled from the big book and published as short stories, essays, sketches, lyrical celebrations of America or a season, satiric commentaries, dramatic interludes, and scenes of America and its people inspired by cinematic techniques. For this reason, *The Complete Short Stories of Thomas Wolfe* presents the many styles and voices of Wolfe and reflects most of his thematic concerns.

As in the longer works, a basic theme here is loneliness and man's inability to break out of the prison of the self and open ways of communicating with other people. Here, too, is Wolfe's focus on mankind's hunger for experience, desire for fixity amidst change, and dream of winning fame and love. Also here are the aspirations to find a father, to become a bardic singer for America, to discredit or demolish artistic aesthetes, and to explore the mysteries of man's movement through time. To this list may be added Wolfe's concern for rootlessness, man's capacity for violence, the conflict of artists with an unsympathetic public, the continuing clash between youth and age, and the dangers of greed and selfishness. Finally, here also is Wolfe's belief that few things matter as much as capturing the sights, sounds, smells, flavors, and textures of American life.

The Foreword to this volume is by James Dickey. Besides revealing what Wolfe meant to him when he first read him, Dickey shows why something kind can be said for Wolfe's insistence that some writers succeed best as putter-inners, as practitioners of the copious style. He also shows why Wolfe's practices lead to boredom and satiety. Simply put, Wolfe often didn't know when to stop. His rhetorical flights could be his undoing.

No critical estimates of this volume had appeared when this analysis was written. The best available references, therefore, are Dickey's Foreword and Skipp's Preface.

THE CORRESPONDENCE OF THOMAS WOLFE AND HOMER ANDREW WATT.

Edited by Oscar Cargill and Thomas Clark Pollock. New York: New York University Press, 1954.

Because Homer Watt liked to have a few men with the creative impulse on his staff, and because the frankness of Wolfe's letter of application pleased him, Wolfe enjoyed his professional relationship with the department head at New York University when he came there to teach English in 1924. Most of the letters blend business and personal matters, Wolfe sharing news of his travels abroad, Watt sending word about some of Wolfe's acquaintances. The tone is cordial, open, trusting. Although Wolfe was to blast some of his colleagues at NYU and scornfully rename the proud institution the School for Utility Cultures, he left Watt off his list of persons to bombard.

Reference: See *Thomas Wolfe at Washington Square*, by Thomas Clark Pollock and Oscar Cargill. New York: New York University Press, 1954.

THE CRISIS IN INDUSTRY.
1919. Reprint. Winston-Salem, NC: Palaemon Press, 1978.

A prize-winning undergraduate essay calling for a larger role of labor in meeting the industrial needs of the nation in the period following World War I, this piece reveals not so much political or philosophical astuteness as a social consciousness that would manifest itself in Wolfe's early plays and in the materials he was working on at the time of his death.
References: 40, 82.

THE FACE OF A NATION: POETICAL PASSAGES FROM THE WRITINGS OF THOMAS WOLFE.
Selected, with an Introduction by John Hall Wheelock. New York: Scribner's, 1939; published for the Literary Guild from the same plates, 1939.

Some seventy passages from FDTM, LHA, OT, and SN were chosen by Wheelock, himself a distinguished poet, to give Wolfe's lyrical prose as proof that Wolfe had indeed earned the right to be called a poet, a designation which Wolfe desired above all others. The subject of most of Wolfe's poetic prose was the sight, sound, smell, taste, and feel of America, hence the appropriateness of Wheelock's title. Wheelock chose passages capable of standing alone as prose lyrics, seeing in them and in Wolfe something close to the spirit and artistry of Walt Whitman. Edward Shenton illustrated the volume. Although reviews of it were largely favorable, critical attention has been practically nil. As one of Scribners' most handsome technical efforts on Wolfe's behalf, the book merits a closer look than it has thus far received.

FROM DEATH TO MORNING.
New York: Scribner's, 1935.

A collection of fourteen previously published stories and sketches, most of them appearing in *Scribner's Magazine* as Wolfe's publishers sought to keep his name before the public while he tried to complete a second novel, this undervalued book contains some of his best writing. His southern Appalachian background, captured appreciatively and beautifully in "The Men of Old Catawba" and "The Web of Earth," stands in revealing contrast to Brooklyn and Manhattan as presented in "No Door," "Death the Proud Brother," "Only the Dead Know Brooklyn," and "In the Park," the last being based on recollections of Aline Bernstein and Wolfe's research into New York City during Aline's childhood. The book also returns to the theme of loneliness and the buried life in "Gulliver" and contains some episodes cut from LHA, among them "The Circus at Dawn" and "The Face of the War." Wolfe's European travels and observations, now yielding many pieces, are represented by the sensitive "Dark in the Forest, Strange as Time" and the satiric "One of the Girls in Our Party." Critics agree with Wolfe and Perkins about the artistic mastery revealed in "The Web of Earth." Perkins instantly saw that not a word needed changing, and Wolfe confidently asserted that his Delia Hawke (or Pentland) deserved to be ranked with Joyce's Molly Bloom. In this short novel, Delia is yet another character based on Wolfe's mother, who wove stories out of her experiences as a child, wife, and mother in the southern Appalachians as she visited her son in his Brooklyn apartment. The richness of the story is best expressed in Wolfe's letter to his mother explaining that he had used one of her tales: "The story is about everything that goes to make up life—the happiness, the sorrow, the joy, the pain, the triumph and the suffering . . ." (LTM 181).

The book's reception was mixed, but unfavorable comments outweighed the favorable. It has retained enough commercial appeal to remain in print as a Scribner's paperback.
References: 14, 38, 40, 46, 68, 82, 87, 88.

THE HILLS BEYOND.
    New York: Harper and Brothers, 1941.

Another collection of materials, some previously published and some intended for works Wolfe did not live to finish, this book was edited by Edward Aswell, whose appended "A Note on Thomas Wolfe" provides a chronological background for each piece and explains some of Wolfe's working habits as a writer. Aswell briefly describes the state of the "mountain of manuscript" left with him before Wolfe departed for Purdue University and points west.

Included in the collection are ten chapters meant to serve as introductory matter to Wolfe's new surrogate families, the Joyners, mountain folk much like the Pentlands, and the Webbers, who resemble the Gants. Although he borrows heavily from his mother's family, the Westalls, Wolfe turns to one of western North Carolina's most colorful men, Zebulon Vance, who served the state as both governor and United States senator, for a model. Combining these traces from the Westalls and Vance with a few touches similar to the personality of maternal kinsman Davy Crockett, Wolfe gave the forebears of George Webber a link to the raw, witty, ribald, energetic, superstitious, clannish, and myth-generating days of frontier America.

Other stories in this volume also draw upon the Westall family. The best of these is "Chickamauga," a vivid account of a Civil War skirmish narrated by Wolfe's great-uncle John Westall. The other, "Kinsman of

His Blood" (earlier entitled "Arnold Pentland"), should be read as a companion to "The Portrait of Bascom Hawke," since Arnold is Bascom's son.

One story reaches back to Eugene Gant's boyhood, telling an episode that evidently once belonged to LHA. Wolfe likewise looked back to an earlier episode from LHA in "The Lost Boy," a poignant recasting of his brother Grover's death following Wolfe's visit to the St. Louis house in which Grover died in 1904. Grover's twin, Ben, receives new literary life as one of the newspapermen in "Gentlemen of the Press," a dramatic skit meant to be a part of Wolfe's vignettes of nighttime America, *The Hound of Darkness*. Also, Wolfe's autobiographical pieces entitled "The Return of the Prodigal" and "God's Lonely Man" add substantially to our understanding of his attitudes toward and uses of materials drawn from Asheville and the nearby mountain villages, and to our insight into the theme of loneliness.

The other pieces in this volume shed either direct or deflected light upon Wolfe's writing career. "On Leprechauns" provides an opportunity to satirize the nation's eager embrace of Irish literary critics and their views of American writing, and "Portrait of a Literary Critic" examines how someone like Henry Seidel Canby could learn to straddle fences as the old guard tried to find a way to accommodate the franker, blunter new authors. The deflected light came from an editorial decision to avoid using names and situations that betrayed Wolfe's satiric handling of stories about the Scribner house, passed along to Wolfe by Perkins.

The reviewers found much to praise in this volume, seeing both new directions and better artistic control. The fact that the book has gone through several paperback editions and remains in print suggests that common readers agreed with its earliest critics. Anthologists and students of narrative art have singled out "The Lost Boy" as a special favorite, perhaps because it can be effectively used to demonstrate a masterful handling of point of view. A paperback edition by the New American Library is available.

References: 2, 14, 17, 20, 22, 38, 40, 46, 47, 54, 56, 61, 62, 67, 68, 76, 82, 86, 87, 88, 89.

HOLDING ON FOR HEAVEN: THE CABLES AND POSTCARDS OF THOMAS WOLFE AND ALINE BERNSTEIN.
 Edited by Suzanne Stutman. Athens, OH: The Thomas Wolfe Society, 1985.

In the dawn of their relationship, Wolfe wrote a postcard to Aline Bernstein telling her how much he valued her letters and cables: "Your letters and cables are the chief events of my life." The cables and cards help to chronicle their affair, from its idyllic beginnings to its stormy climax and resolution into a tactfully managed friendship.

Often the cables and postcards provide only information about travel plans or arrival and departure dates, but occasionally they offer glimpses of the depth of their love, Wolfe's fear of Aline's infidelity, Aline's concern that Wolfe might not be keeping faith with his work, and their realization that their personal and professional needs would prevent a life together. The postcards helped them share, from the beginning of their affair until its breakup and beyond, their love of the visual arts. They sent each other reproductions of favorite artworks on postcards and sometimes commented briefly on the work reproduced. These cables and postcards also give information about the progress of LHA.

The arrangement of the cables and postcards follows the plan of Professor Stutman's edition of the Wolfe-Bernstein letters, published under the title *My Other Loneliness*. Here, as there, headnotes and footnotes explain what was going on in the lives of Wolfe and Bernstein when these postcards and cables were written. More than a dozen of the postcards and a half dozen of the cables have been photographically reproduced for his collection.

A limited number of copies are available from The Thomas Wolfe Society.

THE HOUND OF DARKNESS.
   Edited by John L. Idol, Jr. Athens, OH: The Thomas Wolfe Society, 1986.

A collection of vignettes about American nighttime life, this volume contains materials written (or recast from earlier materials) after Wolfe attended a writers' conference in Boulder, Colorado, in 1935. He announced his plans for the project to Maxwell Perkins by proclaiming, "I have got hold of an immense, rich, and absolutely true thing about ourselves, at once simple, profound, and various—and I know a great and original book . . . can be written on it—and I don't want some fool to get hold of it and write some cheap and worthless thing . . . I think it will be a great tone-symphony of night—railway yards, engines, freight, dynamos, bridges, men and women, the wilderness, plains, rivers, deserts, a clopping hoof . . . " (LTW 489). He launched the project by picking up a fresh ledger and scrawling on its first page "The Hound of Darkness." In the months that followed he gave much thought to the new book and started writing vignettes and making lists of vignettes he wanted to write. His plan was simple: he would capture and celebrate his nation by presenting her mountains, rivers, plains, cities, and citizens at work and play during the night under a blazing moon, while hounds bayed nearby or in the distance. As he wrote, the vignettes took the form of dramatic skits, complete with stage directions and descriptions of settings, except for a couple of pieces done at an earlier time in the fictional mode, "Night Piece" and "Walpurgisnacht," and a story, roughly sketched out, about a telephone conversation that the narrator has with a woman named Adelaide.

He found use for much of the material when the editor of *Vogue* asked him for a piece. Wolfe turned to his vignettes, recast them as a collection of prose lyrics, and sent off his typescript to the magazine, calling the piece "The Hound of Darkness," a title deemed too gloomy by its editors. What emerged from the editorial request for cuts and a new title was "A Prologue to America," published in the February 1938, issue of *Vogue*. But he had additional plans for the material: if he did not realize his dream of a separate book of vignettes he would at least work many of them into the Webber story. True to his lifelong practice, he began making lists of where he could place the vignettes. One section of the Webber story would bear the title "The Hound of Darkness," and, according to some lists, much of the stuff he had put into "A Prologue to America" would serve as a Prologue to the Webber-Joyner chronicle then in progress. As Edward Aswell took up the task of sorting and assembling that chronicle, he headed one of the sections of WR "The Hound of Darkness" and placed some of the material from Wolfe's vignettes in that novel and in YC, and one self-contained unit about newspapermen, which he entitled "Gentlemen of the Press," in HB.

The source of the materials printed by the Thomas Wolfe Society is a typescript in the William Wisdom Collection at Harvard University labelled "The Hound of Darkness," numbered b MS Am 1883 (743–747) and containing 102 pages. That typescript contains a tentative outline and many pages of text left over from the piece shaped for *Vogue* as "A Prologue to America." It also has a shorter version of that piece and thirteen vignettes: "The House at Malbourne," "The Lovers," "The Mexicans," "The Newspaper," "The House in Boston," "The Whores," "[The Boy in Bed]," "The Drug Store," "The Seaman: Dere Ain't No Decent Air in Brooklyn," "The Fantasies: Clara Kimball Young," "The Wind from the West," "The Pencil Merchant," and "The Rock in Maine." An additional scrap is a song called "The Whorehouse Rag."

Wolfe's unifying theme is nightlife in America. Somewhat like a movie script writer, Wolfe presents scenes of America in panoramic shots before zooming in on scenes of Americans talking, reading, visiting with friends, ordering something cold on a hot night, recalling the past, or making love. This approach gave him liberty to move at will and to vary the moods and actions of his characters. He could also contrast the cadences and tones of their voices as he sought to create his tone-symphony of the night.

To ensure objectivity—and, possibly, to escape the nagging charge of his inability to do anything other than autobiographical fiction—he wrote these vignettes in the dramatic mode. A couple of them, "The House at Malbourne," and "The Rock in Maine," give ample reason to regret Wolfe's decision to give up writing for the theatre. The first of these is a delightful comedy of manners featuring Foxhall Edwards amidst some strongly delineated Virginians, the second a haunting bit of lyrical drama involving a pair of lovers on the seacoast of Maine.

Also regrettable is the fact that Wolfe did not have time to complete his "Book of the Night," as he sometimes called it, for here is something experimental in Wolfe's canon, a work not written to conform to some editor's notion of what and how he should write. The design perfectly suited his talents and would have allowed him the chance to realize a favorite dream, to write a book "about the chemistry of darkness, the strange and magic thing it does in our lives, about America at night" (LTW 489).

A limited number of copies remain available from The Thomas Wolfe Society.

K–19: SALVAGED PIECES.
Edited by John L. Idol, Jr. Akron, OH: The Thomas Wolfe Society, 1983.

In the fall of 1932, Scribner's announced the publication of Wolfe's second novel, a work to be called *K–19*, and prepared a publisher's dummy for the use of the sales department. The title was taken from the number of a Pullman car on which Wolfe rode when he traveled from New York to Asheville. The novel, in progress at the time of the announcement, would have treated the lives, thoughts, and deeds of business, political, and social leaders as they returned home from a visit to New York, and would have shown what events occurred in their city as it moved from an economic boom to a bust. Too much space (roughly 180 pages) spent on one character wrecked Wolfe's design and led Perkins to advise him to turn his attention elsewhere. The dummy survived, as did the material Wolfe had been working on. Wolfe and Perkins worked some of the material into OT, and Aswell picked up much of it for YC. One of the pieces not chosen for either of these novels, an essay on the Pullman car itself, was selected for publication with a facsimile of the dummy by The Thomas Wolfe Society as its special project for 1983. A few copies remain available from The Thomas Wolfe Society.

THE LETTERS OF THOMAS WOLFE.
Edited by Elizabeth Nowell. New York: Scribner's, 1956.

This collection of selected letters, postal cards, and cablegrams covers roughly thirty years of Wolfe's life, the first letter dated 1908, the last 1938. Over 700 pieces were chosen to tell the story of his life. The letters included were addressed to members of his family, excluding those to his mother, to his teachers, friends, admirers of his work, to Perkins and Aswell, and to Elizabeth Nowell. Only a few sent to Aline Bernstein appeared in this volume. Even though Wolfe's major work is autobiographical, these letters provide a virtual mine of information about his plans for plays, stories, and novels, and they give the reader more glimpses of Wolfe's buried life, since they reveal his dreams, frustrations, joys, turmoil over breaking with Perkins and Scribner's and signing with Harper and Brothers, and his discovery of America as a central theme in his writing. Several pieces printed here were never mailed, some are first drafts of letters, more forthright or angry than the version eventually mailed, and some are not letters at all but, rather, statements or synopses for the benefit of a publisher's reader or Perkins and Aswell. Few are dull or tiresome, for Wolfe is an engaging letter writer whether musing on his next creative project or recounting his adventures while traveling.

THE LETTERS OF THOMAS WOLFE TO HIS MOTHER.
> Edited by C. Hugh Holman and Sue Fields Ross. Chapel Hill: University of North Carolina Press, 1968.

This edition supersedes John Skally Terry's *Thomas Wolfe's Letters to His Mother*. Unlike Terry, Holman and Ross reproduced the letters as Wolfe wrote them, preserving his errors in spelling, grammar, and punctuation. Included are 225 letters covering a time span from 1909 to 1938. Besides trying to keep his mother abreast of the state of his health and finances, Wolfe often told her what ideas for creative projects were running through his head, especially during his years at Harvard. He calls upon his mother to save copies of his father's letters when he realizes that fictional use might be made of his father's voice and character. He announces to his mother his sense of his inevitability as a writer, he expresses concern for her health and her losses in business ventures, and he shares with her his discoveries about his father's family in Pennsylvania.

This edition contains a calendar of the letters, a detailed chronology, and a chart of family members mentioned in the letters. It provides solid information in the footnotes.

LOOK HOMEWARD, ANGEL.
> New York: Scribner's, 1929; London: Heinemann, 1930, with textual differences.

Begun as "The Building of a Wall" in June, 1926, in England, the novel grew from an as yet unpublished "Autobiographical Outline," and was submitted to various publishers under the title "O Lost" before Wolfe settled on Milton's lines from "Lycidas" as the main title, and "A Story of the Buried Life," taken from Arnold's poem, "The Buried Life." Dedicated to Aline Bernstein, whose artistic, emotional and financial support helped him to finish the work, this autobiographical novel begins the interlinked stories of the Gants, a mountain family from Altamont in Old Catawba, Wolfe's fictional names for Asheville and North Carolina, respectively. Although the artistically inclined Eugene Gant is the central consciousness in most of the novel, the work has two "essential movements—one outward and one downward. The outward movement describes the effort of a child, a boy, and a youth for release, freedom, and loneliness in new lands. The movement of experience is duplicated by a series of widening concentric circles, three of which are represented by the three parts of the book. The downward movement is represented by a constant excavation into the buried life of a group of people, and describes the cyclic curve of a family's life—genesis, union, decay, and dissolution" (LTW 129). Eugene's story covers the period from his birth to his decision to leave for further studies at Harvard. The family's story starts somewhat earlier, since Eugene is its youngest member, and follows, in varying degrees of breadth and depth, the events having the greatest bearing on Eugene's mind and heart. Wolfe explores the forces uniting and dividing the family and examines the attitudes and beliefs of citizens in a southern Appalachian town, sometimes in the manner of Sinclair Lewis and H. L. Mencken but more often in the manner of James Joyce, the chief influence on this work, which Wolfe openly called his *Ulysses* book.

Wolfe's debt to Wordsworth, Coleridge, Milton, Byron, Keats, and Sherwood Anderson is also considerable. To this list the names of Jonson, on whose dramatic art Wolfe wrote a long paper at Harvard, and Dickens should be added, for Wolfe learned much about humor characters and tag lines from them.

The major themes of the novel are isolation and loneliness, two concerns carried over from MH and repeated in practically everything he wrote thereafter; the buried life; bondage to property, to the past, and to family; sibling rivalry; love, hate, freedom, preexistence, philistinism, and death.

A stone (permanence amidst change), a leaf (the decay and changing aspects of life), a door (the opening to both a new life for earthbound men and a return to a life before an earthly sojourn), and an angel (the creative urge within mankind) are the major symbols. The firmest tie between symbol and theme appears in Wolfe's letter to Margaret Roberts, the mother of his spirit: "I am telling the story of a powerful creative element trying to work its way toward an essential isolation; a creative solitude; a secret life . . . In a way, the book marks a progression toward freedom; in a way toward bondage—but this does not matter: to me one is as beautiful as the other" (LTW 111).

Structurally, the novel has three parts: Part I, chapters I–XIII, focuses on the family and Eugene's developing sense of his place in it; Part II, chapters XIV–XXVII, broadens to include the townfolk, the travels of various members of the Gant family, and Eugene's discovery of the beauty and power of the word under the guidance of his teacher, Margaret Leonard; Part III, chapters XXVIII–XL, takes Eugene away to college and brings him home to Altamont to fall in love with Laura James, to witness the death of his brother Ben, and to make a decision about his future after graduation. Wolfe's own image of concentric circles is the best way to visualize the structure. For most critics, the outer circle holds the least interest, largely because Eugene's college life lacks the verve, power, and conflict of his earlier experiences, but that circle does contain one of Wolfe's greatest scenes, the death of Ben.

As Wolfe knew and as his readers quickly discovered, the characters in LHA created a vortex, the compelling force that took the place of plot and suspense in holding the attention of readers. Caught in the swirl of conflicting needs and drives are W. O. Gant, more often drunk on rhetoric than whiskey, whose love of food, a roaring fire, and great passages from plays and poems puts him at odds with his wife, Eliza, whose stinginess, obsession with buying and selling property, and decision to run a boardinghouse threaten to break the family asunder. The Gant children find themselves characterized as either Gants or Pentlands, Eliza's mountain clan, as they grow up, or they begin to choose sides and berate their siblings for showing traits of one family line or the other. Steve, the eldest, inherits his father's wanderlust but not his love of steady, productive work; Daisy, the older daughter, has something of her mother's studiousness and quiet manner; Helen, tall and fun-loving and frustrated by her inability to push her singing career further, has a special knack for reaching W. O. during his binges; Ben, laconic, satiric yet idealistic, cursed by poor health and eager to help Eugene see that he must escape the family's narrow views and bickerings if he is to become the artist he longs to be, looks beyond the family and tries to avoid taking sides; Grover, Ben's twin, has a spiritual quality, almost an angel-like air about him, and his death, by typhoid in St. Louis, takes something very precious out of Eliza's life, a void she tries to fill by dealing in real estate and running Dixieland; Luke, a happy-go-lucky Gant with a Pentland's joy in wheeling and dealing, laughs loud and often, serves as peacemaker and clown, and lacks the power to look inward; Eugene, kept a baby by Eliza, a partner in her bed until his ninth year, keenly feels the split in the family when Eliza leaves W. O.'s roof to run Dixieland, and he discovers a mother of his spirit,

Margaret Leonard, when his writing ability enables him to enroll in her private school. Because Wolfe tried hard to catch something of Joyce's Stephen Dedalus in Eugene and to present him as a potential aesthete and artist, Wolfe eventually came to detest the "Eugene Gant-i-ness" of this character and created other surrogates to take his place.

These family members were, in Wolfe's view, epical and tragic, grand and petty, loathsome and loveable, in short, very human if somewhat larger than life, but they were not the only sharply etched characters in the novel. Its pages are crowded with other memorable names: Queen Elizabeth, town madam, Horse Hines, the undertaker, Hugh McGuire, a drunken surgeon, Margaret Leonard, the frail teacher whose love of poetry leads Eugene to a sense of beauty that otherwise might never have been his, and Laura James, whose summer romance with Eugene enables him to see that love is not raw lust.

Generically, LHS can be typed with almost equal ease as a lyric novel, a *Bildungsroman*, a prose romance, and an autobiographical novel. Wolfe's disclaimer in "To the Reader" that "all serious work in fiction is autobiographical" should be taken as a blatant example of begging the question.

After a slow start in the marketplace, LHA began to enjoy steady sales in the 1930s and reached its peak in the 1960s, averaging over 43,000 copies a year during that decade. it has never been out of print. Deluxe editions by Franklin Mint and Oxmoor House and economical paperbacks are available.

References: 1, 6, 13, 14, 21, 22, 24, 28, 29, 31, 33, 34, 35, 36, 38, 40, 41, 43, 44, 46, 47, 49, 50, 51, 52, 54, 55, 56, 58, 61, 62, 63, 64, 65, 67, 68, 70, 72, 74, 76, 78, 79, 81, 82, 83, 86, 87, 88, 89.

MANNERHOUSE.
> Edited by Louis D. Rubin, Jr., and John L. Idol, Jr. Baton Rouge: Louisiana State University Press, 1985.

A significant stage in Wolfe's creative growth, MH appeared in 1948, cut from four acts to three by Edward Aswell and slightly altered to make the play easier to produce. For example, an old dog used as a symbol of servitude and loyalty is given the boot. Wolfe has Eugene read this play to his wealthy Hudson River friends and allows him to do a critique, faulting the play for its derivative qualities (from Shakespeare, Rostand, Chekhov) and taking pride in its satiric blows at southern "falseness, hypocrisy, and sentimentality" and its treatment of the conflict between youth and age (OT 546).

Begun in 1921 and based partly on a story told by his father about the sale of timberland in the Reconstruction Era by an impoverished western North Carolina family, the play went through several drafts, bearing such titles as "The Heirs," "The House," "The Wasters," and "The House at Belmont" before receiving its present one. A version carried to Paris disappeared when Wolfe's valise was stolen. He rewrote the play in France and made shifts in time, theme, and characterization.

His letter accompanying the play when he submitted it to the Neighborhood Playhouse in 1926 spells out his change of plans: "I wanted to write a play that should describe a cycle in our native history—I should show it by the rise and fall of a powerful Southern family. I was going to call it "The Wasters." I made a draught of it and destroyed it. Later, still significant, I called it 'The House'—my house was to be the symbol of the family's fortune—you saw it put up and torn down." As rewritten in Paris, the play "became the mould for an expression of my secret life, of my own dark faith, chiefly through the young man, Eugene. If you would know what that faith is, distilled, my play tries to express my passionate belief in all myth, in the necessity of defending and living not for truth—but for divine falsehood" (LTW 103–4).

The new element alluded to here is Wolfe's belief in preexistence, a theme he would treat much more fully in LHA. Much remained, however, from his earlier concerns about the South and the reasons for its rise and fall. Early drafts of the play show Wolfe's efforts to turn some of the doctrines of the New South as absorbed at the University of North Carolina to use, sometimes seriously, sometimes sardonically, by having the aristocratic Ramsays, as he finally called his symbolic family, try to carry on the old manner of living amidst the ruins of the South. Thinking themselves too good to labor in the soil, some of the Ramsays opt to sell off timberland to raise cash, but Eugene argues for holding on to the land and working it by himself or together with sharecroppers. In time, Eugene becomes like Hamlet, unable to act in the face of the great challenge before him. He, too, becomes one of the wasters. He begins to believe with his father and brother that some providential plan decrees that there be masters and slaves. Not all of this material found its way into the final draft of the play, but it surely helps to understand his further remark to the Neighborhood Playhouse producers: "I tell you again, this thing came out of me—even in its fierce burlesquing of old romanticism, it defends the thing it attacks" (LTW 104).

The setting of the play is the Ramsay plantation home, except for the Prologue, which shows the house under construction by newly imported slaves; the time, again except for the Prologue, is the eve of the opening of the War Between the States and a few years of Reconstruction. The chief persons in the play are General and Mrs. Ramsay, their sons, Ralph and Eugene; Major Patton and his daughter, Margaret; Tod, a loyal slave, and Porter, a Snopes-like white man whose industry and thrift enable him to buy the Ramsay estate, but whose uncouthness and greed doom the New South to philistinism of the worst hue, for it is he and his kind who will shape the region's future.

The military mind of the South and its hankering after the medieval world as created by Sir Walter Scott are the chief targets of Wolfe's burlesque. Major Patton, founder of, and commander at, a military academy where Eugene has received his training and has watched his classmates volunteer en masse to fight for the honor and glory of the South, draws upon himself all the barbs that the disillusioned Eugene is capable of hurling.

General Ramsay's creed owes much to Thomas Carlyle and those antebellum Southern preachers who believed that God created some men to rule, others to serve. Eugene rejects the creed but marches off to war because he follows the man. In short, like many Rebels, Eugene fought out of loyalty to blood, not to creed.

Loyalty is indeed a central issue in the play, figuring prominently in the Prologue and remaining as a major force in the climax, when Tod, a descendant of the sullen, rebellious Black subdued and mastered in the Prologue, comes to Eugene's aid as the pillars of the old home are pulled down in the final scene.

Clearly foreshadowing a major theme of LHA, Wolfe attempted both to reveal Eugene's buried life and to pose the question of preexistence. Considered as the stuff of theatre, Wolfe's treatment of this material is not effectively handled, largely because the expressionistic elements used to present this theme sit uncomfortably among the realistic scenes making up the bulk of the play. Seeing this difficulty, Aswell chose to cut out an expressionistic interlude in the edition published in 1948.

The trimmed version almost came to the boards when Aswell sold production rights to a company called "New Stages" in 1948, but the only American performance to date occurred May 5–7, 1949, at Yale University. A German translation using a narrator to link the elaborate stage directions and the dramatized portions enjoyed considerable success in post-World War II Germany. The Prologue brought Wolfe much praise at Harvard when he was writing the play and still makes good theatre. It is his best piece of dramatic art.

The edition published by LSU Press is based on the face copy of the play, the typescript Wolfe sent to various producers and apparently gave to Aline Bernstein when no one wanted to stage his play. It is still in print.

References: 21, 34, 40, 46, 54, 68, 76, 82.

THE MOUNTAINS: A PLAY IN ONE ACT and THE MOUNTAINS: A DRAMA IN THREE ACTS AND A PROLOGUE.

> Edited by Pat M. Ryan. Chapel Hill: University of North Carolina Press, 1970.

Although it was produced at Harvard, *The Mountains* owes much to the folk play and to Wolfe's work with the Carolina Playmakers. Its reception at Harvard disheartened him and left him open to mockery because he had made such an issue out of mountains as physical barriers to the outside world. But he had started the play with high hopes.

He told his mother, "It is the real thing and deals with a great tragedy, the tragedy of a fine young man who returns to his mountains with fine dreams and ideals of saving his people. It is not a feud play altho the feud is used. The tragedy of the play is the tragedy of this fine young man fighting against conditions that overcome him and destroy him in the end" (LTM 17).

The setting is western North Carolina, the major characters a young doctor and his family, and grudge-bearing neighbors who cannot forget a dispute over property lines, and the time is the present. The action centers around Richard Weaver and his goal of rendering treatment to everyone needing the attention of a physician, and his eventual choice to stand with his kinsman when fighting breaks out once again.

The short version was produced by the 47 Workshop on 25 January 1921, the long version on 21–22 October of the same year. Evidently, Wolfe never tried to find a commercial producer.

Compared to his early plays at Chapel Hill, MTS shows marked improvement in structure, a firmer sense of plot, a deeper grasp of character, and more ease and naturalness in handling dialogue.

Reference: The Introduction of Pat Ryan is the best source of information and critical evaluation.

MY OTHER LONELINESS: LETTERS OF THOMAS WOLFE AND ALINE BERNSTEIN.

Edited by Suzanne Stutman. Chapel Hill: University of North Carolina Press, 1983.

Only four of the approximately sixty letters by Wolfe had been previously published in the Nowell edition of his letters. This edition contains no postal cards or cablegrams, which are published separately as a special project of The Thomas Wolfe Society. The correspondence offers a record of a love affair that moved from near rapture to recrimination to restive acceptance of separate lives. Beyond that, it provides particularly valuable information on the writing of LHA, revealing how Wolfe conceived and wrote the novel and showing how Bernstein's financial and artistic support helped him to see the novel through from conception to publication. These letters also give glimpses into Bernstein's own fictionalization of the affair and Wolfe's critical response to her efforts.

More so than WR and YC, this correspondence reveals that both Bernstein and Wolfe ignored or undervalued early danger signals in their relationship. For example, Wolfe wrote within a few months of meeting Bernstein: "Whoever touches me is damned to burning. You are a good great beautiful person—as faithful here as this hot life has let you be— but eternally true and faithful to yourself and all others in the enchanted islands where . . . our real ages tick out their beautiful logic." She wrote to him: "I will most likely have to stay at home to see the New Year in with what is left of my family, they would be frightfully hurt if I didn't, but I could be with you the rest of the time, and if we had the facilities I would cook you a New Year dinner."

The correspondence strengthens the charge of caddishness on Wolfe's side, but it gives support also to the charge of possessiveness on Bernstein's. These letters supplement the fictional accounts of both writers by going behind the joy, hope, rewards, and inspiration of their early love and the anguish, resentment, anger, and despair triggered by forces, internal and external, too strong to allow their love to fulfill itself.

A NOTE ON EXPERTS: DEXTER VESPASIAN JOYNER.
New York: House of Books, 1939.

A satiric portrait of a pretentious young man named Dexter Vespasian Joyner and a sketch of a sports writer published in a limited edition of 300 copies, this fragment comes from the cycle of Webber-Joyner materials on which Wolfe was working before his death. Perkins selected the material.

Presumably, Wolfe intended to show how one of the Joyner clan became a snob and aesthete after leaving the farm for town and gown. References: See my article in *Studies in Short Fiction* 11, no. 4 (Fall 1974): 395–98.

THE NOTEBOOKS OF THOMAS WOLFE.
Edited by Richard S. Kennedy and Paschal Reeves. Chapel Hill: University of North Carolina Press, 1970.

Beginning in 1926, Wolfe kept pocket notebooks, recording a wide variety of experiences, snatches of overheard conversation, lists of books bought or read, numbers of cities and countries visited, miles traveled, women slept with or on the list to be slept with if the opportunity arose, names of authors he admired, drafts of letters he planned to write, schemes for organizing material already written and schemes for organizing material yet to be worked up, portions of episodes underway or planned, lists of paintings seen in museums, reminders of chores to be done or engagements to be kept, and descriptions of persons and places.

The notebooks reveal both the man and the artist and are essential reading for anyone wanting to understand either or both.

OF TIME AND THE RIVER.
New York: Scribner's, 1935; London: Heinemann, 1935.

Wolfe's only bestseller, OT brought him the fame for which he yearned and high praise from important critics, many of whom called him the worthy successor of Whitman and Melville, but it also stirred up his foes, especially after Wolfe's account of how he and Maxwell Perkins worked together to reduce Wolfe's heaps of material to publishable limits. The account appeared in *The Saturday Review of Literature* as "The Story of a Novel," and served as the horse that Bernard DeVoto chose to ride when he tilted against Wolfe's creative methods and editorial dependence. Better than his critics, Wolfe knew how far he had missed doing all he had planned for the work, fighting his editor at every turn over suggested cuts or desired additions, not wanting to go to press for another season, and feeling put-upon when Perkins sent the novel to the printer without his consent. Without the help of Perkins and John Hall Wheelock, the novel would not have seen print, for Wolfe stopped reading galley proofs and undertook correcting errors only when the book was within covers. For all his doubts about it and its numerous faults, OT confirmed Wolfe's standing as a major American writer. Modern critics now find in it some of Wolfe's best writing, and much of his worst.

It is thematically akin to LHA in tracing the development of Eugene's loneliness, buried life, desire to be an artist, and his hope of finding the resources within himself to make his own way in the world. It also resembles LHA in its concern for boosterism, the conflict between youth and age, the restless, wandering spirit of Americans, and death. To these themes Wolfe adds a Faustian hunger for knowledge and experience, the dreams and foibles of aspiring playwrights, the adventures and misadventures of American expatriates in Paris, the inarticulateness of some Boston youths, and a young man's discovery of love. However, the most important thematic discovery is something suggested by Perkins, the search for a father, which Wolfe saw as appropriately applying both to a father of spirit, mind, and heart and to a fatherland, in this case, America. That theme would link him not only to Joyce, and beyond Joyce to classical and Renaissance myth, but also to Walt Whitman. Now that his theme embraced a young man's odyssey for knowledge and self-understanding and the face of a nation as well, Wolfe could sing as much as he liked and cram his catalogue as full as he wished.

That thematic expansiveness accounts in part for the loose and open structure of the novel. Eugene's odyssey provides the narrative thread, a major exception being the death of W. O., which Eugene does not witness. The journey motif is broken down into eight unequal parts: Book I, chapters I–VI, entitled "Orestes: Flight Before Fury," narrates Eugene's departure from Altamont, train ride across Virginia, visit to his father's hospital room in Baltimore, and his farewell to W. O.; Book II, chapters, VII–XXXVIII, "Young Faustus," tells the story of Eugene's meeting of Francis Starwick, his study of playwriting with Professor Hatcher (George Pierce Baker) and a group of aspiring dramatists, some of them of the aesthetic sort, visits with Uncle Bascom Pentland, and the manner of W. O.'s dying from Helen's mouth; it also describes Eugene's hunger for knowledge and experience; Book III, chapters XXXIX–XLV, "Telemachus," recounts Eugene's return to Altamont while he awaits word on a play being considered for production in New York, and a drunken ride through South Carolina that leads to a brief incarceration and a transcendent moment of vision about the role of the writer; Book IV, chapters XLVI–LXVII, "Proteus: The City," covers Eugene's efforts to establish himself as a playwright and teacher in New York City, which he finds both exhilarating and intimidating; his friendship with a rich young man from the Hudson River social circles, Joel Pierce, stands in contrast to his relation to a poor Jewish student in Eugene's literature course; Book V, chapters LXVIII–LXXXIX, "Jason's Voyage," follows Eugene's trip to England, where he sees London and Oxford, and to France, where he encounters Francis Starwick and two Boston women, with one of whom, Ann, he falls in love. Starwick's decadence leads Eugene to cast his old friend aside, declaring him and his kind to be the mortal enemies of the true artist, whose highest joy is his work. Book VI, chapters XC–XCV, "Antaeus: Earth Again," brings Eugene to the French countryside where he encounters, first, a peasant family and then a countess and marquise who take him for a newspaper reporter; Book VII, chapters, XCVI–CI, "Kronos and Rhea: The Dream of Time," reveals an important discovery, an epiphany, occurring in Tours: if he would be a writer, Eugene must record the memories and images flowing like a river from his childhood onward and marking his unmistakably as an American; his work must be a tireless, honest attempt to present those moments in time that created his store of images and memories of home, of America. Book VIII, chapter CII, "Faust and Helen," describes the ship taking Eugene back to America, and gives a brief glimpse of the woman destined to become his lover.

The mythological names, once intended to enter more fully and meaningfully in the fabric of the story both as an echo of and tribute to Joyce, and also as a device to suggest the universality of his protagonist's odyssey, are mostly suggestive of parallels. Richest in their suggestiveness are Faust and Telemachus, whose hunger for knowledge and search for a father, respectively, have the most direct bearing on Eugene's quest.

Although it is plotless in the usual sense, the novel does have a unifying narrative flow, a movement describing "the period of wandering and hunger in a man's youth" (SN 77). This flow corresponds to both the title and the pattern of symbols. The movement through time has, in Wolfe's words, three elements: "The first and most obvious as an element of actual present time, an element which carried the narrative forward, which represented characters and events as living in the present and moving forward into an immediate future. The second element was of past time, one which represented these same characters as acting and being acted upon by all the accumulated impact of man's experience . . . In addition . . . there was a third which I conceived as being time immutable, the time of rivers, mountains, oceans, and the earth; a kind of eternal and unchanging universe of time against which would be projected the transience of man's life . . . " (SN 51–52). In this context, the river is clearly a symbol of change and flow, having both a temporal and spatial significance.

Not even LHA is so densely packed with memorable characters as is this crowded novel, which adds to the epical, humorous, and tragic Gants a host of other vividly drawn characters: Francis Starwick, Professor Hatcher and his fledgling playwrights, Uncle Bascom Pentland, Robert Weaver, Jimmy Murphy, Genevieve Simpson, Miss Potter, Miss Flitcroft, Mr. Cram, Abe Jones, Joel Pierce and his family, Elinor, Ann, the Countess, the Marquise, and Altamont leaders and university students in New York. Like Jonson and Dickens, Wolfe found the telling feature, the identifying verbal tag for his minor characters and pushed beyond the reach of Sinclair Lewis, another of his literary forebears, to render his major characters with a far greater depth of insight and understanding. If unwilling to grant him success on any other count, most critics admit that Wolfe's skill in characterization shows to best advantage in this long novel.

Whether to call it a novel or something else has been an enduring problem. On its appearance, a reviewer for *Time* said, "In form it is variously a narrative, an epic, a diatribe, a chronicle, a psalm, but in essence it is a U. S. voice." Other early critics called it a "patchwork of stories," a "picaresque novel," a "rhapsody," and a series of notes from which a novel might have been developed, this last remark coming from Robert Penn Warren. Attempting to list all its generic variety as he sought a better descriptive term, which he finally offered as "thesaurus," Richard S. Kennedy wrote, "The generic mixture . . . is remarkable: novel, essay, choral ode, descriptive travelogue, oratorical discourse, dramatic vignette, cinematographic montage" ("Thomas Wolfe's Fiction: The Question of Genre," in *Thomas Wolfe and the Glass of Time*, edited by Paschal Reeves. Athens, GA: University of Georgia Press, 1971, p. 25). Since it is a sequel to LHA, it might also be profitably considered a lyric novel or a *Bildungsroman* at its core, with other elements added. Like *Moby-Dick*, the novel assumed the form it had to have for the story and impressions Wolfe had to share.

In style OT is more varied than LHA, which had poetic touches blended with oratorical overtones that reminded readers not only of Joyce but of some of the Elizabethan masters as well. Some readers of the first novel had found Wolfe verbose, copious, rhetorical, and repetitive. Complaints on all these counts became louder and more frequent when OT appeared, for Wolfe seemed to want to try practically every stop in both prose and poetry. He now seemed Joycean, Elizabethan, Whitmanesque, Melvillian, DeQuinceyian, and Rabelaisian as critics sought to label his writing. These labels were just other words for the verve, energy, sonority, power, fullness and richness of metaphor, taste for new coinages and combinations, and use of chants and catalogues in the book. These comparisons were not meant to suggest that Wolfe's style was a derivative hodgepodge; rather, they pointed to the traditions within which Wolfe worked as he developed a distinctive style of his own, one now most often censured for its prolixity and unevenness. By now everyone knew that Wolfe was a "putter-inner" and not a "taker-outer," as he later described himself to Scott Fitzgerald.

OT is still available in paperback from Scribner's.

References: 6, 9, 11, 13, 14, 22, 25, 27, 30, 38, 39, 40, 42, 44, 46, 51, 52, 54, 57, 58, 64, 65, 68, 71, 76, 82, 85, 89.

THE RETURN OF BUCK GAVIN: THE TRAGEDY OF A MOUNTAIN OUTLAW.

In Frederick H. Koch, ed. *Carolina Folk-Plays*, Second Series. New York: Holt, 1924.

Written "on a rainy night . . . in three hours" (LTW 68), When Wolfe was seventeen, this folk play stands as Wolfe's first publication since leaving behind the magazines and the newspaper at the University of North Carolina. It was published together with other pieces done by members of the folk-play group working under Frederick Koch.

Wolfe acted the role of the title character when the play was staged at Chapel Hill. Inspired by a newspaper clipping, Wolfe tells the sentimental story of an outlaw risking his life to place flowers on the grave of a friend. He uses the dialect of southern Appalachia, and he tries to capture something of the flavor of life in a backwoods mountain home. Both characterization and and action are shallow.

Except for *The Streets of Durham*, like other plays written at Chapel Hill, this play has not been reprinted.

References: 34, 40, 83.

THE SHORT NOVELS OF THOMAS WOLFE.
>   Edited by C. Hugh Holman. New York: Charles Scribner's Sons, 1961.

Five of Wolfe's short novels appear in this collection, three of them as they first appeared in *Scribner's Magazine*: "A Portrait of Bascom Hawke" (April 1932), "The Web of Earth" (July 1932), and "The Party at Jack's" (May 1939). A major portion of "No Door" had also appeared first in *Scribner's* (July 1933) under the title "No Door" and the rest of the story as Wolfe had written it came out in *Scribner's* under the title "'The House of the Far and Lost" (August 1934). The fifth work, "I Have A Thing To Tell You," was published by *The New Republic* in its issues of March 10, 17, and 24, 1937.

In his introductory remarks and headnotes, Holman gives background information about each piece, explaining when they were written and where Wolfe intended to put them in the "big book" he was writing. Holman reassembles "No Door" and presents it as Wolfe meant it to be published. He finds it an impressive accomplishment, an achievement distorted by the fact that the work was broken up for publication. Readers who want to experience this short novel as Wolfe conceived and wrote it must turn to this collection if they want a convenient source. Holman also here makes his case, a persuasive one indeed, that Wolfe's forte was the short novel. This collection is still in print.
Reference: 28.

A STONE, A LEAF, A DOOR: POEMS BY THOMAS WOLFE.
>   Selected and arranged in verse by John S. Barnes. New York: Charles Scribner's Sons, 1950.

Akin in spirit and intent to John Hall Wheelock's collection of poetic passages from Wolfe's novels, this volume of "found" poems draws upon both the Gant and the Webber cycle. The book represents Wolfe's themes and moods fairly. Reviewers reacted favorably to the book, finding the arrangement into lines largely consistent with Wolfe's cadences and rhythms. To the reviewers, Wolfe most obviously resembled Whitman and the Hebrew mystics.

The hardback edition is still in print.

THE STORY OF A NOVEL.
>   New York: Scribner's, 1936.

An outgrowth of a forthright and stirring speech given at the University of Colorado Writers' Conference on 6 August 1935, this bit of autobiography ranks as one of the best records of Wolfe's creative strengths and weaknesses, and as one of the most revealing statements about the creative process in general. A trimmed version of the talk, as edited for publication by Elizabeth Nowell, appeared in three installments in *The Saturday Review of Literature*, December 14, 21, 28, 1935. For the Scribner's edition of the following year, Wolfe restored the full text of the address and did some polishing. A mild argument with Perkins arose when the price set for the book was higher than Wolfe thought it would be.

The book reports Wolfe's struggle to write a worthy successor to LHA, reveals much about his working habits, describes how his family viewed the life of a writer, and narrates how Maxwell Perkins showed him how to knit a mass of material together to continue the story of Eugene Gant. It goes on to express Wolfe's gratitude to Perkins for the advice and editorial help in preparing OT for the press.

Wolfe's candor left him open to attack, the most pointed of which came from Bernard DeVoto, whose review of the book charged that Wolfe was an incomplete artist who had become a part of an assembly line at Scribner's.

The book was published together with Wolfe's speech at Purdue University as *The Autobiography of an American Novelist*, as edited by Leslie Field for Harvard University Press, 1983. The version as published by Scribner's is still in print.

References: 3, 6, 11, 13, 14, 16, 22, 27, 40, 46, 54, 58, 70, 71, 76.

THE STREETS OF DURHAM OR DIRTY WORK AT THE CROSS ROADS: A TRAGEDY IN THREE MUDDY ACTS.
Edited by Richard Walser. Raleigh, NC: Wolfe's Head Press, 1982.

A reprinting of a humorous undergraduate skit first published in the *Tar Baby*, a humor magazine at the University of North Carolina, this high-spirited farce pokes fun at the street system in the town where Wolfe carried newspaper and magazine copy to be printed and where Trinity College, now Duke University, was located. Filled with topical as well as literary allusions, the farce shows why Wolfe was a popular speaker and humorist during his days at Chapel Hill.

THE THOMAS WOLFE READER.
Edited by C. Hugh Holman. New York: Charles Scribner's Sons, 1962.

An anthology of Wolfe pieces drawn from his four novels, and two collections of stories and essays together with SN and Wolfe's final letter to Maxwell Perkins, this volume attempts to present Wolfe's various talents: descriptive powers, ability to depict character, mastery of lyrical prose, skills as a writer of humor and satire, cataloguer in the Whitman tradition, and shaper of powerful narrative episodes.

Holman also provides a brief biography and succinct comments on Wolfe's artistic aims and practices.

THE TRAIN AND THE CITY.
Edited by Richard S. Kennedy. Akron, OH: The Thomas Wolfe Society, 1984.

An episode originally planned for *K–19* and published in *Scribner's Magazine* (March 1933), this reprinting shows Wolfe as both poet and mythmaker. It also reveals something about his plan to leave Eugene Gant behind and to develop a new protagonist, John Hawke.

A few copies are available from The Thomas Wolfe Society.

THE WEB AND THE ROCK.
New York: Harper and Brothers, 1939.

Reacting to charges that he drew far too heavily on his own life in creating Eugene Gant, Wolfe experimented with other fictional counterparts, among them Paul Spangler and Joseph Doaks, before deciding, "Let him be called Webber." As finally put together by Edward Aswell, WR picked up a large chunk of material that had been written for "The October Fair," a segment of Wolfe's hexapartite scheme to trace the development of an artistic consciousness and the struggle of the artist to find a way to express himself in America; to become the bard and seer. "The October Fair" would have covered the years of Eugene's grand but turbulent love for an older woman and his attempt to fulfill his artistic goal of writing his first novel, a period corresponding to Wolfe's experiences from 1925 to 1928.

Wolfe's unexpected death forced Aswell to depend on a hastily compiled outline of the Webber material and the memories of Maxwell Perkins and Elizabeth Nowell, whose earlier work on Wolfe's manuscripts and conversations with him about his intended use of them had prepared them to see where the various parts belonged. Since Wolfe had not come to the stage of weaving the scores of episodes together and writing the transitional passages, recasting some older material in the more objective style he had come to favor, and fleshing out those sections needed to complete the narrative, Aswell had to assume a role of co-author and editor alike, a status he never fully acknowledged. For that reason, careful critics and readers must preface their interpretations of both WR and YC with something like, "The posthumous novels as prepared for publication by Aswell . . ."

The shift to a new protagonist and a smaller family to see him develop in brought only slight differences in themes, for Wolfe once more focussed on the growth of an artistic temperament in an environment often hostile to the needs and sensitivities of a potential writer. Together with this familiar theme Wolfe brought back the themes of loneliness, wandering, clannishness, idealism versus reality, small-town narrowness, superstitiousness, youth versus age, North versus South, and puritanical religious and social values. Mixed in with all of these was a continuing concern for aestheticism, but now some new notes were to be added to that line: creativity and the parasitism of persons wanting to live in the reflected glory of the artist; creative solitude and the price the artist had to pay to do his work; and the relation of the creative life to such goals as wealth, fame, and love. Another old theme given added emphasis was the provincial youth in the city, a theme Wolfe thought of making central to this cycle when he drafted an oafish Joe Doaks as a bumpkin among city slickers. He also returned to the theme of freedom versus possessiveness, and he explored racial differences more fully than in the earlier works. He hoped to bring unity to these many themes by making the novel deal with "one man's discovery of life and the world . . . through a process of finding out . . . through error and through trial, and through fantasy and illusion, through falsehood and his own damn foolishness, through being mistaken and wrong and an idiot and egotistical and aspiring and hopeful and believing and confused, and pretty much, I think, what every damned one of us is and goes through and finds out and becomes" (LTW 711).

This was to be his version of an American *Gulliver's Travels*, but he listed other forerunners, too: *Don Quixote, The Pickwick Papers, Candide, The Idiot,* and *Wilhelm Meister's Apprenticeship.* Yet, for all of the impressive models, he once again wanted to place his protagonist just as he had Eugene Gant, in the midst of concentric circles capable of conveying "a widening, ever-enlarging picture of the whole thing" (LTW 714).

Structurally, WR follows Wolfe's plan for the Webber cycle as closely as completed portions could guide Aswell. To tie all the various finished episodes together, Aswell wrote connecting links, drawing upon Wolfe's letters and upon Perkins and Nowell when he could, but not revealing that the italicized transitions came from his hand. He broke the novel into seven books, the first three of which represented new materials expressly written for the Webber cycle (pp. 1–278), and a fantasy on the life of a literary man of leisure that had been cut from OT. The remaining four books came from the Gant cycle, a sequel to the love story hinted at in the final scene of OT.

Book I, "The Web and the Root," chapters 1–4, narrates Monk Webber's background and reports his boyhood musings, recounts some of the strange ways and beliefs of his mountain-bred kin, and describes his visions of his father's land, the North, and dreams of wealth, fame, and love.

Book II, "The Hound of Darkness," chapters 5–9, provides more details about George's kin, Aunts Maw and Mag and Uncle Mark, gives scenes of life in Libya Hill, including the stories of a butcher's family and the violent behavior of Dick Prosser, a black man whose calm and affectionate ways suddenly explode into a shooting spree and result in his being hunted down by a posse, and ends with George's recognition that he could be heir to the Joyner clan's mad streak of superstitiousness and fanaticism. (The title of this book was taken from a work that Wolfe had wanted to publish separately, a series of vignettes about America at night.)

Book III, "The Web and the World," chapters 10–16, covers Monk's college days as a student at Pine Rock College (another version of the University of North Carolina) and his relationship with a football hero, Jim Randolph, and Gerald Alsop, the leader of a literary discussion group; describes the preachments of the college president, a Presbyterian cleric; and a professor, who predicts that Monk will go through hell but emerge a poet; and concludes with Monk's move to New York City. Here he shares an apartment with Jim Randolph and other Southerners and sees Alsop from time to time before leaving to find a place of his own, where he fantasizes about the grand life that could be his if he could find the right woman and become the writer he would like to be.

Book IV, "The Magic Year," chapters 17–28, traces his shipboard meeting with Esther Jack, their many adventures in New York City together, their celebration of his twenty-fifth birthday, his trip to Esther's home; their search for an apartment to share, where she can do her work as a theatrical designer and he can write his novel; and reveals that he finds a job, much despised and berated, at the School for Utility Cultures.

Book V, "Life and Letters," chapters 29–35, treats George's efforts to complete his novel, entitled "The End of the Golden Weather"; his awareness that he possibly shares the fanatic madness of Rance Joyner; his submission of his novel to the firm of Rawng and Wright, which rejects it, and his encounter with the outspoken Irish critic Seamus Malone (Ernest Boyd).

Book VI, "Love's Bitter Mystery," chapters 36–43, presents the turmoil and anguish of a love affair turning sour and the remorse stemming from the realization that something precious is being lost, and offers the consolation that both Esther and George have their work to give their lives meaning and joy. It also describes their parting.

Book VII, "Oktoberfest," chapters 44–50, recounts George's travels to Paris and to Munich, where he receives a head wound during a drunken brawl while celebrating Oktoberfest, and pauses to reflect on his life and what he wants to do with it as he lies in a Munich hospital room.

The major symbols of WR appear in the title. Wolfe uses the web to suggest Monk's entanglement with his Joyner kin and, as his experiences widen, with humanity at large and Esther Jack in particular. As Richard

Chase says in his foreword to the Laurel edition of WR, the web also "suggests the quality of Wolfe's mind and art. He is ruminative, retrospective, encompassing, omnivorous" (14). The rock symbolizes, first, Monk's father and then the city of New York. As part and parcel of the city, Esther Jack also comes to represent the rock. The other important symbol of the novel is a door, which retains the meaning it has in LHA.

The characterization of WR is marked by a far greater use of naturalistic detail, as in the presentation of the Lampley family, and by deeper psychological probing, as in the portrait of Esther Jack. Wolfe is also far more objective than he had been in the Gant cycle, especially in his handling of his surrogate, perhaps because he came to think of Eugene as bothersomely egocentric. Looking back on his first protagonist, Wolfe wrote, "The Eugene Gant type of character becomes a kind of romantic self-justification, and the greatest weakness of the Eugene Gant type of character lies in this fact" (LTW 714). Hence, WR would remove all traces of Eugene Gantiness, Wolfe added. But Eugene does not disappear. The physical appearance becomes ungainly and simian, provoking the nickname "Monk," but the spiritual and intellectural changes are few. Some of the other Gants reappear with essentially only name changes. John Webber, for example, is another fictional manifestation of Wolfe's father, who had served as the model for W. O. Gant. Eliza Gant returns as Aunt Maw, who is a far less sympathetic rendering of Wolfe's mother and her mountain heritage. Aunt Maw and her kind seem to be the direct descendants of the iron-willed Puritans that punished Hester Prynne in seventeenth-century Boston.

Monk Webber is too skimpily drawn in the first three books, more of a reflector of action than an actor, a circumstance that surely would have been corrected had Wolfe lived to complete the work, and presumably Wolfe would have tackled the job of scrubbing out the Eugene Gantiness in the novel.

But had he done so, he could well have lost something of the beauty, force, power, and drama of the love affair treated in the final four books. Esther seemed destined to love Eugene, seemed the kind of mother, muse, mistress, and mentor Eugene needed to find himself as a man and artist. In fulfilling all her roles, Esther grew to be one of Wolfe's richest, best realized characters, becoming one of the best portraits of a lady in the whole canon of American fiction, and taking her place alongside Hester Prynne, Isabel Archer, Sister Carrie, and Edna Pontellier. Wolfe catches her vivacity and wit, her love of the theatre, art, and cooking, her belief in the nurturing of genius, her depth of knowledge of the city, her capacity for work, her ability to move gracefully and charmingly among many kinds of people, and her possessiveness, sentimentalism, and emotional excesses. This portrait finds an interesting and satisfying complement in Aline Bernstein's fictionalization of the love affair in "Three Blue Suits" and *The Journey Down*, both of which also provide a depiction of Wolfe as a lover.

Because WR is a scissors-and-paste job, it has greater stylistic variety than any of its predecessors, for Aswell had Wolfe in both the copious and leaner vein to patch together. Smarting from critical objections to his heaping up of modifiers, to his strings of nouns and verbs, and to his pillaging of a thesaurus for fresh words, and having developed a taste for the leaner manner of Hemingway, Wolfe had turned to a more concise style when he left the Gant cycle. The most costly result to the Wolfean voice was the loss of much of the poetry of the earlier work.

Although the remark applies with more force and justice to YC, the assertion in the "Author's Note" aptly describes Wolfe's intent to express himself with "satiric exaggeration" in WR. He claimed that the nature of the story, " 'the innocent man' discovering life," justified his use of satire and that "satiric exaggeration . . . belongs to the nature of life, and particularly American life." All of this is simply a way of saying that he needed the help of satire to attack the faults and vices he had discovered when his social consciousness once again mattered more than his narcissism, when he could stop casting himself and his surrogates in the role of the aesthete, the wounded faun. This satiric voice meant a more frequent turn to parody, irony, degrading portraiture, and rambunctious denunciation than most of his earlier works had contained. As a result, his style became even more varied if not better controlled. The pressures of living and loving thus thrust Wolfe more deeply into the camp of Lord Byron and Sinclair Lewis, and markedly pulled him from the tents of Keats, Shelley, and DeQuincey. The cathartic value of satire, however, was obviously something leading him to evoke the names of Swift, Dickens, Voltaire, Cervantes, and Goethe as he tried to list titles of works most closely resembling his. Thus in WR, the poet yielded ground to the satirist. But this is not to say that the poet died.

Stylistically, then, WR is more varied than any other work by Wolfe, ranging as it does from the sparseness of Hemingway to the grand sonority of Robert Burton and Sir Thomas Browne, and the amplitude of Whitman and the Hebraic psalmists. Not surprisingly, the patchwork nature of WR and its smorgasbord of styles led to a mixed critical reception, prompting some critics to argue that Wolfe had one great work in him, LHA, and that all the fiddling around with style was a mistake, the surest way to undermine his distinctive voice. Other critics saw promise in his turn to a more objective or satiric manner and lamented his untimely death, suggesting that Wolfe was on the verge of discovering how to write as a mature artist. However slanted, the reviews helped WR garner well over 30,000 customers when it was issued. It is still readily available in both hardback and paperbound editions.

References: 13, 14, 22, 26, 36, 38, 40, 43, 46, 48, 51, 54, 59, 63, 65, 68, 76, 83, 86, 89.

WELCOME TO OUR CITY: A PLAY IN TEN SCENES.
Edited by Richard S. Kennedy. Baton Rouge: Louisiana State University Press, 1983.

If for no other reason, this play is important because it marks Wolfe's discovery that Asheville offered suitable material for his pen. This discovery occurred during his return to his native city for his father's funeral (June 1922). As he later told his beloved mentor, Margaret Roberts, he found in Asheville a world-old evil, greed, "masking itself under the guise of civic associations for municipal betterment" (LTW 33–34). In the spirited, debunking manner of Sinclair Lewis and H. L. Mencken, Wolfe began to fashion a play, first called "Niggertown," about the efforts of civic boosters and nostalgia-bound heirs of southern plantation life to buy up desirably located property owned or inhabited by blacks, for development or restoration. The banner under which the boosters march bears the potent word "Progress." Wolfe wanted to fling the word back in the face of Asheville, as he wrote his mother during the time he worked on the play: "I will step on toes, I will not hesitate to say what I think of those people who shout 'Progress, Progress, Progress'—when what they mean is more Ford automobiles, more Rotary Clubs, more Baptist Ladies Social Unions . . . What I shall try to get into their dusty little pint-measure minds is that a full belly, a good automobile, paved streets, and so on, does not make them one whit better or finer,—that there is beauty in this world—beauty even in this wilderness of ugliness and provincialism that is at present our country, beauty and spirit which will make us men instead of cheap Board of Trade Boosters, and blatant pamphleteers" (LTM 42–43).

To present a town vigorously trying to boost itself as a mecca for everyone, from artisans to artists, Wolfe discarded the conventional division into acts and developed his play by scenes, maintaining something like a plot in the dream of Will Rutledge to buy his ancestral home from its present owner, a light-skinned Negro named Dr. Johnson. Altogether, he finally settled on ten scenes as the version to be produced by the 47 Workshop on 11 May 1923 at the Agassiz Theater in Cambridge, a production running to Wagnerian lengths, but impressive enough to drama historian Oliver Saylor to cause him to find the play as "radical in form and treatment as the contemporary stage has yet acquired" (LTM 56). With trimming, suggested and requested by both George Pierce Baker and interested New York producers, the play had a fair chance of reaching the commercial stage, but Wolfe broodingly delayed picking up a blue pencil and finally lost that chance. Although a shortened version was published in *Esquire* (October 1957), the play never appeared on stage and was not to be shared with an audience again until it was given a reading by a drama group at Harvard University, for members of the Thomas Wolfe Society in 1983. The edition prepared by Richard S. Kennedy is a reconstruction of the work as it was seen by the group attending the Agassiz Theater production.

The structural arrangement into ten scenes combines both realistic and expressionistic elements, the former dominating, the latter the more compelling because they show Wolfe pushing American theater in directions being taken by European dramatists. The opening scene is surely one of his most original pieces of writing, and the fact that American drama has not had an opportunity to share Oliver Saylor's excitement over this and other expressionistic elements of the play is regrettable. The scenes have sufficient glue to hold them together, although removing most of two or three scenes would not cause the whole structure to topple; for example, Scenes Three and Six where Wolfe, respectively, flings darts at an escapist teacher and a woman trying to write a play as part of the town's efforts to promote the arts. Had he been willing to focus his attention on the racial conflict, centering his play on the boosters and their drive to remove blacks from land now deemed extraordinarily valuable, he would have shown more of the instincts of a dramatist and less those of a novelist or satirist, but as he was to remark when the play provoked requests for cutting, he yearned to find a vehicle for presenting a whole town. That vehicle, of course, was to be the novel, but even there he would strain the form. The structure finally chosen allowed him the freedom to portray a cross section of Altamont society and its interaction with certain outside forces, such as Preston Carr, a candidate for governor; Sykes, a black from Boston promoting equal rights; and Mr. Jordan, a tubercular writer looking for a home to buy. As Jordan comes to understand the city, he sees that no citizen, whatever his age, color, or background, can stand in the way of progress, a word on the march in town. The municipal and statewide goal of becoming bigger and better seemed to Wolfe but a mask of greed, hence his emphasis in the play on false appearance, something shown best in his portrayal of Governor Carr as a wimpish little man concealed artfully beneath padded clothing and high-sounding slogans. The boosters could not, however, reach their goals without clashing with people holding opposing notions about how Altamont should shape its future. By the time Wolfe gave every faction, including blacks who wanted to push for equal rights under the law or through violence, a voice concerning the future direction of Altamont, his play had reached a densely crowded ten scenes, and he cried out for more space. At such moments as these he surely thought of the novel as the only form capable of the scope he desired, unless he conceived of his future in drama as the creator of scene heaped upon scene until everything somehow drops into place. Work on this play was slowly and painfully revealing to him that his genius demanded a medium allowing a larger canvas.

Besides the theme of progress, Wolfe treated community reaction to the teaching of the theory of evolution, agitation for the advancement of equal rights for blacks, Babbittry within political and educational circles, miscegenation, promotional campaigns by civic clubs and chambers of commerce, packaging of political candidates, little theater groups, and, most important, the dream of returning to the manner of life enjoyed in the days of plantations.

Resembling Jonson's *Bartholomew Fair* in both the number and variety of characters, WTOC moves at too brisk a pace to allow much time for probing characterization. Like Jonson, Wolfe counted on action to help him give dimension if not depth to his characters. Some of Wolfe's Altamontians would feel right a home among a few of Jonson's humor types. Much of the shallowness of characterization can be explained by Wolfe's satiric and comedic needs, for a writer of satiric comedy, as much of this is, does not want the audience to forget the fault or forgive the wrongdoer. Satiric characters exist to be puffed up and pricked. Measured by this standard, Wolfe's Joseph Bailey, Governor Carr, Old Sorrell, Hutchings, and Mrs. Rutledge aptly forecast the crowd of Wolfean characters to be depicted through caricature, for which he has few American peers of note except Sinclair Lewis and Ring Lardner.

Presented with some depth but not much sympathy are Will Rutledge and Dr. Johnson, whose clash of hopes, dreams, and wills could have been the stuff of tragedy if not of a problem comedy. Both suffer from illusions, one thinking that he can recapture the mode of antebellum life if he can buy and restore the ancestral home, the other believing that a self-made man can hold out against the power of whites and the desertion of blacks. Had Wolfe been willing to do more with the predicament of Dr. Johnson and Rutledge, as he was advised to do by producers in New York, he could have at once possibly achieved a contract and a significant social drama. In any case, his play very early touches on a question that would in time become one of consuming interest for Southern writers, the question of race relations. The play seems to cry out for a fuller, more understanding presentation of Rutledge and Dr. Johnson than Wolfe was either willing or able to give. The spirit of Mencken and Lewis flowed too freely through his pen to permit him to make serious use of his insight into the representative problems of a black man seeking respect through his leadership and good services to his community and a white man blinded to the worth of a decent, well-trained black man because he could not rid himself of a plantation mentality.

That Wolfe was fully aware of having seized upon something representative of Southern life is evident in his use of the old Rutledge mansion as a symbol of the planters' society. The play has no other important symbols, but this one was good enough to carry straight into *Mannerhouse*.

Indeed, Wolfe finally carted much of WTOC into later works, bodily moving Joseph Bailey, Preston Carr, Preacher Smallwood, and Henry Sorrell into the pages of LHA, after cutting away much of their bulk and waiting until HB to give Old Sorrell a new life as a perky Civil War veteran pointing to a hole in the roof of his mouth and shouting, "Looky Thar." The most significant use of WTOC material, however, was thematic, for boosterism, land speculation, wheeling and dealing, greed, and an unthinking allegiance to the idea of progress became major concerns in much of Wolfe's fiction.

For a reason apparent in the preceding paragraph, most critics consider WTOC a more important work than MH. His cannibalism of the former is more obvious, it's true, but the latter is the one Wolfe chose to have his surrogate read and weigh as an example of his growth as an artist, and MH marks Wolfe's discovery of the buried life as the most pervasive of themes in modern literature.

The style of WTOC is as close to a straightforward, disciplined prose as Wolfe was ever to write, except in the months preceding his death when he began to use a concise mode again, even turning to dramatic dialogue from time to time. Despite the fact that the characters are from a Southern mountain town, only Old Sorrell among the whites speaks in a South Midland dialect; the other native whites might as well have hailed from Lewis's Zenith or Fitzgerald's East Egg. The blacks are, however, given a conventional literary dialect similar to the one used by Joel Chandler Harris and Mark Twain. In general, Wolfe's style calls little attention to itself except when he parodies the high-flown passages of purple prose used in promotional flyers or the language of politicians. In a word, his style is serviceable.

The play is still in print.

References: 4, 22, 34, 36, 40, 46, 54, 65, 76. See also the thesis of Janis Ashley on WTOC, Clemson University, 1976, and articles on the play in TWR, the first by Jerry L. Rice (Fall 1981), the second by Phyllis H. Lewis (Spring 1984).

A WESTERN JOURNAL: A DAILY LOG OF THE GREAT
PARKS TRIP JUNE 20– JULY 2, 1938.
      Pittsburgh: University of Pittsburgh Press, 1951.

An impressionistic record of a swift-paced tour of national parks in Oregon, California, Arizona, Utah, Wyoming, and Washington, with

Roy Conway and Edward M. Miller by motor car, this journal combines the mundane facts of eating, sleeping, and gawking with vivid, sensitive, and telling observations of places and people seen on the 5,000 mile dash spread over just thirteen days. The hand of Wolfe the poet and novelist often pushes aside the hand of Wolfe the harried tourist, who often felt that his companions were holding a stopwatch and begrudging his attempts to linger and talk with some of the interesting people met along the way. In themselves, these quick jottings do not often reach the level of good travel writing, but, in view of Wolfe's accustomed use of notebook materials, the words scrawled here were meant to be mere jogs to his legendary memory. For Wolfe and American literature, the payoff would have come later. In any case, this jumble of facts and rapid and poetic sketches of roughly a third of the geographical face of the nation stands as Wolfe's last words on a theme close to his heart, the American landscape and the American people.

A paperback edition is still in print.

References: 40, 54, 76, 89, and Brian F. Berger's *Thomas Wolfe: The Final Journey*. West Linn, Oregon: Williamette River Press, 1984.

YOU CAN'T GO HOME AGAIN.
New York: Harper and Brothers, 1940.

The most-often quoted words of Wolfe are no doubt those from the title of this novel, but, as Wolfe had the honesty to say, he heard them from the lips of Ella Winter, the widow of Lincoln Steffens. They aptly phrased for him a lesson he had learned about life since he had left home to follow the craft of a writer: no one, he thought, could go "back home to one's family, back home to one's childhood, back home to the father one has lost, back home to romantic love, to a young man's dreams of glory and of home, back home to exile, to escape to 'Europe' and some foreign land, back home to lyricism, singing just for singing's sake, back home to aestheticism, to one's youthful ideas of the 'artist,' and the all-sufficiency of 'art and beauty and love,' . . . back home to the old forms and systems of things that once seemed everlasting, but that are changing all the time . . . " (LTW 711–12). To dramatize this discovery, he turned from the egocentric Eugene Gant to the more objective George Webber, who would be presented as "a naturally innocent man" whose story would be "a kind of fable, constructed out of the materials of experience and reality" (LTW 700). Rather than following in the footsteps of Stephen Dedalus, as Eugene Gant had done, the protagonist Wolfe now wanted to create would be more like Gulliver, Candide, or Wilhelm Meister. The story he would therefore tell would draw upon the tradition of the fabulists and put a kind of Everyman figure through a linked series of more or less allegorical adventures or misadventures. The hero would thus be shown trying to win fame, glory, or love for himself and then discovering that, more than these, brotherhood is the worthiest of all goals. The fable within which Wolfe would embody the story of Monk's passage through life would allow, stylistically, a mixture of tones and modes of expression, something that would permit him to write in his accustomed vein even if he now fancied himself a wielder of a less fluid pen.

The book as we know it is not an American *Gulliver's Travels*, or *Candide*, and surely not a *Wilhelm Meister*. It is another scissors-and-paste job by Edward Aswell, who worked from a synopsis left by Wolfe and from suggestions about Wolfe's intended use of the Webber materials garnered from Elizabeth Nowell and Max Perkins. The links between books are Aswell's but not acknowledged as such, and Aswell's hand in the structure and style of the book is not small. As Richard S. Kennedy and John Halberstadt and others have found, Aswell assumed more than an editor's role, behaving more like a George Kaufman reworking a play by another author than an Ezra Pound helping a T. S. Eliot with a promising poem, to borrow Kennedy's comparison. Careful critics and scholars have consequently stated that their comments and interpretations of the work are based on the novel as edited by Aswell. Knowing what the situation is, some scholars have called for another edition of the Webber cycle, one that would present the materials as Wolfe left them. The countering argument that the two posthumous novels now have a critical heritage and a niche in American letters has so far kept anyone from launching a serious effort to edit the Webber cycle again. If and when Wolfe is accorded the attention other major writers are receiving in the nation's attempt to publish definitive standard editions, the question must be resolved.

The thematic core of YC is tersely and quotably stated in the title, but, as usual, Wolfe found many topics to help him dramatize and illustrate his unifying theme. As in WR, he treats discovery and growth, illusion and reality, hope and despair, dreams and the loss of dreams, the hunger for success, freedom and possession, the integrity of the individual, and loneliness. Coming in for new or renewed attention now are boosterism, class structure and rank and privilege in a supposed democracy, love of the soil, American business practices, international politics, economic depression and its attendant ills, man's inhumanity to man, and brotherhood. But more important than any of these new or renewed themes are fame and the artist's role in relation to the rest of humanity. John Milton's sage insight that mankind's noblest infirmity (fame) would plague him to the end furnished Wolfe with the psychological profile that would help him depict George Webber as one of the enduring types of mortals.

As arranged by Aswell, the structure of YC follows a series of discoveries, each ending in a rejection of someone, something, or some idea. In Book I, George rejects an insane hunger for material success; in Book II, the life of a privileged class and the love of one of its members, Esther Jack; in Book III, glory and praise as offered by lionizers; in Book IV, social isolation; in Book V, fame; in Book VI, man's inhumanity to man, and in Book VII, fatalistic determinism.

Book I, "The Native's Return," chapters 1–9, narrates Monk's decision to follow his heart and not his head, and resume his affair with Esther upon his return to New York from Germany, and recounts his thrilling discovery that James Rodney & Company will publish his first novel, *Home to Our Mountains*. While the novel is being readied for publication, Monk meets various employees at the House of Rodney (one of them, Foxhall Edwards, is an editor with whom he will develop a close relationship [Maxwell Perkins]), and becomes acquainted with a Japanese sculptor, Katamoto, who has a room beneath his. News of his Aunt Maw's death takes Monk back to Libya Hill. Returning home on a Pullman car numbered K 19 with other Libya Hill citizens, Monk encounters some civic boosters, the thoroughly evil Judge Rumford Bland, and his childhood friend, Nebraska Crane, now nearing the end of a fame-filled career as a professional baseball player. Back in Libya Hill, almost everyone seems caught up in a real estate boom, its chief prophet being the town drunk, Tim Wagner. But Libya Hill's press does pause to note that Monk's book will be issued soon. Monk's stammered interview about his book is twisted into a glowing recommendation of Libya Hill as a mecca for artists. Monk learns about the ugly side of American sales practices by overhearing David Merrit scold Monk's friend Randy Shepperton for not meeting his quota. Monk becomes concerned about the economic health of his home town when he learns about the failure of a local bank.

Book II, "The World That Jack Built," chapters 10–21, picks up Monk's life again in New York and describes in much detail the hosts and the Park Avenue apartment (the house that money or "Jack" built). The employees of the Jacks as well two elevator operators are presented, too, before the story moves on to the party itself, where Piggy Logan (Alexander Calder) came to perform his celebrated wire circus act, and where many of New York's richest, most intelligent, deeply and broadly cultured, and influential people gathered to drink, converse, flirt, and watch Piggy Logan's avant-garde act. A fire interrupts the party and forces the Jacks and their guests and other residents of the apartment house into the street, where master mingles with servant on an equal footing. The fire does little damage, but the elevator operators die when they become trapped. Monk now quietly decides that he must forsake Esther and her life among the privileged class if he is to be free to write of American society as he sees it unfolding before him.

Book III, "An End and a Beginning," chapters 22–26, reports Libya Hill's outraged response to Monk's novel, which he comes to see as not fully truthful, despite his effort to be wholly honest. He realizes his lack of truthfulness because he learns that he has behaved as an aesthete, as a Joycean kind of wounded faun, seeing himself ultimately in a false light since he thought of himself as somehow better and finer than others.

Book IV, "The Quest of the Fair Medusa," chapters, 27–31, recounts Monk's decision to leave Manhattan and its allurements and settle in Brooklyn, where he observes the demoralizing and devastating effects of the Great Depression on good and decent men and women, and begins to feel that something must explain why such people must suffer a bitter end to their dreams. He is not yet ready to give an answer. Meanwhile, he thinks of his friend Foxhall Edwards and how he rises to greet the day and a house filled with womenfolk. As Foxhall reads the morning paper he sees an account of the suicide of a man named C. Green, who asserted his individuality in the act of death by leaping from the window of a hotel and disrupting the normal flow of city life. Monk now has further thoughts about the promise of America. A vision of the American landscape, a passage taken from "The Hound of Darkness" and previously published in *Vogue* as "A Prologue to America" also appears in this book.

Book V, "Exile and Discovery," chapters 32–37, contains two episodes, the first treating the humorous ways of a London charwoman named Daisy Purvis, a talkative, plump soul who stoutly defends the rights and deeds of British aristocracy. For her, the class system seems just, as long as she can rattle on about the goings and comings of royalty. The second episode reports Monk's escapade with the famous American novelist, Lloyd McHarg (Sinclair Lewis). Monk discovers that fame failed to soothe the restless, tortured, and wild spirit of McHarg.

Book VI, " 'I Have a Thing to Tell You'," chapters 38–44, opens with Monk's own taste of glory and fame in Germany, where he now enjoys a round of parties and the love of a beautiful woman. Something dark and evil is spreading across the face of Germany, however, a malign force that Monk is led to identify with Hitler. To the hints of his friends about the cruelty of the Nazis, Monk must painfully add the story of a Jew trying to escape to France, for Monk becomes involved in the Jew's attempt to flee. Outraged by the sense of terror he sees aroused in the Jew, Monk bids farewell to Germany, a land and people he had come to love.

Book VII, "A Wind is Rising, and the Rivers Flow," chapters 45–48, takes the form of a letter to Foxhall Edwards and serves as a summary of many of Monk's reflections on his life and his thoughts about the problems and promises of his country. To underscore where he now stands he contrasts his views, which are a blend of Populism and southern conservatism, with those of Edwards, which Monk perceives as being a kind of fatalistic determinism. Edwards sides with Ecclesiasticus, but as an artist Monk must stand with Man-Alive, affirming both growth and change as the vital elements of life, believing that the way of the world can be bent to the will of man. Continuing in a philosophical and sociological mood, Monk pinpoints the cause of the nation's present ills as "single selfishness and compulsive greed." Somewhere around the time of the Civil War, a time also chosen by literary historian Vernon Parrington, the nation went wrong, but Monk believes that Americans will refuse to let despair destroy their dreams. He states his faith in the much-quoted passage beginning, "I think the true discovery of America is before us. I think the true fulfillment of our spirit, of our people, of our mighty and immortal land, is yet to come" (YC 741).

The episodes making up the novel are without a plot and derive their structure instead from the presence of a person whose character and discoveries were intended, in something of the manner of epic writers, to represent national traits and experience-gained insights.

That concept of structure grew up alongside Wolfe's choice of a naive Everyman as his protagonist, who "comes to realize that he is in no fundamental sense different from other people: he is compacted of the same clay, filled with the same blood, breathes the same air, has the same passions, appetites, joys, fears, hopes, and aspirations as the rest of humanity" (YC 715–716). Monk is a quieter, more reflective and introspective man than Eugene, and, after realizing that the true artist is not an aesthetically self-protective wounded faun, Monk stops building walls around himself and starts constructing bridges instead. More than anything else, he now wants to be an honest writer, just as willing to reveal the truth about himself as he does about others. As Wolfe had hoped, critics found George more mature and objective and capable of growth.

Esther Jack's character also undergoes enrichment and enlargement, for she is revealed as wife, mother, and hostess in these pages, not just as George's mistress. Better than in WR, the reader senses how graciously and forcefully she moves in the world of gifted and privileged people, but the reader also learns that the faddishness and decadence of her circle thrust her and her friends into a role like that of Francis Starwick, an enemy of art. At least that is how Monk comes to see her, perhaps because thinking of her as such will make his separation from her less painful, for he does pledge eternal love to her.

Esther's husband, Frederick, joins a list of Wolfean sketches done by a pattern: the routine of awakening and starting a new day, a method he used with Foxhall Edwards, Esther, and with the protagonists of "The Lion at Morning," James Wyman, and "Old Man Rivers," Edward

Rivers. A parasite of sorts, since he produces no wealth of his own but instead makes his living by playing the stock market, Frederick Jack enjoys his rank among the privileged and takes pride in his wife's artistic triumphs. As Lady Brett might have said, "He's really not a bad sort once you get to know him." His most glaring fault is that he condones the thievish, lying conduct of his servants.

Monk's friends and the editor of his work appears in both a Jonsonian and biblical light. His life in a house filled with females assumes something markedly Jonsonian, for Foxhall Edwards is a humor character. Later, he is Ecclesiasticus, the fatalist. Also decidedly humorous is Lloyd McHarg, whose restless energy pushes him and Monk to exertions beyond the reach of ordinary men. Daisy Purvis might also have marched straight from the pages of Jonson if democracy had been in vogue when he lived. Back in Libya Hill, Delia Flood becomes still another manifestation of Wolfe's mother.

Just how far Wolfe had moved in his ability to create characters appears best in his depiction of Nebraska Crane and Judge Rumford Bland, the first a model of the wise man whose love of a simple life on his own farm is far more precious than fame or wealth, the second the embodiment of cynical wisdom gained through suffering, making him something like Tiresias. Altogether, Wolfe seemed to be moving from caricatures to rounded characters in the Webber cycle, though oddly enough Monk often comes off as flat.

Wolfe's shift to a more objective, less poetic, protagonist brought about marked changes in style. The most obvious one is the sharp cutback in lyricism. Also much reduced are his strings of adverbs and adjectives, his catalogues, and his bombast. The "strong element of satiric exaggeration" promised in the Author's Note in WR adds salt, spice, barbs, acid, and hammer blows, all of which help Wolfe to perform more as a social critic than a poet in this work. Seen in relation to Whitman's career and work, YC is Wolfe's *Democratic Vistas*, whereas the Gant cycle and the second half of WR are *Song of Myself*. Although Wolfe's talent for mimicry remains good, he more often chose a forward, workmanlike reportial style, a result, perhaps, of his practice of dictating rather than writing during the final months of his work on the Webber materials. The upshot is, however, a loss of more sharply etched characters like Bascom Pentland and W. O. Gant, whose voices gave them fictional immortality. The epistolary style employed in the final four chapters does not match Wolfe at his best as a letter writer. Had he lived to finish the work, he surely would have dramatized George's differences of opinion with Foxhall Edwards on matters of personal philosophy and the nation's faults and promises. To achieve any closure at all for the Webber cycle, Aswell was forced to adapt one of Wolfe's letters to Perkins, a letter filled with more special pleading and self-justification than

Wolfe would have used, since he had partially overcome his habit of playing the role of the wounded faun.

In summary, Wolfe's style is still a mixed bag in YC, but it is simpler, quieter, drier, and more cramped than in any other novel. In short, his style almost comes back again to the manner of WTOC, with glaring exceptions like the long and labored letter at the end of YC.

Some of the symbols of WR still function in YC: Esther is both web and rock; New York remains a rock; Monk's craft still resembles that of a weaver, and Foxhall Edwards as a father figure can be linked to the rock. Entirely new to this novel is Wolfe's use of the Jacks' apartment building and its subterranean structure as a symbol of American capitalism as it had evolved to the period of the late 1920s and early 1930s. The occupants of the building represent a privileged class, people who produce little or no wealth themselves, making their money, instead, by dealing with money earned by those who toil and sweat. The apartment also houses a serving class, made up of cooks, housekeepers, chauffeurs, maids, and elevator operators. Some among these, like Nora Fogarty, are corrupted by the system because of its lax attitude toward morality, and the ready availability of whiskey. Others, like John Enborg, defend the system, since it provides work and a livelihood. Still others, like Henry, argue that the workers must organize if they are to receive fair wages. Besides representing a microcosm of a class system, the building, honeycombed as it was by the subway beneath and elevator shafts along its length, reflected both the potential vulnerability and weakness of capitalism. When a fire breaks out, the privileged and the serving class alike are forced to stand on equal terms in the street. But serving the system did exact a price. With much too heavy irony, Wolfe has the system's staunchest defender, John Enborg, die in the fire.

This symbol gave Wolfe the chance to bring to his fiction a concern about American economic and political questions that he had wanted to voice as early as OT. Perkins had argued that any inclusion of Depression Era politics would be foisted upon Eugene, and had finally won his point. The discussion eventually helped Wolfe to see essential differences between him and Perkins on how best to deal with the problems of the time. Always more liberal than Perkins, Wolfe saw a need for change and strongly backed the New Deal reforms advocated by Franklin D. Roosevelt. Wolfe also was willing to listen to the suggestions of reformers to Roosevelt's left, a stance which would eventually result in the translation of YC into Russian because Wolfe was perceived as having Marxist leanings. A more exact label would be a southern Populist with some vestiges of southern conservatism.

One of the reasons for the largely favorable critical reception of YC was the fact that some reviewers saw it as a tract for the times, joining the novel with *Grapes of Wrath* as an expression of the nation's need to deal more justly and humanely with socioeconomic problems. But the appeal of the novel was not limited to its treatment of social themes. Many reviewers saw it as evidence of, and testimony to, Wolfe's growth as an artist. Some applauded its leaner style, some its more mature protagonist, others its powerful, moving close. The consensus about its rank placed it second only to LHA, though most critics thought of the first novel as a finished work and of YC as a splendid fragment.

Both a hardback and a paperbound edition remain in print.

References: 5, 6, 13, 14, 16, 19, 22, 26, 28, 37, 38, 40, 42, 45, 46, 48, 51, 54, 60, 65, 68, 69, 76, 82, 88, 89.

Glossary of Characters and Places

The glossary excludes the actual names of towns and cities serving as settings in Wolfe's work, such as Boston, St. Louis, New York, London, and Paris; and the names of characters who appear as members of a group and play no part in the development of a story, drama, or novel, for example, guests rocking on the porch at Dixieland, students in Eugene Gant's or George Webber's classes who merely occupy desks and take no part in classroom activity, and passers-by doing nothing more than going to work or to school. Major characters are analyzed as well as identified, and references to helpful secondary sources are given. If a character or place appears in two or more of Wolfe's works, that fact will be signified by the appropriate abbreviations. The page citation given with each entry indicates the first appearance of a character or place name. In the case of CSS, some characters appear in more than one story or sketch; each page citation indicates the first appearance of a character or the first mention of a place. Alternate forms of names are cross-referenced.

Abramson, Jake. A rakish old man attending the Jack's party; "old, subtle, sensual, weary." YC 236

Adamowski, Johnnie. A passenger on a German train who is returning to America after a visit to Poland. YC 672

Adzigian, Vladimir. A literary critic in "On Leprechauns" who comments on George Webber's style. HB 142, CSS 537

Alec. A young Frenchman with whom Francis Starwick has a homosexual relationship. OT 725

Alexander, Martha. A mountain woman about whom Rance Joyner is teased. WR 73

Allan, Robert C. An Altamont judge. LHA 334

Allen, Ken, Jr. Son of Ken Allen, Sr., a Chicago meatpacker. "He looks lean . . . well-conditioned and proportioned." HD 109

Allen, Ken, Sr. A Chicago meatpacker and friend of Gracie, a meatpacker's daughter. "He is a big man, tall and large of limb and feature, heavily built, still powerful, with a bald head, a red face, a kind of coarse openness of countenance touched with a prairie flatness, and a just perceptible porcine complacency." HD 109

Allen, Mrs. Ken. "She is a strong, plain-featured, somewhat buxom-looking female of late middle age, with plain manners, plain flat speech, plain broad features touched with complacency." HD 110

Alsop, Gerald (Jerry). A fat, priestly childhood friend of George Webber who later, in college, chides him for placing Dostoevski above Dickens. Known as "Mother Machree of Pine Rock College," Jerry re-enters George's life in New York. The model for this character was John Skally Terry, who edited Wolfe's letter to his mother and never made progress on a biography he was planning to do of Wolfe. WR 33.
References: 13, 14, 22, 40, 46, 54, 82, 83.

Altamont. The setting of the action in WTOC, LHA, OT; a mountain town in Old Catawba. Wolfe's fictional name for Asheville, NC, his home town. WTOC 16, LHA 7, OT 25, CSS 542

Anderson, Herbert. An elevator operator in the Park Avenue apartment building where the Jacks live who is trapped and killed when a fire breaks out. YC 200

Andrews, Albert. A boy killed when struck by a car in George Webber's neighborhood. WR 106

Andrews, Johnny. Brother of Albert Andrews. WR 108

Andrews, Moses. A burglar in Altamont who is killed by Jefferson Flack, a rival for the love of Molly Fiske. LHA 184

Andrews, Mr. and Mrs. A Libya Hill couple whose son Albert is killed when hit by a car. WR 108

Ann. A Boston woman traveling in Paris and other parts of France with her friend, Elinor, and Francis Starwick with whom Eugene falls in love but who does not return Eugene's affection.

Reference: See Richard Walser's "Boston's Elinor in Paris." TWR (Fall 1982). OT 687

A. P. Man. The operator of the wire news service for an Altamont newspaper where Ben Gant works. HB 50, HD 49, CSS 522

Appleton, John S., III. See, Appleton, Paul S., III. CSS 401

Appleton, Paul S., III. President of Federal Weight, Scale, and Computing, Co. and founder of the Hundred Club. YC 131, CSS 401

Armstrong. Principal of the public elementary school which Eugene attends. LHA 92

Arthur, Julius. A classmate of Eugene at the Altamont Fitting School. LHA 224

Avery. An elderly, deaf, and paralyzed Altamont scholar. LHA 335

Axe-Face. A vulture-like whore in a Paris brothel, The Mysteries of Asia. WR 646

Baer, Philip J. A cinematic potentate who insists that he must retrieve valuable records from a burning Park Avenue apartment. YC 296

Bahr, Fraulein. The operator of the Pension Burger in Munich and sister of Heinrich Bahr. WR 654

Bahr, Heinrich. A native of Munich who accompanies George Webber to the Oktoberfest. WR 654, CSS 308

Bailey, Joseph. A Babbitt-like secretary of the Altamont Board of Trade; a booster and babbler. WTOC 19, LHA 336

Bailey, Rosalind. A fashionable New York poet much celebrated for her sonnets. Reputedly based on Elinor Wylie. WR 469

Ballatyne, Joseph. A college student elected president of the freshmen class at Pulpit Hill. LHA 425

Barnes, Bessie. An elementary school classmate of Eugene and sister of Honest Jack Barnes. LHA 92

Barrett, Mrs. A Baltimore landlady in whose house the Gants stay during W. O.'s radium treatment at Johns Hopkins. FDTM 258

Barton, Hugh T. An employee of the Federal Cash Register Company and husband of Helen Gant. Based on Wolfe's brother-in-law Ralph Wheaton. LHA 377

Barton, Mrs. A large, opinionated woman; mother of Hugh Barton. LHA 380

Baskett. A cotton merchant from Hattiesburg, MS, and boarder at Dixieland. LHA 184

Battery Hill. A hilly section of Altamont; in reality Battery Park in Asheville. LHA 185

Beals, Clyde. A debt collector for Judge Rumford Bland. YC 72

Beals, Ellen. Sister-in-law of W. O. Gant and wife of John Beals; in the parlance of mountain speech, "Eller." FDTM 232

Beals, John. Brother-in-law of W. O. Gant. FDTM 232

Becker. A Munich surgeon who treats the wound George Webber receives at Oktoberfest. WR 675

Bell, Mrs. The owner of the St. Louis house to which Eugene returns to visit the scene of Grover Gant's death. HB 35, CSS 378

Bellamy, Monty. A young southerner who shares a New York apartment with George Webber and others. WR 224

Bendien, Cornelius. A Dutch friend of the American novelist Lloyd McHarg; a kind of Dutch Babbitt. YC 547

Benson, Edward Pettigrew ("Buck"). A dandified bachelor who taught Eugene Gant's Greek class. LHA 401

Bickett. The assistant chief of the Altamont Fire Department and baseball fan. OT 204

Bixley-Dunton, Major. George Webber's landlord on Ebury Street in London. YC 511

Black, Joe. A street-car foreman in Libya Hill who comforts Johnny Andrews after a car hits him. WR 107

Blackstone. South Carolina town (Greenville) where Eugene is jailed for public drunkenness. OT 341.

Blake, Emmet. The nephew of a famous automobile manufacturer and Eugene's companion during a drunken ride to Blackstone, SC. OT 363

Blake, Miss. A midwestern schoolteacher on a European tour in "One of the Girls in Our Party." FDTM 155, CSS 195

Bland, Judge Rumford. A blind, greedy, sinister usurer in Libya Hill who plies his trade among ignorant blacks and who sees deeply into the corrupt hearts of his fellow townsmen. A kind of Tiresias, he foresees the economic woes Libya Hill will suffer.
References: 14, 16, 22, 46, 88. YC 70

Blankenship. A mountain community in Zebulon County. WR 78

Bowden, Malvin. A boyhood friend of Eugene Gant. LHA 357

Bowden, Mrs. An Altamont woman who takes a group of Altamont teenagers to Charleston, SC. LHA 358

Boy in Bed, A. A dark-haired boy who awakens to ask what is stirring in the night. HD 78

Bradley, G. T. Adversary of Eugene Gant at Pulpit Hill and son of Eugene's first landlady. LHA 403

Bradley, Hazel. Promiscuous daughter of an Altamont grocer. LHA 234

Bradley, Mrs. Eugene Gant's first landlady at Pulpil Hill. LHA 403

Bradshaw, Mrs. An unhappy American tourist in Paris. WR 638

Bragg, General Braxton. The leader of Confederate forces fighting at Chickamauga. HB 77, CSS 393

Brandell, Richard. Theatrical producer and actor who is the friend of Esther Jack's father, Joe Linder. WR 415, CSS 451

Brant's Mill. A small town in Pennsylvania near the birthplace of W. O. Gant. OT 263

Briggs, Dexter. A drunken friend of George Webber's friend Jim Randolph. WR 268

Brill, John T. A partner in the realty firm with Bascom Pentland (or Hawke) who revels in lewdness and vulgarity. An enormous man at once rapacious and innocent. OT 119

Brill, Muriel. The eldest daughter of John Brill who works as a typist in her father's realty firm. OT 116

Brown, Gertrude. One of Helen Gant's high school chums. LHA 146

Brown, J.H. A sportsman and publisher of the *Altamont Citizen*. LHA 185

Brown, Josephine. A childhood friend of Daisy Gant, with whom she studied Latin. LHA 40

Brown, Miss. A whorish boarder at Dixieland who takes Eugene's medals in lieu of money. LHA 463

Brownlow, Clifford McKinley. A young Altamont pilot killed in action while flying for the Lafayette Escadrille. HB 63, HD 64, CSS 531

Bruce, Lola. A dental asistant in Doctor Smathers' office. LHA 330

Bryan, William Jennings. The Great Commoner who visits Doak Park in Altamont (Grove Park in Asheville). LHA 337

Buckles, Mrs. One of the permanent residents at the Hotel Leopold. OT 433

Bull. One of the hoboes in "The Bums at Sunset." FDTM 153, CSS 274

Burgin, John. The man shot by Ed Mears and Lawrence Wayne in "The Web of Earth." FDTM 280

Butler, The. An English servant in the household of Earle Williams. HD 98

Bynum. A young slave in the Ramsay family who finds work with a railroad following the end of the Civil War. MH 89

Cadet. A young Civil War volunteer mocked by Eugene Ramsay. MH 50

Calhoun. A South Carolina town, the site of Charlie Evans's drug store. HD 84

Candler, Frank. An Altamont politician traveling north on a train carrying Eugene Gant to Harvard. OT 41

Candler, Jack. A classmate of Eugene Gant at the Altamont Fitting School. LHA 224

Cardiac. The Altamont doctor who helped deliver Eugene Gant. LHA 3

Carleton, Amy. "A dollar princess, kept, costly, cabined, pruned, confined." The Medusa and Circe of a jaded society who attends the Jacks' party. One of the most decadent of Wolfe's flappers. YC 245

Carpenter, The First. A bawdy-minded man hired by Porter to help dismantle the Ramsay house. MH 139

Carpenter, The Second. A man who helps raze the Ramsay house and who considers Eugene Ramsay a lazy, shiftless tramp. MH 139

Carr, Governor Preston. Substantial in appearance but hollow in reality, Carr is campaigning in Altamont during a real estate boom and race riot. He later advises W. O. Gant to send Eugene to the state university. WTOC 13, LHA 316
References: 33, 35.

Catawba House. Wolfe's name for Biltmore House, the chateau of George Vanderbilt near Asheville. Also called Biltburn. OT 228

Cathcart, Joe. One of Helen Gant's beaus. LHA 144

Cathcart, Miss. Drawling, honey-toned brunette who orders soda at Charlie Evans's drug store. HD 83

Caux, La Comtesse de. An elderly Frenchwoman, called Little Mother by her American friends, who drinks horse's blood and forces Eugene Gant to pretend that he is a reporter for *The New York Times*. OT 808

Chakales, George. A cook on the night shift at the Athens Cafe in Altamont. LHA 300

Chapman, John. A Libya Hill policeman killed by Dick Prosser. WR 149, CSS 343

City's Child, The. A customer in Leo's bar in "Gulliver." FDTM 146, CSS 247

Clapp, Jake. A widower rooming at Dixieland who pays court to Miss Florry Mangle and joshes Eugene Gant about the loss of Laura James. LHA 463

Coggins, Ed. A red-faced man shopping in Charlie Evans's drug store. HD 82

Coker, J. H. A doctor described as a "lung-shark" at the Uneeda Lunch in Altamont. LHA 171

Collingswood. A Harvard graduate who turns Communist and then Humanist. YC 409

Collins, J. T. An Altamont businessman. LHA 46

Colton, Sam. An alumnus of Eugene Gant's university who asks him to speak at an alumni rally. HB 136

Community Guild. A theater begun as a place for the poor to enjoy and express themselves. An adjunct to settlement work. Based on The Neighborhood Playhouse in New York City. WR 322

Conroy, Hunt. A member of the Lost Generation of writers and friend of Foxhall Edwards. Probably F. Scott Fitzgerald. YC 715

Copeland, Dr. Royal S. A writer of a syndicated medical column who is cited by Eliza Gant. OT 240

Cordoza, Pete. A Mexican who, while drunk, wrecks his car in the Sangra di Cristos Mountains of New Mexico and appeals to Dr. Ferguson for help. HD 42

Corpening, Ella. One of the subscribers on Eugene Gant's paper route. Apparently the same person as May Corpening. LHA 303

Corpening, Essie. A black prostitute working the streets of Altamont. WTOC 13

Corpening, Joe. An orderly at an Altamont hospital. OT 234

Corpening, May. A sultry Negress on Eugene Gant's newspaper route. Apparently the same person as Ella Corpening. LHA 167

Cottswold. A popular literary critic in New York City. WR 399

Coulson, Edith. The daughter of Eugene Gant's landlady near Oxford. OT 621, CSS 148

Coulson, Mrs. Eugene Gant's landlady during his stay in Oxford. OT 648, CSS 148

Covington. A town near Pine Rock College where George Webber visits some whores. WR 205

Cram, Mr. A Cambridge musician who delighted in sneering at people and reporting hostile reviews to them. OT 295

Crane, Captain John. A policeman of Cherokee blood working in Libya Hill and doubling as a professional wrestler; father of Nebraska Crane. WR 47, CSS 338

Crane, Myrtle. Nebraska Crane's wife; "small and plumb, and pretty in a dull-like way." YC 60, CSS 472

Crane, Nebraska. A childhood friend of George Webber who becomes a major league baseball player and retires happily to a mountain farm when his legs go bad. A man close to nature and unspoiled by fame, he stands in direct contrast to the evil Judge Rumford Bland and the money-grubbing civic and business leaders of Libya Hill. Although he is cut from cloth woven by Ring Lardner, he is Wolfe's creation in his belief in holding on to traditional values. Wolfe drew upon no single player to create this character; he is a composite and a reflection of what Wolfe found good in baseball and southern Appalachian ethical values. WR 30, YC 57, CSS 332, 469
Reference: See my article in TWR (Fall 1981).

Creasman, Nurse. The night superintendent at Altamont Hospital. OT 223

Creech, Jay. The part-Negro brother of an Altamont butcher. LHA 188

Creech, Michael Walter. An Altamont butcher. LHA 187

Crestville. A mountain town through which Confederate volunteers march in "Chickamauga." HB 83, CSS 383

Crockers, The. Operators of the candy store into which Grover Gant hungrily peers. They merit the wrath of W. O. Gant when they doubt Grover's story about how he earned the postage stamps used to pay for candy. HB 3, CSS 360

Croswell, Cecil. A pompous actor in the Community Guild Theater. WR 393

Cynthia. W. O. Gant's wife who dies from tuberculosis. LHA 5

Daddy. An actor who frequents White's Restaurant with his daughter in "In the Park." Esther Linder Jack's father, Joe Linder. FDTM 170, CSS 250, 451

Dave. A mountaineer who bears news to Tom Weaver that his son Sam has been killed. MTS 170

Davin, Father. An old guard priest and foe of modernism invited to attend parties given by the Misses Potter and Flitcroft. OT 290

Davis, Dr. A prosperous physician and father of Laura Weaver. MTS 97

Davis, Tom. One of Eugene Gant's classmates at Altamont Fitting School. LHA 218

Dempsey, Jack. A heavyweight champion boxer whose match with Firpo George Webber goes to see. WR 251

Depot Lil. A whore in Covington, near Pine Rock College, with whom George Webber loses his virginity. WR 205

Deshaye, Grace. A friend of Helen Gant and daughter of an Altamont plumber. LHA 146

Dexter [Patton]. An early name for Margaret Patton in MH; left unchanged in one instance in the final typescript of the play. MH 73

Dick. A dexterous, joking, soda-jerker working in Charlie Evans's drug store in sultry South Carolina. HD 82

Dingley, Ira. A lower-class boy from the Doubleday section of Libya Hill. WR 54

Dixieland. The name of the boarding house run by Eliza Gant and called the "old barn" by W. O. Gant. In reality, the Old Kentucky Home and not The Thomas Wolfe Memorial in Asheville, NC, Dixieland provides much of the setting for LHA, including Ben Gant's death. Here is where W. O. also dies. LHA 127, OT 213

Doak, Guy. A native of New Jersey and classmate of Eugene Gant at Altamont Fitting School. LHA 318

Doaks, Jim. Brother of Joseph Doaks. CSS 397

Doaks, Joseph. At one time Wolfe wanted to use this name for his central character but later retired it in favor of George Webber. However, it survived in two places: first, as the name of the young novelist whose work is considered, unfavorably, by the firm of Rawng and Wright; second, as the name of the young American writer who meets the Irish critic Seamus Malone in a story published as "Mr. Malone" in the *New Yorker* (29 May 1937). When the story became part of WR, Joe Doaks became George Webber. Joe Doaks was to be Wolfe's version of Everyman. WR 494, CSS 300, 997
Reference: 39.

Doaks, Kate. Sister of Joseph Doaks. CSS 397

Dodd, Hugh. One of the student playwrights in Professor Hatcher's playwriting course at Harvard. OT 114

Dolan, Father Dan. A priest who frequents White's Restaurant with Father Chris O'Rourke in "In the Park." FDTM 171, WR 435, CSS 251

Dorgan, Miss. Secretary at the publishing firm of James Rodney & Company. CSS 587

Dorothy. A society woman who lionizes George Webber. YC 346

Doubleday. A section of Libya Hill where lewd and raucous mountain white trash lives. WR 53

Duke, John. An Altamont man killed by a hotel detective. LHA 317

Dunbar, J. C. A tailor caught up in Altamont's real estate. WTOC 13

Duncan, James. An Altamont man who sometimes helped to put the drunken W. O. Gant to bed. The father of childhood friends of the Gants, Fergus and Sandy Duncan. LHA 28

Duncan, L. K. One of Eugene Gant's college roommates. LHA 482

Duncan, "Teeney." A high school classmate of Helen Gant. LHA 146

Dunn, L. B. A public school principal in Altamont. LHA 340

Eager, Cash. A merchant whose store is broken into by the mob pursuing Dick Prosser. CSS 340

Eaton, Jack. The advertising manager of the newspaper where Ben Gant works. LHA 292

Ebbs, Mrs. Richard Jeter. The highest ranking socialite in Altamont and the envy of Helen Gant. OT 229

Edith, Miss. Eugene Gant's fourth grade teacher and the object of his sexual fantasies. LHA 109

Edwards, Billie. A guest at Dixieland and a liontamer for Johnny L. Jones Combined Shows. LHA 183

Edwards, Foxhall. "A little past his thirtieth year; already a little deaf, holding his head a little to one side as he listens, the whole head and face . . . as shrewd and subtle as a fox—strange mixture of gentleness and granite, innocence and wisdom, simple directness and maddening deviousness, delicacy and strength, the poet, the shrewd Yankee all combined." A friend of the Latimers. A reserved yet warm and kindhearted man with New England roots who works as chief editor at the publishing firm of James Rodney & Co. He becomes a friend to and the spiritual father of George Webber, who finds him grand and admirable and slightly laughable, especially when Foxhall tries to keep his composure in a house filled with women, his wife and four daughters. He has a tragic sense of life, siding with the Preacher and disagreeing with the more hopeful outlook of George. Wolfe based this character on Maxwell Perkins, his editor at Scribner's, a man he came to rely upon heavily in both his creative and personal life. When Wolfe left Scribner's, one reason for breaking with the firm was his desire to prove his ability to do his creative work without Perkins' help. HD 9, YC 16, OMR 96, CSS 582

References: 3, 6, 11, 14, 27, 40, 43, 54, 57, 58, 70, 71, 76, 82.

Edwards, Ruth. The literary-minded daughter of Foxhall Edwards who discusses a term paper with him. Her sisters are named Martha, Eleanor, and Amelia. YC 448

Efird, Maggie. The first wife of W. O. Gant, whom he divorces. FDTM 235

Elinor. A native of Boston and former World War I ambulance driver, who is seeing Paris and France with her friend Ann and Francis Starwick. She obviously belongs to the Lost Generation. OT 687

Reference: Richard Walser's "Boston's Elinor in Paris." TWR (Fall 1982).

Eliot, Wade. Doctor at Johns Hopkins who treats W. O. Gant. FDTM 296, OT 240

Else. A passenger in a Munich train station in "Dark in the Forest." FDTM 100, CSS 167

Enborg, John. The elderly elevator operator in the apartment building where the Jacks live. A defender of the American economic system, he sees little or no wrong in the existence of a privileged class in a democratic society, arguing that each person is given the right to rise by ability. He is killed when trapped in his elevator after having brought many rich people to safety. YC 197

Ettinger, Jack. A friend of the Jacks who brings both his wife and his mistress to the Jacks' party. YC 233

Ettinger, Margaret. The wife of Jack Ettinger and friend of the Jacks. YC 233

Evans, Charlie. Owner of a South Carolina drug store; "a youngish-looking man, a little under forty, of medium height, trim-figured, just slightly inclined to corpulence." Some of his customers call him "Ivans." HD 81

Everett, Lon. See Pilcher Lon. CSS 335

Exeter. A small town near Pulpit Hill; the fictional name of Durham, NC. LHA 396

Fairfields. A town toward which Dick Prosser flees. WR 151

Faithful Dog. "A big shag beast, with comically sentimental eyes." A symbol of loyalty in MH. MH 45

Fame. The goddess sought by writers who comes to call on George Webber when his novel makes a big splash. CSS 290

Far Field Farm. The name of the Hudson River estate of the Pierce family. OT 515

Farley, Roy. An actor in the theatre with which Esther Jack is associated. WR 334

Farrel, Mr. A dance instructor rooming at Dixieland. LHA 462

Fay. A prostitute in Newport News in "The Face of War." FDTM 78, CSS 235

Feeney, Mr. A lodger at Mrs. Murphy's house on Trowbridge Street in Cambridge, MA. OT 160

Feinberg, Sadie. A student in the class taught by Eugene Gant. OT 426

Ferguson, Dr. "A physician, a cadaverous, tall man" who came to the aid of car-wrecked Mexicans in New Mexico. HD 41

Ferguson, Mrs. Wife of Dr. Ferguson traveling with him when they come upon wrecked car in New Mexico. HD 41

Fetzer, Samuel. A theatrical colleague of Esther Jack. YC 232

Finch, Mr. The chief checker at the Newport News job where Eugene Gant finds summer work. LHA 525

Firkins, Mr. and Mrs. Clarence. The hosts in their home, named Snotwood, for the coming-out party of their daughter, Gladys. Among the guests are Catherine Hipkiss, Aline Titsworth, Lena Ginster, Ophelia Legg, Beatrice Slutsky, Mary Whitesides, Helen Shockett, Lofta Barnes, I. C. Bottom, O. I. Lovett, U. B. Freely, R. U. Reddy, Cummings Strong, and Samson Horney. LHA 179

Firpo. "The Wild Bull of the Pampas" whose fight with Jack Dempsey George Webber attends. WR 253

Fishbein, Harry. A student in the class taught by Eugene Gant. OT 477

Flack, Parson. A kingpin of Libya Hill politics and feverish Campbellite. YC 53

Flack, Tom. A hack driver in Altamont. LHA 24

Flint, Seth. "Sour and withered ex-reporter" studying playwriting in Professor Hatcher's class; a prolific writer of cliché-ridden plays, who is considered a misfit by his classmates. OT 171, CSS 181

Flitcroft, Miss. A friend of Miss Potter who helps plan Friday afternoon gatherings of artistic people in Cambridge, MA. OT 287

Flood. The owner of the newspaper where Ben Gant works. OT 36

Flood, Delia. A friend of Aunt Maw and the Joyner family; she shares traits with Eliza Gant, and, therefore, with Wolfe's mother. YC 97

Flood, Jim. A passenger on the train heading north when Eugene Gant leaves home for Harvard. OT 36

Fogarty, Mike. A building contractor and friend of the Gant family in Altamont. OT 160

Fogarty, Nora. An often tipsy Irish maid at the home of the Jacks on Park Avenue. YC 8

Foraker, Wayne. Final victim in Dick Prosser's killing spree. WR 152, CSS 344

Fortescue, Hugh. An English sea adventurer who tried to plant a colony in Old Catawba in 1594; its disappearance gave rise to the legend of the Lost Colony. HB 201

Foxey. Ben Gant's helper at the newspaper office who posts scores telling the progress of a baseball game Ben is listening to on a radio. OT 203

Fried. A Jewish Rhodes scholar. OT 631

Friedman, Samuel. "A meagre-looking little Jew" who works for the Brill Realty Company in Boston. OT 117

Fuss-and-Fidget. A Jewish lawyer from Germany who is arrested by the Nazis during an attempt to flee Germany. YC 681

Gaffney, Pickens. A black loafer in Altamont and friend of Slew-foot. WTOC 94

Gall, J. Brooks. An Altamont preacher. LHA 338

Gallatin, George. The mayor of Libya Hill during Dick Prosser's rampage. WR 144. See McNair, Hugh. CSS 340

Gambell, Joe. A native of South Carolina and husband of Daisy Gant. LHA 151

Gant, Benjamin Harrison. The twin brother of Grover Cleveland Gant; the "quiet one" of the Gants who is much admired by his younger brother Eugene, who learns from him that he must look within himself and go his own way if he is to become what he wants to be. Ben is honest, laconic, and energetic of spirit, though weak of body. His death is one of Wolfe's acknowledged masterpieces. He

seems to appeal to an angel when he wants a witness to some human deed or word, and his ghost becomes the angel to whom Eugene turns for succor. He works as a newspaperman in Altamont and elsewhere. The model for this character was Wolfe's brother Benjamin Harrison Wolfe, to whom he dedicated FDTM. FDTM 213, HB 23, HD 50, LHA 18, OT 47, CSS 523
References: 13, 14, 16, 22, 24, 38, 40, 41, 46, 45, 51, 53, 54, 56, 61, 68, 72, 76, 78, 81, 82, 83, 88, 89.

Gant, Bessie. Ben Gant's nurse during his fatal illness. LHA 541

Gant, Daisy. Eugene Gant's older sister; dutiful, quiet, married to a South Carolinian. LHA 18

Gant, Eliza. Daughter of Major Thomas Pentland and wife of W. O. Gant. Her children are named Steve, Daisy, Helen, Grover Cleveland, Benjamin Harrison, Luke, and Eugene; another child, a daughter named Leslie, died in infancy. Eliza comes from a mountain family, sharing its shrewdness, independence, mystical leanings, ambition to overcome the deprivation caused by the Civil War and Reconstruction, and clannishness. More than anything else, she shares her family's superstitiousness and love of storytelling. Except when pursing her lips or winking her eye, both potent means of body language for her, she never falters in recounting some tale about her own life or some story about an ancestor, cousin, or neighbor. Her manner of talking resembles the flow of associative thought in Molly Bloom's stream of consciousness, not merely by happenstance, since Wolfe knew Joyce well and considered his depiction of Eliza in "The Web of Earth" Molly's equal if not better (LTW, 339). Her talkativeness can both fascinate and exasperate, and the depth and exactness of her memory amaze everyone around here. She has to endure the shame of her husband's drunken sprees and the sting of his words when he rants against her kin, her greed for more land, and her decision to leave his bed and board to run Dixieland. Strong enough to stand any abuse heaped upon her by W. O. and any of their offspring, she becomes a successful businesswoman, buying and selling lots in Altamont and elsewhere. Her industry wins approval, but her frugality turns into stinginess. She saves everything, even short pieces of string. She is proud of her family but has problems showing her love outwardly. She keeps her youngest child, Eugene, at her breast long past the normal weaning time and sleeps with him until his ninth year. She figures prominently in two death scenes, Ben's and W. O.'s Wolfe's mother, Julia Westall Wolfe, served as the model for this character. FDTM 212, HB 15, CSS 533, 550

References: 8, 13, 14, 16, 17, 22, 24, 29, 38, 40, 46, 53, 56, 61, 65, 68, 82, 83, 88, 89.

Gant, Eugene. The central character of LHA and OT and son of W. O. and Eliza Gant, Eugene is in large measure Thomas Wolfe outwardly; inwardly, the correspondence is sometimes close, but enough differences exist to prevent the knowing reader from proclaiming Wolfe and Eugene one and the same. Wolfe, to take only two instances, was far more outgoing and fun-loving than Eugene. Eugene suffers keenly from isolation, neglect, family squabbles, the selfishness and greed of certain family members, and the taunts and charges of favoritism hurled by other siblings, charges usually resulting from the fact that Eugene is sent to a private preparatory school and later to Harvard. Creatively inclined, he spends much time reading and fantasizing and comes under the influence of a sensitive teacher, Margaret Leonard, who heightens his love of poetry, something he had begun to admire from the lips of his father, who likes to quote poems or passages from Shakespeare's plays. Eugene likes the warmth and hospitality of his father but loathes his mother's closefistedness. A sometimes happy but often tormented student, Eugene becomes a hopeful and then failed playwright, a harried teacher, a wanderer, and an aspiring novelist, realizing while in France that his major theme is to be America. As a hopeful writer, he tends to be somewhat like Stephen Dedalus or Lord Byron, though impulses like those of Jonson, Swift, H. L. Mencken, and Sinclair Lewis bring a sting to what he says. Eugene is on a troubled mission of self-discovery and is prone to cast himself in the role of the misunderstood artist. Wolfe was ready to turn to a new surrogate after LHA, but came back to Eugene as a way of tying together materials written after the publication of his first novel. At last, tired of the subjectivity, the Eugene Gant-i-ness of his first surrogate, Wolfe turned to George Webber. LHA 34, OT 3, HB 108, FDTM 213, CSS 222, 533, 542
References: 13, 14, 22, 23, 24, 25, 28, 29, 31, 33, 38, 40, 41, 46, 50, 51, 53, 56, 61, 65, 68, 69, 72, 78, 81, 83, 85, 88, 89.

Gant, Gil. The older brother of W. O. Gant who stands beside him as soldiers march on Gettysburg and who later becomes a plasterer. LHA 74, FDTM 240, OT 79

Gant, Grover Cleveland. The twin brother of Benjamin Harrison Gant. Grover is a family favorite, everyone admiring his gentle ways and good spirits. His death in St. Louis from typhoid fever hits the family hard, especially his mother, who never seemed the same after his passing. He is the subject of one of Wolfe's best and most widely known stories, "The Lost Boy." He is based on Wolfe's brother

Grover Cleveland Wolfe. HB 1, LHA 18, OT 266, FDTM 303
References: 14, 22, 29, 40, 46, 61, 68, 72, 83, 88, 89.

Gant, Helen. The younger daughter of W. O. and Eliza Gant. She is rawboned, energetic, ambitious, magnanimous, and sociable. Her dream is to be a celebrated singer, but she sings professionally only a short while with Pearl Hines before becoming the wife of Hugh Barton, a salesman. Better than anyone else in the family, she could control W. O. Gant during his drunken escapades. She became a substitute mother once Eliza began to operate a boarding house. "There was in Helen a restless hatred of dullness, respectability. Yet she was at heart a severely conventional person, in spite of her occasional vulgarity, which was merely a manifestation of her restless energy." Like her father, she had a thirst for whiskey. She is based on Wolfe's sister Mabel. LHA 18, OT 3, HB 22
References. 13, 14, 22, 29, 68, 81, 82, 83, 88, 89.

Gant, Leslie. First-born child of W. O. and Eliza Gant; died in infancy. LHA 70

Gant, Luke. A stuttering, stammering, humorous, energetic, aggressive and sometimes clownish son of Eliza and W. O. Gant, Luke makes his mark as a salesman and organizer of a sales force of Altamont boys. A gregarious person, his greatest fear is loneliness. He and Helen have a special affinity. Sometimes he appeared to be possessed by a demon, especially when he laughed. Wolfe modeled Luke on his brother Fred. LHA 18, OT 14, HB 24, FDTM 213
References: 72, 88, 89.

Gant, Lydia. Consumptive wife of W. O. Gant who died after she moved with him to Altamont in search of better health. FDTM 231, OT 250

Gant, Ollie. W. O. Gant's nephew, Ollie is a plasterer and the husband of W. O.'s nurse. OT 228

Gant, Steve. The swaggering, restless, unstable, and whiney eldest son of W. O. and Eliza Gant, Steve is inclined to both excessive drinking and self-pity. He has all the character flaws of W. O. and none of his redeeming virtues. He marries a midwestern woman of German descent. Wolfe's model for this character was his brother Frank. LHA 18, FDTM 213, OT 9, HB 23

Gant, W. O. A kind of dynamo aswirl with gusto, rhetoric, lust, love of hot fires and heaped tables, and a frustrated desire to carve an angel, W. O. is a blend of the demonic and angelic. When drunk, he lets his demon rip into Eliza and deride her for leaving his bed and board to run Dixieland. If the boarding house is not the cause

of his outrage, one of Eliza's real estate deals is. Sober, he is a respected stonecutter, caring father, and concerned, if hypocritical, citizen. (His hypocrisy seems limited to drinking. He signs a temperance pledge but backslides often.) A wanderer, he came to Old Catawba from Pennsylvania, married twice before coming to Altamont, where his second wife died of tuberculosis, and took trips to New Orleans and the Pacific coast before being struck by prostate cancer. He enjoyed the theater as a lad, admired Shakespeare, surrounded himself with good books, and longed to carve an angel like the ones shipped in from Italy to his tombstone shop. His battle against cancer was both heroic and bathetic, the latter stemming from his urge to dramatize his self-pity. His destiny is to remain something of an outsider in Altamont, the man from the north arousing the suspicion of Eliza's family and mountain-bred neighbors, but inspiring Eugene's visions of a golden land. His big hands, large mustache, and alert eyes give his lanky body a physical presence felt by everyone around him. Wolfe drew upon his father for this character. Long before writing LHA, Wolfe told his mother, "There has never been anybody like papa. . . . He is headed straight not for one of my plays, but for a series. He dramatized his emotions to a greater extent than anyone I have every known—consider his expressions of 'merciful God'—his habit of talking to himself *at* or *against* an imaginary opponent. . . . I verily believe I can re-create a character that will knock the hearts out of people by its reality" (LTM, 39–40). LHA 3, OT 12, HB 2, FDTM 114, CSS 535
References: 13, 14, 22, 24, 29, 38, 40, 46, 51, 53, 55, 56, 61, 65, 68, 72, 81, 82, 83, 88, 89.

Garfield, Arthur, Harrison, and Hayes. Youthful spectres of Presidents James Garfield, Chester Arthur, Benjamin Harrison, and Rutherford Hayes and part of the memory of W. O. Gant in "The Four Lost Men." FDTM 119, CSS 109

Gates, Bunny. A friend of an unnamed actor (Daddy) in "In the Park." FDTM 173, CSS 252

Gaunt, Gilbert. An English immigrant and ancestor of W. O. Gant. LHA 3

Gavin, Buck. A stall, powerfully built mountain outlaw who appears in Wolfe's first play for the Carolina Playmakers. RBB 33

Gavin, Mary. Sister of Buck Gavin who warns him that the Sheriff is looking for him. RBB 33

Gay, Harold. A college roommate of Eugene Gant. LHA 482

Gely, Madame. Eugene Gant's landlady in Paris. OT 729

Gely, Monsieur. Eugene's landlord in Paris. OT 729

Gertrude. A teacher of handweaving in Zebulon. HB 239

Gibbs, Mr. One of the managers of the Hotel Leopold. OT 448

Gilmer. A boarder at Dixieland who buys a jug of whiskey for the Gant family on the night of his death. OT 262

Glendenning, Bruce. A hero in one of Eugene Gant's fantasies; the beau of Veronica, daughter of J. T. Mullins. LHA 106

Goff, Willie. A happy-go-lucky pencil merchant. HD 127, LHA 342

Gorewitz, Boris. A student taught by Eugene Gant. OT 426

Gorman, Richard. The city reporter for an Altamont newspaper. LHA 340

Goulderbilt. One of the names (the other, Willetts) used for the George Vanderbilt family. LHA 169, OT 228

Grace. The daughter of Gripe, who brought condoms and tuberculosis to Zebulon County. HB 239

Grace. A prostitute in Newport News. FDTM 79, CSS 234

Gracie. Daughter of a Chicago meatpacker; "she is still good-looking, but her looks are somewhat spoiled by a kind of metallic hardness, a kind of feverish nervousness and impatience of manner, a general impression of over-wrought energies, impatient discontent." Rejects American heritage and becomes an Anglophile. Loathes the smell of Chicago. HD 107

Grady, Bob. An Altamont citizen who dropped dead while walking from a bank. LHA 316

Grady, John. A Libya Hill police lieutenant shot by Dick Prosser. WR 147, CSS 342

Grant, Plato. George Webber's philosophy teacher at Pine Rock College. YC 713

Grant, Tom. A college friend of Eugene Gant. LHA 405

Graves, George. A classmate of Eugene Gant at Altamont Fitting School. He is Eugene's companion during the Joyce-inspired walk through the streets of Altamont. LHA 325

Grebenschik, Sol. A student taught by Eugene Gant. OT 426

Green, C. One of the unidentified men of the Great Depression who asserts his individuality by leaping from the Admiral Drake Hotel, refusing to remain a nameless cipher. YC 461, CSS 485

Greenberg, Sol. An Altamont junk dealer. LHA 197

Grey, Mr. A playwright in Eugene's Harvard class. OT 285

Grey, Mrs. A permanent resident at the Hotel Leopold. OT 432

Grimes, Colonel. The head of the militia in Altamont charged with stopping a race riot. WTOC 115

Grinder, Dr. Fairfax. An Altamont lung specialist. LHA 336

Gripe. A mining official who took mica and left the people working the mines with lung disease in Zebulon. HB 239

Grogan, Father. A priest living in Brooklyn. FDTM 13

Grogan, Pat. A customer at Leo's bar in "Gulliver." FDTM 143, CSS 246

Groody, Miss. Eugene Gant's public school teacher. LHA 92

Grubb, Jenny. A kitchen maid in Mrs. Hopper's boarding house. WR 116

Guardsman. A member of the Altamont militia. WTOC 124

Gudger. A neighbor of the Weavers who disputes their claim to some mountain farmland and later kills George Weaver. MTS 90

Gudger, Brock. A rival stonecutter to W. O. Gant. LHA 72

Gudger, Dick. The real estate agent who handled Eliza Gant's purchase of Dixieland. LHA 128

Gudger, Nan. A friend of Helen Gant who worked as a bookkeeper and gave part of her earnings to her loutish brothers for monthly visits to a local brothel. LHA 146

Gudger, Randolph. An Altamont banker who wants to marry Irene Mallard. LHA 472

Gudger, Saul. A pretender to high social standing among Altamont's younger set. LHA 179

Gudger, Saul. A stonecutter and friend of W. O.; perhaps, the same person as Brock Gudger. OT 248

Gudger, Will. A young mountain farmer who becomes an apple grower. MTS 156

Gus. The passenger killed when Pete Cordoza wrecks his car in New Mexico. HD 45

Hake. A flour salesman boarding at Dixieland. LHA 462

Hale, Roderick. A lawyer attending the Jacks' party. YC 232

Harold. Son of Gracie, the daughter of a Chicago meatpacker; "he gives the impression of being sorrowfully undeveloped. He is an ugly child with an egg-shaped head and patchy, close-cropped taffy-colored hair." HD 108

Harris, Mr. A train porter and husband of Pansy Harris who slashes Dick Prosser when he finds him with his wife; shot by Dick Prosser as the first victim in a shooting spree. WR 146

Harris, Pansy. A cook in the Randy Shepperton family who becomes the object of Dick Prosser's affections. WR 136, CSS 335

Hatcher, James Graves. A professor of drama at Harvard University under whom Eugene Gant studies playwriting. Hatcher is suave, urbane, informed, cosmopolitan, and successful. He is noted for his chuckle and for his ability to draw talented writers to his classes. The model for this character was George Pierce Baker, whose English 47 workshop Wolfe attended for three years. OT 94, 130, CSS 177
References: 4, 13, 14, 22, 25, 29, 38, 40, 46, 54, 76.

Hauser, George. A pianist with great sensitivity and alert sensuous powers, but burdened with the habit of repressing all sources of enjoyment except his music. BLL 140, CSS 596

Hauser, Otto. A reader at James Rodney & Company and acquaintance of George Webber. The model for both Otto and George Hauser was Wallace Meyer, a Scribner's reader. YC 21, OMR 102 (Here called George)

Hawke, Arthur McFarlane. Son of Delia and W. O. Hawke and twin brother of Edward Madison Hawke. These names replace those of Benjamin Harrison and Grover Cleveland Gant in LHA and OT. CSS 136

Hawke, Bascom. See Pentland, Bascom.

Hawke, Delia. The name given to the storyteller of "The Web of Earth" in the version printed in *Scribner's Magazine*. She is the wife of W. O. Hawke. Another fictional name for Wolfe's mother. CSS 122

Hawke, Edward Madison. Twin brother of Arthur McFarlane Hawke. CSS 136

Hawke, Helen. See Gant, Helen. CSS 123

Hawke, John. Son of Delia and W. O. Gant. Wolfe chose this name for his surrogate after writing LHA and used it in some periodical pieces before returning to Eugene Gant in OT. CSS 122

Hawke, Lee. See Gant, Luke. CSS 122

Hawke, W. O. Gant, W. O. CSS 137

Haythorpe. An aesthete who supports a variety of artistic forms and causes. He is somewhat like Francis Starwick. YC 409

Heilig, Franz. A German friend of George Webber who works as a librarian. YC 629

Heilprinn, Roberta. A theatrical colleague of Esther Jack. YC 232

Heinrich. A passenger on a German train. FDTM 101

Hendrix, Ralph. A college friend of Eugene Gant. LHA 421

Henry. A doorman in the Park Avenue building where the Jacks live, who spends time as a union organizer. YC 203

Hensley, Dock. A friend of the murderers Ed Mears and Laurence Wayne in "The Web of Earth." FDTM 271

Heston, Mr. One of Eugene Gant's schoolmates at Pulpit Hill. LHA 535

Hewitt, Mrs. Thomas. The comely wife of an Altamont lawyer. LHA 334

Hilliards, The. A family from Charleston, SC, ranking among the highest aristocracy of Altamont. LHA 42

Hill-top Farm. A country house owned by the Coulsons, with whom Eugene stays during his Oxford sojourn. OT 619, CSS 147

Hines, Horse. An undertaker in Altamont whose pride in the makeup job done on Ben Gant sends Fred and Eugene Gant into painful howls of laughter. LHA 171

Hines, Pearl. A ragtime singer and friend of Helen Gant, with whom she toured parts of the South as part of the duet called The Dixie Melody Twins. LHA 146

Hirsch, Lawrence. A New York banker who attends the Jacks' party. He is a "captain of finance, letters, art, enlightened principles" in Wolfe's ironic characterization. YC 231

Hodge, Wellington. A former Methodist preacher from whom Eliza bought Dixieland. LHA 128

Hogan. A hopeful playwright under Professor Hatcher's tutelage at Harvard. OT 303

Hogwart Heights. A local name for the area in which Theodore Joyner's military academy is located. HB 265

Hook, Mary. The sister of Stephen Hook. WR 476, YC 233

Hook, Stephen. A biographer, critic, and friend of Esther Jack. Wolfe's model was Thomas Beer. WR 399, YC 233

Hooton, Carl. A friend of Sidney Purtle and member of a detested group of lower-class boys in George Webber's Libya Hill. WR 35

Hopper, Mrs. Charles Montgomery. A boarding house operator in Libya Hill who had fancy ways and airs. WR 114

Horton, Ed. A student in Professor Hatcher's playwriting class. OT 175, CSS 184

Horton, Effie. The wife of Ed Horton; nicknamed Pooly. OT 310

Hotel Leopold, The. Eugene Gant's residence for a time when he began teaching college English in New York. OT 428

Humperschlagel, Mr. and Mrs. Two disgruntled American tourists in Paris. WR 637

Hundred Club, The. A group formed by Paul S. Appleton III for his top salesmen in the Federal Weight, Scales, and Computing Company. He thought of it as a kind of heaven for salesmen, who would be sent on pleasure cruises at company expense. YC 134, CSS 403

Hunt. A rather bellicose pacifist attending Cambridge University. OT 296

Hutchings, Professor. A political adviser of Preston Carr and head of the Department of Social Welfare at a state university. WTOC 54

Ingram, Billy. A law student at Harvard and friend of Eugene Gant. OT 98

Isaacs, Buster. A cousin of Max Isaacs and occasional playmate of Eugene Gant. LHA 142

Isaacs, Max. A playmate of Eugene Gant. LH 65

Isaacs, Sol. The owner of a Libya Hill clothing store, heading home on K–19 when George Webber returns for Aunt Maw's funeral. YC 53

Isaacs, Sudie. A childhood friend of Daisy Gant. LHA 25

Isaacs, Willie. Younger brother of Max Isaacs. LHA 98

Jack. A customer at a Newport News whorehouse in "The Face of the War." FDTM 79

Jack, Alma. The daughter of Esther and Frederick Jack. YC 227, WR 429

Jack, Esther. A small, brisk, vital, rosy, slightly hard of hearing, good-humored, sensitive, artistically talented stage designer, and wife of a wealthy New York stock broker, Esther becomes George Webber's muse, lover, and millstone. Gracious, open, and gregarious, she enjoys the role of hostess. Her talents in the kitchen match or top those she displays in costume or stage design, and she turns out peerless dishes. Her richly stored mind enables her to converse energetically on many subjects, especially art and literature, which she can also create and inspire. The daughter of a well-known actor, she feels comfortable with everyone in the theater except snobs and bores. Whereas she is at ease, George is not, and the difference

becomes a factor in their breakup. Her work in the theater brings her praise, fulfillment, and torment whenever George derides her for associating with theatrical people. In her behavior, she can be histrionic herself, particularly when she suspects George of cheating on her, or when his slanderous remarks about Jews, actors, or her circle of friends touch her to the quick. Although fine and beautiful in other ways, her love becomes possessive, and her cries of outrage in the throes of jealousy are the ugly match of George's rantings about her unwillingness to let him go his own way. But she lacks George's cruelty and darkness of spirit. Unlike George, she will not intentionally inflict pain, and she is free of the Calvinistic burden of guilt that skews George's perceptions of humanity. Her life and love teach George much about life and how it is to be lived nobly, grandly, intensely, with a healthy respect for the value of play and work. The strongest bond between them, one stronger than food or sex, was their dedication to art and its pleasures. Wolfe based Esther Jack on Aline Bernstein and chose the name as more appropriate and symbolic after trying Rebecca Feitlebaum in early drafts of the love story about his liaison with Aline. The name *Jack* would suggest money, rank, and power, and Esther, which means "star" in Hebrew, would suggest fixity and inspiration. But Wolfe provides this complex character with more than simple name symbolism: she is linked by words and deeds to such heroines as Penelope, Helen, and Eve, and she is a kind of muse as well. Moreover, she stands for the city and its manifold potentials for fame, power, and love. FDTM 169, OT 907, WR 311, YC 5, CSS 300, 430, 451
References: 13, 14, 22, 29, 38, 40, 43, 46, 51, 54, 56, 65, 68, 72, 76, 82. See also Aline Bernstein's fictional treatment of her affair with Wolfe: *Three Blue Suits* (New York: Equinox House, 1933) and *The Journey Down* (New York: Alfred A. Knopf, 1938).

Jack, Frederick (Fritz). A wealthy Wall Street investor and husband of Esther, Fritz likes comfort, fine things, and an orderly life. Believing that the world's moral scheme makes allowance for occasional peccadillos, he does not punish his servants for petty crimes and tolerates Esther's infidelity, and proudly shares her success in the theater. He admires her ability as a hostess and homemaker, for she shows good taste and makes life pleasant for him. Above all, he appreciates what is "solid, rich, and spacious, made to last." WR 434, YC 149

Jackson, J. H. A black owner of an Altamont vegetable stall. LHA 187

James, Laura. A boarder at Dixieland with whom Eugene Gant has an idyllic summer filled with picnics, walks, good talk, and dreams of romance. Laura's relationship is platonic, but tendor and caring nonetheless. She marries soon after leaving Altamont. LHA 427

James Rodney & Co. A New York publishing firm which accepted *Home to Our Mountains*, George Webber's first novel. Wolfe used this name for Charles Scribner's Sons. YC 15

Janie. A maid working for the Jacks. YC 286

Jannadeau, Mr. A jeweller who rented space from W. O. and remained his friend during his drunken sprees. LHA 17, OT 228

Jenny. "A well-developed mulatto girl of twenty-three" who stays on the Ramsay plantation following the Civil War. MH 85

Jeter, Cash. A lawyer who represents Addis Mears in a divorce case and later becomes her husband in "The Web of Earth." FDTM 291

Jeter, Walter C. A judge in Altamont. LHA 346

Jim. One of the debaters in "The Men of Old Catawba." FDTM 196, CSS 216

Joe. An Armenian waiter who tells George Webber a story that will make both of them a fortune if only George will write it. YC 421

Joe. A drunken passenger in a car overturned in New Mexico. HD 43

Joe. One of the debaters in "The Men of Old Catawba." FDTM 195, CSS 216

Johann. Orderly in Munich hospital where George Webber is treated for his head injury. WR 677

John. Lloyd McHarg's valet. YC 572

John. A rich dweller of a well-appointed Manhattan apartment who speaks enviously in "No Door" of the narrator's life in Brooklyn. FDTM 5

John. A wagon driver in "Death the Proud Brother." FDTM 66

Johnson, Annie. The daughter of the black physician Dr. Johnson who secretly sees Lee Rutledge, the son of Will Rutledge, the man seeking to buy the ancestral Rutledge home from Dr. Johnson, its present owner and occupant. WTOC 73

Johnson, Dr. Jim. A mulatto physician in Altamont who has risen from the ranks of the despised and downtrodden to become the owner of the Rutledge plantation home, which he is being asked to sell to Will Rutledge. WTOC 22

Jones, Abraham. A tormented, involuted, melancholy, and loyal student in Eugene's composition class, Abe Jones becomes Eugene's friend and frequent companion. His Jewishness becomes a blend between a pedestal and a millstone; he wants to share the dream of Americans but fears that his faith and looks will be obstacles. His ability to inspire trust and care in Eugene Gant shows his potential for reaching beyond the lonely world of immigrants and misunderstood intellectuals. OT 426

Jones, D. T. A student in George Webber's college philosophy class. YC 709

Jones, Jimmy. The illegitimate son of Sylvia Jones being raised by Abe Jones and his mother. OT 460

Jones, Lily. A prostitute in Exeter with whom Eugene, impotently, goes to bed. LHA 407

Jones, Major Patterson T. An American army officer who made a photograph of Marshal Foch and never sent some promised money to La Marquise Mornaye. OT 845

Jones, Mrs. The mother of Abe, Rose, and Sylvia Jones. OT 492

Jones, Rose. A talented pianist, she is married to a musician; sister to Abe Jones. OT 463

Jones, Sylvia. Sister of Abe Jones and owner of a fashionable dress shop. OT 459

Jordan. A tubercular journalist looking for property to buy in Altamont. WTOC 16

Jordan, Sinker. Eugene Gant's co-worker at Newport News. LHA 517

Josie. A niece of Mrs. Bowden who accompanies her on an outing to Charleston. LHA 358

Joslin, Captain Billy. The locomotive engineer who, in April, 1884, brought the first train to Libya Hill. HB 344

Joyner, Amelia. The daughter of a mountaineer named Lafayette ("Fate") Joyner, she is the wife of John and the mother of George Webber. She is as clannish and provincial as the hill-born family from which she comes. WR 5, YC 96

Joyner, Bill. George Webber's great grandfather. WR 70

Joyner, Dexter Vespasian. An affected dilettante, aesthetic aristocrat, and shallow oracle of wisdom who considers the people from his native region peasants. He is the central character in a rare item in Wolfe's canon, *A Note on Experts: Dexter Vespasian Joyner*. NE 1, CSS 444

Joyner, Drumgoole (Drum). The son of Theodore and Emily Joyner who attends the University of Virginia and returns to teach in his father's military academy. HB 279

Joyner, Earl. Nephew of Mag Joyner and brother of Tad. WR 99

Joyner, Edward. Brother of Mark Joyner who died in his fourth year. WR 167

Joyner, Edward Zebulon. The son of Judge Robert Joyner whose tendency to fantasize links him as a character type to Eugene Gant and George Webber. HB 302, CSS 282

Joyner, Emily Drumgoole. Wife of Theodore Joyner and daughter of a Virginia military academy master. Her bluebloodedness leads her to snub the richest family in town until she discovers a drop of blueblood in Mrs. Willets' forebears. HB 277

Joyner, Emmaline. The daughter of Theodore and Emily who is brought up a snob. HB 279

Joyner, Gustavus Adolphus. The son of Theodore and Emily whose nickname is Silk. Once he finishes his law degree, he migrates to the West. HB 282

Joyner, Harriet (Hattie). The "lusty, gusty" love child of William (Bear) Joyner. HB 228

Joyner, John. The son of Bill Joyner and George Webber's uncle. WR 73

Joyner, Lafayette (Fate). The kinsman under whose roof George Webber actually lives even though his legal guardian is his uncle Mark Joyner. WR 7, YC 95, HB 246

Joyner, Mag. The aunt with whom George Webber lives after his mother dies; she is a tall, gaunt, sneering, bristling Baptist. WR 7

Joyner, Mark. Oldest brother of George Webber's mother and George's legal guardian. WR 7, YC 45

Joyner, Maw. The oldest daughter of Lafayette Joyner and the person most actively involved in rearing George Webber. A woman who epitomizes mountain and mode of behavior, she is, in some ways, another fictional version of Wolfe's mother. WR 8, YC 45

Joyner, Rance. The youngest of Bill Joyner's children, he is known as "Stinkin' Jesus" because of his odor and religious fervor. He is Lafayette Joyner's brother. WR 71, YC 718, HB 246

Joyner, Robert. The son of William "Bear" Joyner who is trained to become a lawyer. HB 228, CSS 283

Joyner, Rufus. The eldest son of William "Bear" Joyner who runs the family store and becomes notorious for his stinginess. HB 225

Joyner, Sam. The son of Bill Joyner and George Webber's uncle. WR 73, HB 246

Joyner, Tad. A nephew of Aunt Maw Joyner. WR 99

Joyner, Theodore. The youngest son of William "Bear" Joyner who fails at law but succeeds as a master of a military academy. Symbolic of southern colonelcy, he lives by outmoded codes of gentlemanly behavior and marries a snobbish Virginia woman, Miss Emily Drumgoole, the daughter of a military academy operator near Winchester, VA. Theodore is heir to Wolfe's satire against military men and schools dating back to MH. HB 228, CSS 514
References: 34, 89.

Joyner, William ("Bear"). An early settler in Zebulon County in Old Catawba, William first marries Martha Creasman and becomes the father of seven children. A legendary hunter in the Davy Crockett mold, he earns the nickname "Bear." After the death of his first wife, he marries another mountain woman and raises a large second family: Betsy, Alice, Melissa, Florabelle, Lafayette, Sam, John, Claudius, Sid, and Rance. Wolfe drew upon his maternal great grandfather, William Westall, for this character. HB 212, WR 70, CSS 514
Reference: See Richard Walser's article in TWR, entitled "Thomas Westall and His Son William" (Spring 1984).

Joyner, Zachariah. A country lawyer and successful politician from Zebulon County in Old Catawba. This colorful, dynamic, crass, bawdy, sly, and humane character was based on Zebulon Vance, one of the most celebrated men from the mountains of North Carolina. He was that state's governor during the Civil War. HB 208, CSS 514
References: 17, 20, 47, 62, 88.

Judson, Mack. A real estate agent in Libya Hill. YC 54

Katamoto. A Japanese sculptor who lives in George Webber's apartment building and complains, good-humoredly, about George's stalking the floor above him. YC 28, CSS 351

Katz, Mr. A student enrolled in Eugene Gant's class. OT 477

Kendall. The editor of an Altamont newspaper. WTOC 117

Kennedy, Baxter. The mayor of Libya Hill who actively boosts the city's real estate boom, but who commits suicide when the boom turns to a bust. YC 53

King's Highway. A major thoroughfare in St. Louis near which Eliza's boarding house is located. The boarding house sits on Edgmont Street. HB 42, CSS 374

Kitchin. A companion during Eugene Gant's drunken ride to Blackstone, SC (Greenville). OT 363

Krause, Otto. A German immigrant and classmate of Eugene Gant. LHA 92

Lampley, Baxter. The son of a Libya Hill butcher and a rapist. WR 122

Lampley, Grace. The searingly sensual daughter of a Libya Hill butcher and sister of Baxter, whose sex drive is uncontrollable. WR 123

Lampley, Mr. An Irish butcher in Libya Hill who marries a big, coarse mountain woman and fathers two sex-driven children. WR 118

Lampley, Mrs. The Amazonian wife of a Libya Hill butcher notable for her "epic animality." WR 119

Lane, Bessie. A gray-haired spinster and director in the Community Guild Theatre. YC 233

Latimer, Amy. "A good-looking woman, not deeply intelligent, but active-minded, amiably and amusingly garrulous, possessing the gift of storytelling, the pleasant humor, that are certainly two of the most agreeable attributes of the Southern temperament." Wife of Andrew Latimer and sister of Margaret Meadesmith. HD 9

Latimer, Andrew. "A spare lean man approaching fifty"; a Virginian opposed to the pacifist policies of Woodrow Wilson; husband of Amy Latimer. HD 9

Latimer, Mr. A consumptive painter of the Impressionist School and husband of John Dorsey Leonard's sister Sheba. LHA 223

Lavender, Doc. One of the victims in Dick Prosser's shooting spree. WR 151, CSS 344

Ledig. The landlord of George Hauser. BLL 157, CSS 611

Leo. The bartender in "Gulliver." FDTM 134, CSS 246

Leonard, Amy. The sister of John Dorsey Leonard and teacher of mathematics at Altamont Fitting School. LHA 222

Leonard, John Dorsey. A public school principal who founds Altamont Fitting School and does an uninspired job of teaching Greek and Latin, being better suited to farming and tending livestock. Based on the husband of Wolfe's spiritual mother, Margaret Roberts. LHA 205

Leonard, Margaret. Eugene Gant's teacher at Altamont Fitting School, who awakened in him a love for poetry and whose encouragement of his speaking and writing ability helped to shape the course his life would take. Wolfe's model for this character was Margaret Roberts, a teacher at the North State Fitting School whom he came to

regard as the mother of his spirit. LHA 208
References: 13, 14, 22, 24, 38, 40, 46, 54, 65, 72, 83, 88, 89.

Leonard, Tyson. The nephew of John Dorsey Leonard. LHA 320

Levenson, Sol. A New York stage designer and friend of Esther Jack. WR 330

Lewald, Karl. The German publisher of George Webber's novels. YC 624

Libya Hill. The birthplace of George Webber, this small mountain town becomes a center for the tourist trade and for people looking for a cool place for summer homes. A need for land fuels a real estate boom, and starts local developers dreaming of riches in a continuously expanding economy. Prosperity comes, but more on paper than in reality. When the bubble bursts, the town suffers greatly, and many of its business and civic leaders kill themselves. The model for this city was Wolfe's hometown of Asheville, NC. HB 241, WR 3, YC 15, CSS 280

Lichenfels. A Jewish boarder at Dixieland suffering from tuberculosis. LHA 141

Liddell, Charles. An electrician in Altamont who serves as the model for Luke Gant's choice for a career. LHA 114

Liddell, Major. A Civil War veteran living in Altamont. LHA 111

Linder, Edith. The sister of Esther Jack and an employee in the fashionable New York store of Stein's and Rosen's. WR 339, YC 166

Linder, Joe. Actor and father of Esther Jack and Edith. WR 406. See Daddy.

Lipinski, Isaac. A Jewish schoolboy harrassed by Eugene Gant and his friends. LHA 96

Little Maudie. A writer of a social gossip column for an Altamont newspaper. LHA 179

Locust Gap. A railroad head to which Confederate soldiers march in "Chickamauga." Wolfe's fictional name for Hickory, NC. HB 83, CSS 383

Locust Street. The address of the Joyners with whom George Webber lives. WR 101

Logan, Piggy. A faddish artist whose performance of a wire-circus goes embarrassingly awry at a party given by the Jacks. Wolfe's model was Alexander Calder, whose fame was yet to be earned when Wolfe saw him perform his act with figures now in the Whitney Museum in New York. YC 218

Reference: See my article entitled "Thomas Wolfe Attends a Performance of Alexander Calder's Circus," in *Thomas Wolfe: A Harvard
Perspective*. Ed. Richard S. Kennedy. Athens, OH: Croissant & Co.,
1983.

Longstreet, General James. One of the Confederate generals in "Chickamauga." HB 77, CSS 394

Louise. An Altamont waitress who goes on an outing to Charleston,
SC, with Mrs. Bowden and becomes involved in a torrid but un-
consummated love scene with Eugene Gant. LHA 358

Luther. A fishmonger with whom Helen Gant trades. OT 228

Lutz, Margaret. An Indiana woman of German ancestry whom Steve
Gant marries. LHA 239

Lyda, Jim. An Altamont sheriff. LHA 55

Lydia. W. O. Gant's second wife and victim of tuberculosis in "The Web
of Earth." FDTM 231; see Gant, Lydia.

Mabley, Nick. A student in Eugene Gant's philosophy class at Pulpit
Hill. LHA 594

McCoy, Hunter Griswold. The liberal president of Pine Rock College
who is considered by some of his admirers to be "the second greatest
man since Jesus Christ." Based on Edward Kidder Graham, the
president of the University of North Carolina during Wolfe's studies
there. WR 202

McGuire, Doctor Hugh. An Altamont physician who is called in when
W. O. goes on one of his binges, and who expresses amazement
at the growth of Eugene Gant's hands and feet in "No Cure for It."
LHA 43, HB 43, OT 210, CSS 533

McHarg, Lloyd. An American novelist and leading figure in letters who
is at "the zenith of his career" when George Webber meets him in
London. McHarg is restless, driven, drunken, and has found no
enjoyment in fame, appearing to George to be a "tormented tene-
ment of fury" in his rapid pacing of his hotel floor and in his refusal
to rest. McHarg praised George's novel during a speech and pre-
dicted a distinguished contribution to American letters by the
younger writer. The two authors undertake a trip in heavy English
fog and rain to the country estate of McHarg's friend, and wander
across much of southeast England before reaching it. Sinclair Lewis
served as the model for McHarg, but Wolfe exercised many liberties
in fictionalizing the junket the two of them made. YC 537, CSS 300
Reference: For a very brief account of the London encounter and

the wild ride across the English countryside, see Mark Schorer's *Sinclair Lewis: An American Life* (New York: McGraw-Hill, 1961), pp. 558–59.

McIntyre. A teacher forced to leave Altamont for espousing Darwin's theory of evolution in his classroom. WTOC 42

McIntyre, Jim. A Libya Hill man shot and crippled for life by Dick Prosser. WR 148

McKissem, Mr. One of the rejected beaus of Daisy Gant. LHA 130

McLendon, Reese. A man beaten to death with a horseshoe by Dock Hensley. WR 271

McMurdie, Reese. One of the mountain grills from the Doubleday section of Libya Hill. WR 54

McNabb, Harley. George Webber's friend in Libya Hill who labels a review copy of *Home to Our Mountains* "pretty frank." YC 330

McNair, Hugh. As the town's mayor, he attempts to stop a mob from lynching Dick Prosser. CSS 340. Called George Gallatin in WR.

McPherson, Hugh. A law-abiding citizen of Libya Hill who attempts to stop a lynch mob in pursuit of Dick Prosser. WR 144

McRae, D. H. The minister of Altamont's First Presbyterian Church. LHA 185

Mad Maude. The narrator's landlady in "No Door." Thinking herself harmed by his depiction of her and her family, Marjorie Dorman, Wolfe's landlady at 40 Verandah Place, in Brooklyn, brought suit against Wolfe and Scribner's for $125,000. Settled out of court, the suit cost Wolfe $2,745.05, half of the amount agreed upon by the attorneys handling the case. Wolfe's unhappiness over the reluctance of Scribner's to let the case come to court was a factor in his decision to break with the firm. FDTM 9
References: 6, 54, 76.

Makropolos. A Greek immigrant who buys a house from Bascom Pentland. OT 183

Mallard, Irene. A roomer at Dixieland who tries to console Eugene Gant after the departure of Laura James. LHA 463

Malone, Seamus. An Irish literary who lashes out at most modern writers, including T. S. Eliot, but who finds a few kind words for George Webber's first novel. Based on the outspoken Irish critic Ernest Boyd. WR 520, CSS 301
Reference: See my "Thomas Wolfe and T. S. Eliot: The Hippopotamus and the Old Possum" in *The Southern Literary Journal* 13 (Spring 1981).

Mandell, Lily. A "tall, smoldering beauty" who attends the Jacks' party. She is the heiress of an American Midas. YC 231

Mansfield. An actor and friend of Esther Jack's father. CSS 251

Man's Voice, The. One of the pair of lovers recalling the past and thinking of the future on the rocky coast of Maine. HD 131

Margaret. A friend of George Hauser who telephones him and tries to persuade him to leave his shell and go out with her. BLL 150, CSS 605

Margaret. One of the prostitutes working in Newport News. FDTM 81

Marple, Mr. George Webber's neighbor in a South Brooklyn apartment house. YC 401

Marriott, John Hugh Williams MacPherson. The husband of the daughter of Altamont's richest family, he travels north on the same train that carries Eugene to Harvard. Wolfe based this character on John Francis Amherst Cecil, the husband of Cornelia Vanderbilt. OT 61 Reference: See "Wealth in Their Midst: Bill Nye and Thomas Wolfe on the Asheville Vanderbilts" by David B. Kesterson and John L. Idol, Jr., TWR (Fall 1983).

Martin, Howard. One of the men who gossips about Ellen Rossiter's fling with a stable boy. OT 517

Martin, Mrs. A permanent resident at the Hotel Leopold. OT 432

Mascari, Pete. The operator of a fruit shop in Altamont. LHA 177

Mason, Mrs. The mother of Lydia and mother-in-law of W. O. Gant in "The Web of Earth." FDTM 232, 252

Mathilde, Marquise de Mornaye. A noblewoman near Orleans with whom La Comtesse de Caux arranges a meeting with Eugene Gant. OT 830

Matthews. A Libya Hill policeman. WR 20

May. A maid at the home of the Jacks. YC 212

May. A prostitute in Newport News in "The Face of the War." FDTM 79, CSS 234

Maysville. A town in Old Catawba on the rail line leading to Virginia. OT 30

Meadesmith, Margaret. "A girl of twenty-five whose manner in conversation is marked by vivacity and humor. In repose, however, ... the expression of the face is touched with sadness, a kind of lonelines and resignation." Sister of Amy Latimer and friend of Foxhall Edwards. HD 9

Mears, Addie. The wife of the murderer Ed Mears in "The Web of Earth" who marries Cash Jeter following her divorce from her husband. FDTM 291

Mears, Ed. An escaped murderer whose story is told, in rambling fashion, by Eliza in "The Web of Earth." FDTM 225–26.

Mears, J. Rufus. A real estate agent, gambler, and drunkard who is considered an infallible adviser on buying and selling property. CSS 124

Mears, James ("Duke"). The beau of Pretty Polly and would-be aristocrat. WR 113

Meeker. A clergyman who comes to the Friday afternoon soirées at the Misses' Potter and Flitcroft in Cambridge. OT 303

Meekins, Zebulon N. A congressman from Libya Hill who spoke at the high school graduation ceremonies of George Webber's class. WR 104

Merrick, Big Bill. A "hog-jowled and red" Altamont policeman; perhaps the same person as Big Bill Messler. LHA 165

Merriman, Henry T. An Altamont lawyer. LHA 334

Merrit, David. Randy Shepperton's boss at the Federal Weight, Scales, and Computing Company; a pink-cheeked Santa Claus of a fellow with "jolly little jokes" and a stony heart. YC 94, CSS 397

Merrit, Robert. See Merrit, David. CSS 397

Messler, Big Bill. A paunchy citizen of Altamont. LHA 76

Michalove, Edward. The effeminate son of a Jewish jeweller in Altamont with only one strike left when he meets the other boys in town. Unmerciful, they throw him curves. LHA 234

Mike. The ambulance driver in "Death the Proud Brother." FDTM 28

Millerton. A community near the Blue Ridge Mountains in Old Catawba; Wolfe's name for Morganton, NC. HB 249

Minister. A preacher who leads prayer for savage heathens and cites biblical passages, a few of them created out of thin air, in support of slavery. MH 30

Mock's. A restaurant in "In the Park." FDTM 170, CSS 251

Monk. A member of an Altamont Boy Scout troop. LHA 338

Monroe and Madison College. The chief football rival of Pine Rock College, loosely based on the University of Virginia. WR 178

Reference: See my note entitled "Easley's Bill Folger: Thomas Wolfe's Football Star," in *Pembroke Magazine*, number 17 (1985).

Moody, Gus. A crony of Steve Grant. LHA 46

Morgan, Mrs. A boarder at Dixieland with suspected Cherokee blood who gives birth to a baby out of wedlock. LHA 227

Moriarty, Frank. An Altamont moonshiner with social pretensions. LHA 332

Morison. An aristocratic Englishman, a kind of prodigal son, with whom Eugene Gant spends time in Oxford. OT 613, CSS 150

Motorman, The. Operator of streetcar on Atlantic Avenue, who challenges a drunken seaman's claim that Brooklyn lacks decent air. HD 93

Mug. One of the hoboes in "The Bums at Sunset." FDTM 153

Mulatto. A furtive overseer helping to build the Ramsay mansion. MH 30

Mullins, J. T. The father of Veronica Mullins, the heroine in Eugene Gant's fantasy starring Bruce-Eugene Glendenning. LHA 107

Mullins, Veronica. The beloved heroine in Bruce-Eugene Glendenning's fantasy. LHA 106

Munson, Victor. One of the loathed mountain grills from the west side of Libya Hill. WR 36

Murphy, Eddy. The son of Eugene Gant's landlady on Trowbridge Street in Cambridge, and a student at Boston College. OT 160

Murphy, Jimmy. The son of Eugene Gant's landlady on Trowbridge Street in Cambridge whose poverty of language is both pitiable and scornful. OT 160

Murphy, Mrs. The wife of a night watchman, mother of sons named Eddy and Jimmy, and Eugene Gant's landlady on Trowbridge Street in Cambridge. OT 160

Myerson, Sylvia. One of the directors of the Community Guild Theatre. WR 330

Myrtis. A girl who worked for Helen Gant. OT 228

Mysteries of Asia, The. A fancy brothel in Paris. WR 647

Nagle, Maurice. A theatrical director and friend of Frank Werner. WR 481

Nast, Harry. One of a gang of lower-class whites that George Webber finds loathsome. WR 35

Neely, Helen. A stenographer for Altamont Development Company, who is described as having sweetness but "little light." WTOC 15

Nelson, Ida. The assistant director of Altamont's Shakespearean pageant. LHA 374

Newton, Miss. Eliza's assistant manager at Dixieland. LHA 529

Nicholl. A former army officer who works in an automobile factory near Oxford, England. OT 624, CSS 151

Night-Eye. A Frenchman who helps George Webber find a ticket for the Folies Bergere. WR 642

Nino. A waiter at Posillipo's who is admired by Francis Starwick. OT 277

O'Boyle, Tim. A childhood friend of Eugene Gant whose mother also runs a boarding house, the Brunswick. LHA 202

O'Donnel, Tim. An Altamont bartender. LHA 23

O'Doul, Mr. A lodger at Mrs. Murphy's home on Trowbridge Street in Cambridge. OT 160

O'Doyle, Tim. An Altamont publican, who along with Major Ambrose Nethersole, claims membership in the Party of the Wets. LHA 284

O'Haley, Father James S. J. A small priest serving a church in Altamont. LHA 332

Old Catawba. A middle Atlantic state with socially pretentious citizens in the eastern section, hard-working middle-class citizens in the Piedmont region, and independent and argumentative dwellers in the mountains. Wolfe's name for North Carolina. OT 3, FDTM 185, HB 109, CSS 214

Old Looky Thar. A Confederate Civil War veteran who boasts of his wound. His real name is Purtle, and he was bestowed upon himself the rank of major. He is another form of Old Sorrell in WTOC 32, HB 323, CSS 284

Old Sir Kenelm. The *nom de plume* of an essayist following in Charles Lamb's footsteps. JB 92, CSS 589

Old Stockade. A mountain village where Confederate volunteers camp on their way to a rail head at Locust Gap. Wolfe's name for Old Fort, NC. LHA 7, HB 83

One-eyed Spaniard. The European discoverer of Old Catawba in "The Men of Old Catawba." FDTM 189, CSS 265

O'Rourke, Father. Lover of the theatre and friend of Father Dolan. WR 435, FDTM 171, CSS 251

Osherofsky, Sidney. A student in Eugene Gant's composition class. OT 426

Otto. A passenger waiting in a Munich train station in "Dark in the Forest." FDTM 100, CSS 167

Packer, Dr. The St. Louis physician from whom Eliza rented a house to be used as a place for boarding visitors to the St. Louis Fair. HB 27, CSS 377

Page, Leonidas Paget. Elderly, bald, mustached, partner of the law firm of Paget and Page. JB 95, CSS 591

Paget, Joe. An acquaintance of Edward Rivers who trades innuendos with him about a prominent preacher who is sued for breach of promise by an actress. OMR 99, CSS 577

Paget, Lucius Page. Elderly lawyer, gentle patrician, and partner in the prestigious firm of Paget and Page. JB 94, CSS 591

Pappas, Mr. The owner of a Greek restaurant in Altamont. OT 228

Park, Johnny. Eugene Gant's friend and a Rhodes Scholar. OT 627

Parker, Hugh. One of Helen Gant's beaus. LHA 144

Parsons, W. Wainwright. A renowned religious writer and Sunday school superintendent whose sexual peccadillos make the headlines and lead to surprise and envy on the part of his peers. HB 180, CSS 510

Paston, Fergus. An Altamont banker who gazes lecherously at Miss Bernie Powers. LHA 334

Paston, Hunter. A Hudson River millionaire who owns a miniature railroad and who has a fireworks show every July 4. OT 578

Patton, Lucindy. A slave owned by Captain Patton in "The Web of Earth." FDTM 215

Patton, Major Robert. The head of a military academy and father of Margaret Patton. Given to bragging and flights of Walter Scott-inspired rhetoric, he represents Age in the contest between Youth and Age featured in MH. He leads his troops off to battle and returns to carry on the militaristic spirit of the South by re-opening his school. An unreconstructed Rebel, he believes that the South was unbeaten though defeated. MH 48
References: 34, 40, 46, and Jerry L. Rice's "Thomas Wolfe's *Mannerhouse*," in TWR (Spring 1982).

Patton, Margaret. The daughter of Major Patton, a military school master. She loves Eugene Ramsay, who seems to think of her as someone he has known as a pre-existing soul. She is hit hard by the Civil War and Reconstruction but has the strength to face the reality of a plebian life after the aristocratic order that produced her has been toppled. In some drafts of MH, Wolfe had her taking up school-teaching as a livelihood. MH 55

References: 34, 40, 46, and Jerry L. Rice's "Thomas Wolfe's *Mannerhouse*," in TWR (Spring 1982).

Patton, Martha. The first wife of Bill Pentland in "The Web of Earth." FDTM 221, OT 253

Patton, Martha. A mountain girl with whom Jim Weaver falls in love. He swears that he will marry her. HB 87, CSS 382

Patton, Thomas ("Bull"). A friend of Lee Rutledge who enjoys parties and the good life of country clubs. He is one of Wolfe's sharpest depictions of a Southern member of the Jazz Age. WTOC 65

Patton, Willy. A slave owned by Captain John Patton in "The Web of Earth." FDTM 216

Pearson, Jim. A customer in Charlie Evans's drug store who enjoys making bawdy remarks to the soda-jerker, Dick, who works there. HD 82

Pearson, Junius. A rich Altamont socialite in whose circles Helen Gant would like to move. OT 228

Pegram, Ernest. A neighbor of the Gant family and a plumber who inherits enough money from a brother to enjoy the good life in Altamont. OT 228, HB 139

Pegram, Scroop. The president of an Altamont bank. OT 355

Pennock, Ernest. Mark Joyner's next-door neighbor. WR 107

Pennock, Sam. A childhood friend of George Webber who becomes a successful real estate agent. WR 107, YC 112

Pension Burger, The. The place in Munich where George Webber was living before attending Oktoberfest. WR 653

Pentland, Arnold. The fat son of Bascom Pentland whose comings and goings are mysterious and whose appetite is enormous. He calls himself Arthur Penn. HB 66, CS 222

Pentland, Bacchus. A religious fanatic and prophet who is seen by W. O. Gant on the Gettysburg road and again in Altamont. He shares with Rance Joyner the unsavory tag of "Stinking Jesus" because of his foul odor and religious fervor. He becomes a Russellite and spends much time calculating and re-calculating the time the world will end. LHA 9, OT 10, HB 78

Pentland, Bascom. Eugene Gant's uncle whose passage from clergyman to a Boston real estate agent took many twists and turns, particularly in the denominations of churches served and theology espoused. He ended by becoming a Unitarian. His mind is keen and stocked with bits of poetry, drama, family history, biblical lore, and legal jargon. Nothing stops his flow of words. When provoked, he can hurl verbal thunderbolts. In conversation, he usually assumes the role of a debater, and a domineering one at that. Except for her stubbornness about playing recordings of the music of her beloved Wagner, his wife shrinks before him. At home and at work, but more so in his office than in front of his wife, his language can be ribald, bawdy, energetically sarcastic. For all his verbal fire, he has a despairing outlook and seems something of a hollow man ready to give in to old age. He serves, in short, as yet another voice in Wolfe's continuing thematic concern for Youth and Age. He is colorful, dynamic, and unforgettable nonetheless, a humorous character in the mold of Jonson and Dickens. He is called Bascom Hawke in the version of the story published in *Scribner's Magazine* and for which Wolfe shared a first prize in a fiction contest. In LHA, he is referred to as Uncle Emerson. LHA 614, OT 15, HB 66, CSS 222 References: 13, 14, 40, 44, 46, 54, 76, 82, 88.

Pentland, Bill. A mountain settler who becomes a hatmaker and father of many children in "The Web of Earth." Wolfe based this character on his great grandfather William Westall. FDTM 219, HB 77, CSS 381
Reference: See Richard Walser's article in TWR, entitled "Thomas Westall and His Son William" (Spring 1984).

Pentland, Crockett. A bookkeeper in his brother's lumber firm in Altamont. OT 246

Pentland, George. Eugene Gant's cousin who comes to see him off to Harvard and who later steals the wife of Emmet Blake. OT 9

Pentland, George. Helped to make effigies of slaves. FDTM 215

Pentland, Greeley. "Congenital scrofulous tubercular, violinist, Pentlandian punster, petty check-forger, and six weeks' jailbird." This is the image W. O. Gant has of Eliza's brother. Wolfe based this character on his uncle Horace Greeley Westall. LHA 13

Pentland Heights. A housing development in suburban Boston built on a "flat and weary waste" by Bascom Pentland. OT 182

Pentland, Joe. Eugene Gant's cousin who accompanies him in his visit to Zebulon County in "Return of the Prodigal." HB 125

Pentland, John. A mountaineer who fights with the Confederate forces at Chickamauga. The story he tells covers his parting from his kin and friends, the march of a rail head, the fierce battle itself, and his return home. Wolfe heard the tale from a kinsman, John B. Westall. HB 77, CSS 381

Reference: See John S. Phillipson's "Thomas Wolfe's 'Chickamauga': The Fact and the Fiction." TWR (Fall 1982).

Pentland, Louise. A music teacher who separates from her husband, Elmer Pentland. LHA 250

Pentland, Louise. The wife of Bascom Pentland and admirer of Wagnerian opera. OT 142

Pentland, Sam. One of Bill Pentland's sons and Eliza's brother in "The Web of Earth." FDTM 219, OT 10

Pentland, Thomas. Eugene Gant's maternal grandfather. He wrote poems, stories, and essays and spent much time exploring religious and philosophical questions. Eliza traces Eugene's gift to him. The model for this character was Wolfe's grandfather Thomas Westall. LHA 13, FDTM 282

Reference: See Richard Walser's "Major Thomas Casey Westall," in TWR (Fall 1984).

Pentland, William. Eugene Gant's maternal uncle who owns a lumber store in Altamont. His flourishing business makes him one of the town's richest men, and his success brings out the competitive spirit of his sister, Eliza. Some of his mannerisms, particularly his habit of flensing his hand and paring his nails, resemble those of Porter of MH. The model for this character was Wolfe's Uncle William. LHA 13, OT 9, FDTM 216

Pentland, Zeb. A prosecuting attorney in "The Web of Earth." FDTM 272

Pert, Marie. An alcoholic guest at Dixieland who becomes Ben Gant's friend. LHA 183

Pettigrew, Colonel James Buchanan. The head of Pettigrew Military Academy in Altamont. He and Major Robert Patton of MH probably were modeled on Colonel Robert Bingham, head of Bingham Military Academy in Asheville, where Wolfe was offered a teaching position after graduating from the University of North Carolina. LHA 347

Reference: 88.

Pettigrew, Edward (Buck) Benson. Eugene Gant's college Greek professor. LHA 401

Phelps, Jim. One of Helen Gant's beaus. LHA 144

Pierce. The father of Joel and Rosalind Pierce who owns an estate on the Hudson River. OT 501

Pierce, Ida. The mother of Joel and Rosalind Pierce. She is a skilled and gracious hostess. OT 516

Pierce, Joel. The scion of a wealthy Hudson River family who becomes Eugene Gant's friend and loyal supporter. He is a talented amateur artist, but his devotion to a quiet, meditative, humane way of life is stronger than his commitment to art. A kind of family Buddha, he never says or does anything to harm anyone. Wolfe drew upon his friend Olin Dows, whom he came to know at Harvard and to whose home at Rhinebeck, NY, he was often a visitor. For a time after the publication of LHA, Wolfe attempted to use materials gathered from his association with Dows and his circle in a book entitled "The River People." OT 500
References: 40, 54, 76.

Pierce, Mrs. Joel. The Kentucky-bred wife of the patriarch of the Pierce family. OT 560

Pierce, Old Joel. The grandfather of Joel and Rosalind Pierce and patriarch of the wealthy Hudson River family. OT 556

Pierce, Rosalind. The sister of Eugene Gant's friend, Joel; she hears Eugene read *Mannerhouse* and generously, if unskillfully, praises it. OT 519

Pigtail Alley. An area of Altamont inhabited by poor whites. LHA 97

Pilcher, Lon. A drunken Libya Hill driver who kills Albert and Johnny Andrews. WR 110. See Everett, Lon. CSS 335

Pine Rock College. A small Baptist-affiliated college attended by George Webber. It is perhaps a cross between the University of North Carolina and the Wake Forest College of Wolfe's era. WR 177, CS 514

Plemmons, Jim. One of George Webber's shipmates during a crossing of the Atlantic. WR 305

Pocallipo, Joe. The owner of a New York speakeasy where George Webber and Esther Jack celebrate George's 25th birthday. WR 352, CSS 432

Polly. A friend of the Pierce family who shares a juicy bit of gossip. OT 516

Porter. A lower-class white who tries to keep his son out of the Confederate army and envies the property and power of the Ramsays, his aristocratic neighbors. After the Civil War, he buys the Ramsay mansion and razes it. He is a Snopes-like character, though he came on the scene, fictionally, before that tribe. He is notable for his nod, wink, and flensing of his hands. MH 69

References: 34, 40, 46, 54, 68 and Jerry L. Rice's essay entitled "Thomas Wolfe's *Mannerhouse*," in TWR (Spring 1982).

Porter, Melvin. A lawyer and friend of Will Gant in "The Web of Earth." FDTM 224

Porter, Rufus. He borrows money from W. O. Gant and does not repay it in "The Web of Earth." FDTM 227

Portia. A maid in the home of Foxhill Edwards. YC 449

Posillipo's. An Italian restaurant and speakeasy in Boston; also called Masillipo's. OT 276

Potter, Miss. A spinster living on Garden Street in Cambridge, MA, who, with her dear friend, Miss Flitcroft, holds parties for artistic and intellectual persons on Friday afternoons. On the guest list are members of Professor Hatcher's playwriting class and an odd mix of other people, some invited because the hostesses want sparks to fly when their guests converse. Both Miss Potter and her friend may safely be described as caricatures, but they are interesting characters nevertheless. OT 286

Potterham, Augustus. A childhood acquaintance of George Webber whose bulldog is killed by Simpson Simms' mastiff. WR 19, CSS 332, 449

Pottle, Tobias. A soda jerker in Altamont. LHA 342

Pounders, Ben. A member of the mob that lynched Dick Prosser; brags about shooting Dick. CSS 346

Powell, C. M. An Altamont undertaker. LHA 331

Powers, Miss. A midwestern schoolteacher on a European tour in "One of the Girls in Our Party." FDTM 160

Pratt, Genevieve. One of Helen Gant's high school friends. LHA 146

Pretty Polly. A singer and pianist for an Altamont theater; she also appears in WR, thereby earning the distinction of a place in both the Gant and the Webber cycle. HD 50, HB 50, WR 117, CSS 523

Price. A Rhodes Scholar and roommate of Johnny Park. OT 629

Prosser, Dick. An athletic, deeply religious, and quiet black man who wins the admiration and respect of those for whom he works and with whom he plays. Apparently harmless and extraordinarily caring, he wins the trust of all who know him. His shooting spree leaves many Libya Hillians dead or seriously wounded. His body is riddled by a gun-happy posse and brought back for display in town. To suggest the mystery of goodness and evil, Wolfe quotes from William Blake's "The Tiger." Wolfe's story of Dick Prosser was the only one he sold to *The Saturday Evening Post*. For an excellent study of Prosser and the story as a whole see Suzanne Stutman's "Technique in 'The Child by Tiger': Portrait of a Mature Artist" *The South Carolina Review* 18, no. 1 [Fall 1985], 83–88. WR 132, CSS 332 References: 40, 46, 65, 88.

Pulpit Hill. The name of the university town where Eugene Gant goes to college. It is a playful renaming of Chapel Hill, NC, where the University of North Carolina is located. LHA 396, CSS 236

Purtle, Mrs. S. Frederick. A socialite in Altamont who calls Theodore Wills with news of a dinner and bridge party at her home. A guest list which she supplies resembles, in its play on names, some of Wolfe's undergraduate humor. The surname "Slagel" appears in "The Newspaper" in HD. HB 61, HD 61, CSS 531

Purtle, Sidney. A member of a group of mountain boys considered coarse and insolent by George Webber. WR 34, CSS 558

Purvis, Daisy. An English charwoman in the employ of the man from whom George Webber takes rooms in London. Garrulous to the core, she rambles on about this and that, but often about the upper classes in England, with whose ways she finds no serious faults. To her way of thinking, a structured society is proper. Her favorite topic is British royalty. She is as much a Tory as any duke or princess. YC 513, CSS 316

Queen Elizabeth. An Altamont madam who buys a marble angel for a deceased girl in her brothel. The episode in which she and W. O. Gant appeared was Wolfe's first piece of published fiction. LHA 24 Reference: See Guy Owen's " 'An Angel on the Porch' and *Look Homeward, Angel*," in TWR (Fall 1982).

Radiker, Ambrose. The owner of a saloon frequented by W. O. Gant and his friends in "The Web of Earth." FDTM 224

Ramsay. The original builder of a plantation house who believes that some men are masters, others slaves. He subdues some slaves, including the kingly figure who most stoutly and intelligently opposes him. He wants his house to endure forever. His son is named Robert. MH 30

Ramsay, Alec. An Altamont stonecutter and friend of W. O. Gant. OT 228

Ramsay, Eugene. The son of William and Mary and brother of Ralph Ramsay. Sardonic, questioning, alienated, lonely, sensitive, not knowing whether he is a ghost or alive, Eugene Ramsay stands as a direct ancestor of Eugene Gant, although the earlier one had traces of Hamlet, Coleridge, George Bernard Shaw, and Cyrano de Bergerac confusedly mingled in. He scoffs at much of what his family holds sacred and lashes out at such southern institutions as privately run military academies. Romantic notions about war arouse his ire, since he sees Walter Scott's glorification of going into battle as an illusion blinding southern leaders to the harsh realities of war. His father's notions about some men being chosen by God to rule while the great masses must obey strike him as self-serving poppycock. His mother's Victorian sentimentalism he finds absurd, but not quite so absurd as the tinsoldierism of Major Robert Patton. He is willing to follow his father to battle and to fight gallantly because he respects the man and the family he represents, a cultivated group of planters who care for many of the finer things of life. He dislikes the attitude of defeatism that infests his father's thoughts and actions during Reconstruction, but he feels powerless to stop his father's moves to hold on to the old ways by selling off part of the estate. At last, he must suffer the indignity of watching the family home fall into the hands of a greedy and crass poor white, Porter. His outrage over Porter's gleeful destruction of the Ramsay mansion finds an outlet in a Samson-like act of demolition and self-sacrifice when he pulls the house down upon himself, Tod, and Porter, an act symbolizing the end of a southern social system based on an uneasy and unacceptable alliance of former slaves, poor whites, and fallen aristocrats. His love for Margaret Patton leaps from Hamlet-inspired faultfinding to Cyrano-like adoration. And if that were not enough, he cannot make up his mind about her reality, for he has a philosophical question about whether he and she are really ghosts. Eugene Ramsay, in short, is a character with many dimensions, a character with fascinating but ultimately confusing facets. MH 44 References: 34, 40, 46, and Jerry L. Rice's "Thomas Wolfe's *Mannerhouse*," in TWR (Spring 1982).

Ramsay, General William. A southern aristocrat representing the plantation society in its defense of its values and the ultimate break-up of that essentially feudal order within a nation subscribing to a democratic system. He believes, with Thomas Carlyle and others, that some men were meant to rule, others to obey. He demands loyalty, commitment, and gentlemanly conduct because the code of behavior that produced him and his kind requires life to be lived in a prescribed manner. Although he is willing to go to war to defend his way of life, he puts up no fight to change the course of Reconstruction. To live in the old manner as long as he can, he sells his land and even the ancestral home. He becomes a man of romantic gestures, earning both pity and scorn from the people around him. He is the husband of Mary and the father of Eugene and Ralph Ramsay. MH 44

References: 34, 40, 46, 68, and Jerry L. Rice's "Thomas Wolfe's *Mannerhouse*," in TWR (Spring 1982).

Ramsay, Mary. The wife of William Ramsay and mother of Ralph and Eugene. She is a sentimentalist who represents the values of southern aristocratic women. Better than her husband, she learns to endure the hardships of Reconstruction, but she never develops into a forceful character. As the play evolved her role became less and less important. Early drafts gave her spunk but left her with a more bitter defeat because, despite her efforts, everything tumbled around her when the men in her family broke under the strain of trying to carry on in ruined circumstances. MH 53

References: 34, 40, 46, 68, and Jerry L. Rice's "Thomas Wolfe's *Mannerhouse*," in TWR (Spring 1982).

Ramsay, Ralph. The younger son of William and Mary and Eugene's brother. He loves uniforms, the thought of glory on the battlefield, and good times. His loyal support of southern aristocracy places him at odds with Eugene; he lacks Eugene's sardonic, questioning attitude. MH 55

Ramsay, Robert. The son of the Ramsay who built the family mansion after moving from Virginia. MH 37

Rand, John. The jailer on duty when Ed Mears and Laurence Wayne escaped in "The Web of Earth." FDTM 278

Randall. A man who talks with some Altamont newspaper boys in Uneeda Lunch. LHA 166

Randolph, James Heyward. A sports hero who leads the Pine Rock College football team to victory over Monroe and Madison, receives an injury in World War I that curtails his athletic career, becomes a sports reporter in New York, and ends by claiming a place among the Lost Generation. The model for this character was Augustine William Folger. WR 174

Reference: See my article entitled "Easley's Bill Folger: Thomas Wolfe's Football Star, in *Pembroke Magazine* (Number 17, 1985).

Randolph, Steve. A citizen of Altamont who marries Emma Smathers. OT 5

Raper, Justin. The son of Bishop Raper and student at Altamont Fitting School who is caught in sexual union with Hazel Bradley. LHA 233

Ravenel, Dr. Dick. An Altamont surgeon who has an aristocratic appearance. LHA 176

Rawls, Mrs. Roland. The wife of a wealthy Altamont manufacturer. LHA 334

Rawng, Hyman. The partner in the New York firm of Rawng and Wright where George Webber submits his novel. WR 488

Ray, Laura. An Altamont nurse who works for Dr. Coker. LHA 352

Reade, Rickenbach. The English host to Lloyd McHarg and George Webber at his country estate and "a writer of sorts." YC 596

Red. A young reporter in Altamont who formerly worked for the *Atlanta Constitution*. He has a great idea, he thinks, for a novel about the true parentage of Abraham Lincoln. HB 53, HD 53, CSS 523

Redmond, Dave. One of Luke Gant's customers for a copy of the *Saturday Evening Post*. OT 45

Redmond, Wilson. A Libya Hill police magistrate who tries to arrest Dick Prosser. WR 148

Reed, Dan. An office man employed by the Altamont Development Company. WTOC 15

Reed, Lillian. The deceased prostitute for whom "Queen" Elizabeth buys a marble angel from W. O. Gant. LHA 265, CSS 6

Reed, "Preacher." The pastor of Pine Rock Episcopal Church who is considered by some students to be the "third greatestman since Jesus Christ." He mixes sports and religion and mingles comfortably with students. He seems to be a forerunner of the type now found in the Fellowship of Christian Athletes. WR 197

Reed, Ted. A mountain cousin of Eugene Gant who guns down Emmet Rogers and warns Eugene not to put the episode in a book. HB 126, CSS 553

Reinhart, Stephen. One of Eugene Gant's classmates at Altamont Fitting School. LHA 218

Revel, Mrs. An Altamont woman who, for a time, rents Dixieland from Eliza to operate as a boardinghouse. LHA 317

Reynoldsville. A mountain town near Altamont; Wolfe's fictional name for Hendersonville, NC. LHA 258, CSS 411

Riggs, Jarvis. A Libya Hill banker headed home on the train when George Webber returns to Libya Hill for Aunt Maw's funeral. YC 53

Rivers, Edward. A self-satisfied, stuffy, Victorian-minded editor retired from *Rodney's Magazine*. Based on Robert Bridges, an editor at *Scribner's Magazine*. He appears in "Old Man Rivers," a story published in *The Atlantic Monthly* (December 1946). The story was part of Wolfe's satirical use of various persons connected with Charles Scribner's Sons. OMR 92, CSS 563

Robert. Young lad who dies of typhoid fever in St. Louis. CSS 359. See Gant, Grover Cleveland.

Roberts, Clem. A mountaineer who calls on Richard Weaver to treat his sick daughter. MTS 77

Roberts, Leslie. An Altamont police patrolman. LHA 174

Rockham, Dr. George B. The Altamont author of the Shakespearean pageant in which Eugene Gant plays the role of Prince Hal. LHA 372

Rogers, Emmet. A mountain man killed by Tom Reed. HB 127

Rolls, Ralph. One of Eugene Gant's classmates at Altamont Fitting School. LHA 326

Rosecrans, Old Rosey (William Starke). The Union general commanding the forces against which the narrator of "Chickamauga" fought. HB 92, CSS 388

Rosen, Mr. The owner of a fashionable New York dress shop where Esther Jack and her sister, Edith Linder, work. WR 400, FDTM 31

Rossiter, Ellen. A rich girl who takes a stable boy as a lover. OT 516

Rountree. A student in Virgil Weldon's philosophy class. LHA 594

Ruth. A cousin of Rosalind and Joel Pierce. OT 553

Ruth. A public school classmate of Eugene Gant and the object of his sexual fantasy. LHA 205

Rutledge, Lee. The pleasure-loving son of Will Rutledge and law student who is secretly seeing the daughter of a mulatto physician in Altamont, Dr. Johnson. WTOC 39

Rutledge, Mrs. The wife of Will Rutledge and member of a local drama group. She is childish and kept that way by a patronizing husband. WTOC 77

Rutledge Park. A prestigious residential area in Altamont. WTOC 18

Rutledge, Will. A nostalgic man from an aristocratic southern family who tries to purchase his ancestral home, now in the hands of a mulatto physician, Dr. Johnson. He is literate, laconic, intelligent, proud, given to dreaming of the past but willing to work with a pushy crowd of philistine business men if need be, to regain access to his family's old place, and capable of condoning violence if his ends are thereby served. WTOC 34

References: 34, 40, and Jerry L. Rice's "Thomas Wolfe's *Welcome to Our City,*" in TWR (Fall 1981).

Saltonstall, Ambrose. A resident of Louisburg Square, Beacon Hill, Boston, who reads a disparagement of a modern literary movement in the Boston Evening *Transcript* with satisfied approval. HD 69

Saltonstall, Mrs. Ambrose. High-toned Boston lady who closes window to a bawled song by an Irishman. HD 70

Sanders, Miss. A blonde-haired, drawling customer and friend of Miss Cathcart who orders a soda at Charlie Evans's drug store. HD 85

Saunders, Captain Bob. The commander of the Confederate unit in which the narrator of "Chickamauga" serves. HB 81, CSS 382

Savage Chieftain. An African king who is subjugated by Ramsay after hurling an ax into a column of the house Ramsay is building; a forerunner of Tod. MH 34

Sawyer, Jim. An Altamont young blood, owner of a Cadillac, and beau of Miss Cutler. LHA 136

Scarsati, Tony. A friend of the Gant family. OT 227

Schmidt, "Nosey." The son of an Altamont butcher. LHA 103

School for Utility Cultures, Inc., The. A large school in New York City where George Webber finds a teaching job. He considers the institution an educational factory where students come to train for high-paying jobs and where teachers follow literary fads and engage in fierce backbiting in their efforts to succeed as academics. Although Wolfe's model here was the Washington Square College of New York University, the satire is more general than specific. Wolfe's idea of a university placed stress on building good minds, strengthening the capacity to enjoy beauty, heightening the ability to perceive and appreciate truth, and keeping the power of the imagination alert and functioning. The shoe Wolfe describes in depicting The School for Utility Cultures, Inc. would have fit many feet in his era and, with the rise of technical and vocational colleges since his death, now fits hundreds more. The defenders of New York University largely chose to view Wolfe's satire as specific, a factor that mars the value of a book that treats Wolfe's years at the Washington Square campus. WR 315

Reference: See *Thomas Wolfe at Washington Square,* edited by Oscar Cargill. New York University Press, 1954.

Scoggins, Roonsworth. Friend of Clara Kimball Young who melodramatically spurns her love when he finds she is married. HD 98

Scoville. A playwright in Professor Hatcher's class; "an elegant and wealthy young dawdler from Philadelphia." OT 114

Scudder, Lulu. The literary agent who places George Webber's novel. Wolfe based this character on Madeleine Boyd. WR 524, YC 15 References: 54, 76, and Boyd's own account, *The Discovery of a Genius,* published by the Thomas Wolfe Society in 1981.

Seaholm, Carl. A guest at the home of Joel Pierce. OT 580

Seaman, The. A drunken Irishman who boards a streetcar in Brooklyn and, while continuing to drink, berates the foul air of that city. HD 91

Selborne, Delia. The pubescent daughter of Mrs. Selborne; Luke Gant fondles her and Eugene has sexual fantasies about her. LHA 259

Selborne, Mrs. A sensual earth goddess from South Carolina who spent the summer at Dixieland. LHA 147

Sergeant. A member of the Altamont militia who tries to help put down a race riot. WTOC 124

Shankworth, Miss. An advocate of free love and birth control, attending party given by the Misses Potter and Flitcroft. OT 290

Shepperton, Margaret. The big, strong, energetic sister of Randy Shepperton who acts as George Webber's hostess when he returns to Libya Hill for Aunt Maw's funeral. YC 47

Shepperton, Randy. A boyhood friend and lifelong supporter and confidant of George Webber. He helps George see himself more clearly and tells him to stop playing the role of the wounded faun. WR 132, YC 47, CSS 332

Shulemovitch, Nathaniel. A student in Eugene Gant's composition class. OT 426

Shulemovitch, Sam. A Communist editorial writer invited to attend the Friday afternoon parties hosted by the Misses Potter and Flitcroft. OT 290

Shytle, Loney. A sluttish poor white girl from Pigtail Alley. LHA 98

Sidney. The capitol city of Old Catawba; Wolfe's name for Raleigh, NC. LHA 419, OT 254

Simms, Simpson. A pock-marked black man and childhood acquaintance of George Webber. WR 18, CSS 448

Simon. A millionaire who boards at Dixieland and keeps two bodyguards, Flannagan and Gilroy, with him. LHA 198

Simpson, Genevieve. A young violinist from Melrose, MA, whom Eugene Gant calls on and begins to treat shabbily in order to assault her family's pretentiousness. OT 194

Simpson, Jimmy. The brother of Genevieve Simpson. OT 196

Simpson, Mrs. An acquaintance of Bascom Pentland and mother of Genevieve and Jimmy Simpson. OT 195

Sinclair, Mr. The mayor of Altamont. WTOC 112

Singvogel, Mr. The tour guide and bus driver in "One of the Girls in Our Party." FDTM 158

Sister Sheba. Wife of tubercular artist and mother of two healthy daughters. LHA 223

Sladen, Mrs. An elderly Altamont woman whose body is prepared for burial by Horse Hines. LHA 171

Slagel, Frederick. See Purtle, Frederick.

Slew-Foot. A black man whose time is spent loafing in Altamont. WTOC 94

Sluder, Fagg. A retired contractor and baseball fan who owns the Altamont baseball park and club. LHA 262, OT 204

Smallwood, John. A Baptist preacher in Altamont. WTOC 112, LHA 339

Smathers, Bessie. One of Richard Weaver's patients. MTS 95

Smathers, Emma. One of Eliza Gant's friends from childhood. OT 5

Smathers, H. M. An Altamont dentist. LHA 330

Smathers, Tyson. A boy who takes over Eugene Gant's old paper route. LHA 561

Smead, Perce. A young Southerner who shares a New York City apartment with George Webber. WR 224

Smike. A lumber thief in Zebulon County. HB 239

Snead. A ballad thief in Zebulon County. HB 239

Snuggerie, Ye. An apartment at Altamont Inn occupied by gubernatorial candidate Preston Carr. WTOC 86

Society of the Sons and Daughters of the Aborigines. A socially pretentious group from the eastern section of Old Catawba claiming descent from the Lost Colony. HB 207

Sorrell. An Altamont fish and oyster man. LHA 187

Sorrell, Henry. A booster, civic leader, and real estate developer in Altamont. WTOC 17, LHA 339

Sorrell, Old. A Civil War veteran and racist from Altamont; the father of Henry Sorrell; essentially the same character as Looky Thar in HB. WTOC 32

Spangler. A client in the law firm of Paget and Page. Wolfe once planned to use the name Paul Spangler for the material now associated with George Webber. JB 96, CSS 592

Spangler, Elly. A neighbor of W. O. Gant in Pennsylvania. OT 259

Spangler, Paul. Another fictional surrogate of Thomas Wolfe. Part of the name remains in the opening pages of WR. See George Webber.

Spangler's Run. A small community in Pennsylvania near where W. O. Gant lived. OT 258

Spaugh, Dr. Jefferson. A handsome physician with country club polish in Altamont who is jocularly called Percy Van der Gould by his medical colleagues. LHA 173

Sprague, Cornelia Fosdick. The wife of an art patron and the pillar of a salon. YC 563

Spurgeon, Chester. An intellectual critic in New York who once taught at the School for Utility Cultures. YC 410

Starwick, Francis. An assistant in Professor Hatcher's playwriting course at Harvard, and son of a Midwestern family. He becomes an aesthete, a dilettante, and collector of Japanese prints. He befriends Eugene Gant and enjoys sharing his knowledge of art and good places to eat with him. He is quick to recognize Eugene's talents and encourages his work. Later, however, after a decadent escapade in Paris with two Boston women and some Parisian habitués of bistros, Eugene declares Starwick his "mortal enemy" because he sees him as someone representing a degenerate rather than a creative approach to art and life. The fact that Starwick's homosexuality moves from a latent to an active stage has much to do with Eugene's bitter denunciation of him. But part of the outrage stems from Starwick's Francophilism, something thrown more into focus since Eugene is now discovering that the great theme he is to treat in his writing is America. Starwick begins to evolve as one of Wolfe's most complex and engaging characters, someone depicted with understanding and sensitivity, but Wolfe ends by portraying him as a monstrous caricature of a Bohemian. Kenneth Raisbeck was the model for this character. OT 94
References: 13, 14, 16, 22, 25, 40, 46, 54, 68, 76.

Stearns, J. T. A railway passenger agent in Altamont. LHA 566

Stein's and Rosen's. A fashionable dress shop in New York where Esther Jack works as a designer, and her sister serves as vice president. WR 432

Sterling. A Rhodes Scholar hailing from the American Southwest. OT 630

Sterling, Bob. A college roommate of Eugene Gant who dies of a heart disease. LHA 480

Stevens, Amanda. A blunt, plain-spoken mountain woman in "The Web of Earth." FDTM 218

Stoat, Donald. A strait-laced English publisher ridiculed by Lloyd McHarg for his pompous pretentiousness. YC 548

Stumptown. A Negro section in Altamont. LHA 579

Suggs, "Fielder." A former professional baseball player who owns two of Libya Hill's cinemas. WR 111

Sykes. A black Bostonian championing the cause of Negroes in Altamont who serves as the traveling secretary of a group called "Society for the Promotion of Brotherly Love, Racial Equality, and Humanitarian Principles Between the Colored and White People." WTOC 103

Tall Stranger, The. The highpockets subjected to jokes and questions in "Gulliver." FDTM 146, CSS 241

Tang. Francis Starwick's dog's name. OT 309

Tarkinton. A neighbor of the Gant's on Woodson Street. LHA 25, OT 228

Tarkinton, Harry. One of Eugene Gant's childhood playmates. LHA 65

Tarkinton, Seth. A childhood friend of the Gant children. LHA 25

Tayloe, Judge Webster. A retired corporate counselor. LHA 181

Teitlebaum, Morris. A Libya Hill pawnbroker who sold a rifle to Dick Prosser. WR 138

Telfair, Margaret. A Hudson River neighbor of the Joel Pierce family. OT 514

Ten Eyck, Oswald. A former Hearst syndicate employee attending Professor Hatcher's playwriting course; his plays are always about food because he is constantly hungry. OT 282

Thelma. A prostitute in Exeter, a town near the college Eugene Gant attends. LHA 408

Theresien Fields. The section of Munich where the Oktoberfest is held, and where George Webber fights with some drunken Germans and receives a head wound. WR 662, CSS 308

Thomas, George Henry. A Union general in the battle at Chickamauga. HB 77, CSS 391

Thomas, Mary. An Altamont prostitute and friend of Helen Gant. LHA 145

Thornton, Dr. A permanent resident of the Hotel Leopold. OT 437

Thornton, George. A guest at the home of Joel Pierce on the Hudson River. OT 518

Thrall, Miss. A student in the women's section of Professor Hatcher's course who reads a translation of a German play. OT 292

Tipton, Sam. The grandson of Amos Todd and a convict just out of prison. WTOC 96

Tod. The loyal servant of the Ramsay family and descendant of the type of character represented by the Savage Chieftain in the Prologue of MH. He stays behind to serve the Ramsay family after other slaves have left. Symbolic of the serving class, he dies when Eugene Ramsay pulls down a column of the Ramsay house being razed by Porter. His loathing of Porter, a poor white, shows that his loyalty lies with the aristocrats. MH 45

Todd, Amos. An elderly black cobbler who is forced to sell his home so that a new development can be built. WTOC 33

Toe River. A shortened form of the Indian word, *Estatoe*; a stream near which the Pentland family lived. HB 77, CSS 381

Tolly, Gus. A drinking pal of W. O. Gant hailing from Seneca, SC, in "The Web of Earth." FDTM 261

Torrington. A literature teacher at Pulpit Hill. LHA 397

Trivett, Jim. One of Eugene Gant's college friends. LHA 404

Trotter, Mrs. The wife of an Old Catawba education professor studying for an advanced degree at Harvard. OT 97

Tugman, Harry. A newspaperman working in the same office as Ben Gant. He enjoys satiric banter and the companionship of Ben. Wolfe returned to him in "Gentlemen of the Press" after having given him a brief role in LHA. LHA 168, HB 51, HD 51, CSS 523

Turner, Dr. Hugo Twelvetrees. A celebrated editor and literary critic. HB 150, CSS 420

Turner, Mrs. A midwestern schoolteacher on a European tour in "One of the Girls in Our Party." FDTM 155, CSS 195

Turner, Mrs. Hugo. The wife of a literary critic and book reviewer. HB 159

Tyson. The president of an Altamont bank. WTOC 112

Uneeda Lunch Cafe. An Altamont eatery where many townsmen gather for coffee or breakfast and engage in lively repartee and ribald jests. It is the scene of one of Wolfe's sharpest renderings of small town American life. LHA 166

Upshaw, Martha. A wealthy woman with whom Robert Weaver has a tempestuous affair. OT 451

Upshaw, Mr. The husband of Martha Upshaw who is cuckolded by Robert Weaver. OT 484

Van Vleeck, Paul. A fashionable writer attending Esther Jack's party. The model for this character was the novelist Carl Van Vechten. WR 469, CSS 300

Van Yeats. Eugene Gant's classmate at Altamont Fitting School and son of a shoe store owner. LHA 326

Vatel, Madame. The wife of a hotel manager in Orleans. OT 813

Vila, Joe. A sports writer working for the *New York Sun*. NE 15, CSS 440

Vogelsang. See Singvogel. CSS 197

Voices. Faint sounds speaking to Eugene Ramsay as he returns to his ancestral home. MH 137

Van Kohler, Else. "A young widow of thirty who looked and was a perfect type of the Norse valkyrie"; she became George Webber's companion in Berlin. YC 624, CSS 462

Vucker, Sam. A student in Eugene Gant's composition class. OT 426

Wade, Emmet. A swarthy Altamontian on the train carrying Eugene Gant to Harvard. OT 37

Wagner, J. Timothy. The Libya Hill drunkard who becomes the respected oracle on when to buy and sell real estate, acting as "the high priest of prophet of [the town's] insanity of waste." YC 93

Wakefield. A Civil War veteran and neighbor of George Webber living in South Brooklyn. YC 405

Walters, Hen. A friend of Piggy Logan. YC 275

Wang. A Chinese student at Harvard who takes a room next to Eugene Gant's at Mrs. Murphy's home on Trowbridge Street. OT 166

Ward, Stanley P. A foppish real estate salesman employed by the John Brill Realty Company in Boston. OT 118

Ware, Jennings. A newspaper carrier whose route in Niggertown Eugene Gant assumes. LHA 298

Ware, Randolph. A scholar and teacher at Pine Rock College addicted to digging up facts. He was based on the famous Spenserian scholar Edwin Greenlaw. WR 216

Warren, Hattie. A gray-haired spinster and director of the Community Guild Theatre. YC 233

Warren, Mr. Nicknamed "Sugarlips," he is the butler of James Wyman. HB 171, CSS 501

Watson, Genevieve. The sister of Hugh Barton, the husband of Helen Gant. LHA 382

Wayne, Laurence. An escaped murderer who figures in Eliza's recollections in "The Web of Earth." FDTM 226

Weaver, Ben. A farmer and Tom Weaver's father. MTS 89

Weaver, Dick (Richard). See Richard Weaver.

Weaver, Doctor. "A heavy florid-faced man of medium height" and the father of the young physician Richard Weaver. MTS 64

Weaver, Grandpa. A mountain farmer who is shot in a dispute over property boundaries with his neighbor, a man named Gudger. MTS 88

Weaver, Jim. A mountaineer fighting with the Confederacy in the Civil War; the best friend of the narrator of "Chickamauga." HB 77, CSS 381

Weaver, Laura. The wife of Richard Weaver; also the name of Richard's daughter. MTS 54, 95

Weaver, Mag. A mountain girl working as a housemaid for Laura and Richard Weaver; she marries Tom Weaver. MTS 70

Weaver, Reese. The son of Tom Weaver described as a "heavy looking lout of eighteen." MTS 130

Weaver, Richard. An idealistic physician who returns to his native mountains upon finishing his training, to work among the backward and medically neglected people from which he sprang. His hope is to serve all the people well and avoid getting caught up in a feud between his family and another mountain clan. He marries the daughter of another physician, who wants him to leave the mountains for a better career in town, where all the family will also be safe from any of the occasional squabbling that breaks out. Despite his vow to have no part in the senseless feuding, Richard cannot desert his family when the fight comes. MTS 54

Reference: Pat M. Ryan's Introduction to *The Mountains*, published by the University of North Carolina Press in 1970, is the best source.

Weaver, Richard. Son of Richard and Laura Weaver. MTS 134

Weaver, Robert. A classmate of Eugene Gant in Altamont and at Pulpit Hill, who goes on to study law and to enter into the society of fabulously rich people by becoming the lover of Martha Upshaw. He is restless, destructive, violent when drunk, and impetuous. In his family there runs an insane streak, and he did not escape it. Wolfe meant to use Robert Weaver in "K-19" and wrote 180 typed pages of copy entitled "The Man at the Wheel" to tell Weaver's madcap passage from boyish highjinks to Lost Generation desperation. OT 16, CSS 128
Reference: See my Foreword to *K-19: Salvaged Pieces*.

Weaver, Sam. The youngest son of Tom Weaver. MTS 129

Weaver, Tom. A mountain farmer. MTS 87

Webb, Burton. A lawyer and publisher caught up in Altamont's real estate boom. WTOC 13

Webber, George Josiah. The central character of WR and YC whose simian-like traits lead to the nickname "Monk." This was the name Wolfe finally settled on after trying John Hawke, Paul Spangler, Joe Doaks and others in his attempt to replace Eugene Gant as his fictional surrogate. George is something of a Southern grotesque, though Wolfe was working not so much in the tradition followed by Faulkner and Flannery O'Connor as that of Jonson, Swift, and Dickens. Wolfe wanted George to be an American Gulliver, a rather naive, trusting, well-intentioned person who discovers the difference between the ideal and real world. To achieve the kind of detachment he needed for the element of satire planned for the work that he began after the publication of OT, Wolfe wanted someone far more objective than Eugene Gant and someone far less under the sway of James Joyce's Stephen Dedalus. He also wanted a character whose looks would help him gain the fullest impact from his intention to prove once again that appearance isn't reality. Like Socrates or any number of grotesques from fiction and drama, George's physique would belie his actual or potential spiritual beauty. (Wolfe had wanted to bring Socrates into the Gant cycle to make precisely this point, by describing Eugene's thoughts upon seeing the heavy, ugly face of Socrates as portrayed in a bust in the Boston Museum of Fine Arts, but the episode was cut as he and Perkins put OT together.) Like Eugene, George would have forces tugging at him, the two strongest being the culture of his mother's hill-bred folk and his father's tales of the farms and cities of the

North. The first seemed dark, oppressive, life-denying; the second, golden, liberating, life-affirming. Escape from the fanatical, superstitious, clannish ways of his maternal heritage seemed to be essential if George hoped to become a writer. But he came to see that he could not be a whole artist until he could somehow reconcile the dark Helen of his blood (the South) with his golden vision of the North. As he grew older and as the nation changed, he saw that he must try to speak for the common man everywhere, not for any one section of the country. George would have a social and political awareness denied to Eugene Gant, denied for aesthetic and logical reasons in OT, when Perkins finally convinced Wolfe that ideas fueled by the Depression were not a part of Eugene's consciousness.

George would struggle with personal problems as well as those confronting the nation, but they would ultimately be linked in George's mind. He desired fame and love, seeking them as the twin pinnacles of happiness, but finding them both far less satisfying than he thought they would be. George also wanted to speak out on the state of morals and art in the nation, believing them to be decadent. A traditionalist in both, he found the old values and forms worth preserving and following.

In his love for Esther Jack, George is a provincial cad, a singer of golden love lyrics, a mean-spirited ingrate, an eager and appreciative devotee of great art, food, and stories, a pool of swirling and dark passions, a buoyant companion, a distrustful lover, and a host of other contradictory things.

Some traits of George's character betray egocentrism, especially when he casts himself in the role of the aesthetic wounded faun, but compassion for the downtrodden and the poor eventually leads him to choose the role of spokesman for his unlettered brothers and sisters. Unlike his fatalistic friend Foxhall Edwards, George wanted to be "Man-Alive" and work to make the American social, economic, and political system better. His hope for change rested on his faith that Americans could find what had gone wrong and then make the needed repairs. George saw greed and selfishness as the chief ills. WR 3, YC 3, CSS 447, 459, 469

References: 5, 10, 13, 14, 16, 19, 22, 28, 30, 38, 39, 40, 43, 44, 45, 46, 48, 51, 54, 63, 68, 76, 82.

Webber, John. The father of George Webber and native of Pennsylvania who becomes a builder. He marries Amelia Joyner, a mountain woman, when he comes to Libya Hill. WR 3, YC 105, HB 294

Webster. A publisher in Altamont. WTOC 117

Weisman, Bessie. A student in Eugene Gant's composition class. OT 426

Weldon. A young Confederate officer whom Eugene Ramsay considers a "faultless ass" and tries to embarrass. MH 61

Weldon, Virgil. Eugene Gant's philosophy professor at Pulpit Hill who espouses a personalized form of Hegelianism. Wolfe based this character on Horace Williams, a revered philosophy teacher at the University of North Carolina. LHA 594, OT 65
References: 40, 83, 88.

Werner, Frank. A literary buff attending Esther Jack's party. WR 468

Westerman, Andy. The roommate of Robert Weaver and son of a vacuum cleaner manufacturer. OT 307

Wheeler, Mary Todd. A friend of Lee Rutledge attending a dance at the Altamont Country Club. WTOC 69

Wheeler, Mrs. The mother of Mary Todd Wheeler and chaperone at a dance at the Altamont Country Club. WTOC 70

White's Restaurant. A favorite dining place for actors and lovers of the theater in "In the Park." FDTM 170, CSS 251

Wilson, Mrs. Long. Mother of one of Eugene Gant's schoolmates. CSS 558

Willetts, George. The head of a rich family from the North who chose to settle in Libya Hill and build a fine home. Wolfe drew upon George Vanderbilt in creating this character. HB 288, WR 3

Williams, Earle. The sneering, villainous, vindictive husband of Clara Kimball Young. HD 100

Williams, Harvey. A South Carolina native who shared a New York apartment with George Webber. WR 224

Willis, Sam. A Libya Hill constable sent to investigate the trouble started by Dick Prosser; Prosser shoots him. WR 147, CSS 342

Willis, Mr. A philosophy student at Pulpit Hill. LHA 593

Willis, Theodore. A reporter in Altamont and fellow worker of Ben Gant. HB 49, HD 49, CSS 523

Withers, Dr. A permanent resident at the Hotel Leopold. OT 433

Woman's Voice, The. One of the young lovers on the rocky coast of Maine recalling the past and looking to the future. HD 131

Wood. A modernist playwright in Professor Hatcher's course. OT 115

Wright, Jimmy. The publisher partner of Rawng and Wright, the firm (actually Liveright) rejecting George Webber's *Home to Our Mountains*. WR 488

Wright, Miller. A friend of Eliza Gant who suffers reale state losses in "The Web of Earth." FDTM 300

Wyman, James. A banker whose early morning ritual in his Central Park mansion reveals his desire to assert himself and his willingness to forgive the peccadillos of an acquaintance who strays from the straight and narrow. He is a disguised version of Charles Scribner. HB 162, CSS 499
Reference: See my article entitled "Wolfe's 'The Lion at Morning' and 'Old Man Rivers' " in TWR (Fall 1977).

Young, Clara Kimball. A wealthy, beautiful woman whose love for her friend Roonsworth Scoggins arouses the spite of her vindictive husband. HD 99

Young Man. A newspaper reporter covering the Altamont race riot. WTOC 126

Yvonne. A hotel maid in Orleans. OT 811

Zebulon County. A county in the mountains of Old Catawba where the Pentlands and the Joyners settled and reared their families before some of them moved to neighboring towns and counties. Yancey County, located in the Blue Ridge Mountains of North Carolina, was the seat of Wolfe's maternal ancestors. HB 124, WR 5, CSS 381

Genealogical Charts

Gant Genealogy*

Gilbert Gaunt

W. O. Gant   =   Eliza Pentland

(1851-1922)   (1860-

[William Oliver Wolfe]   [Julia Elizabeth Westall]

Unnamed girl	Daisy	Steve	Helen	Benjamin	Grover	Luke	Eugene
(1885-1886)	(1887)	(1888)	(1890)	(1892-1918)	(1892-1904)	(1894)	(1904)
[Leslie]	[Effie]	[Frank]	[Mabel]	[Benjamin Harrison]	[Grover Cleveland]	[Fred]	[Thomas]

*The names of the Wolfe family are bracketed and the birthyear is the correct one for the Wolfe children. The year of death for the deceased members of the Gant family is also the correct one for the Wolfe family. In the fictional family, Steve is older than Daisy.

I am indebted to Richard Walser for help with the genealogical charts.

Pentland Genealogy

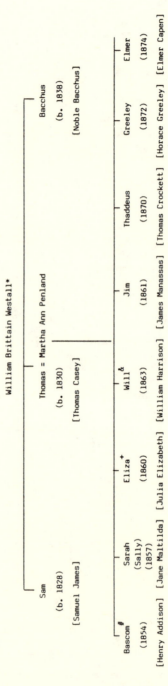

Unnamed Scotch-English mining engineer

William Brittain Westall*

Thomas = Martha Ann Penland
(b. 1830)
[Thomas Casey]

Sam
(b. 1828)
[Samuel James]

Bacchus
(b. 1838)
[Noble Bacchus]

Bascom#
(1854)
[Henry Addison]

Sarah
(Sally)
(1857)
[Jane Maltilda]

Eliza+
(1860)
[Julia Elizabeth]

Will&
(1863)
[William Harrison]

Jim
(1861)
[James Manassas]

Thaddeus
(1870)
[Thomas Crockett]

Greeley
(1872)
[Horace Greeley]

Elmer
(1874)
[Elmer Capen]

*Not all of the family is used.

#Also appears as Uncle Emerson in LHA and Bascom Hawke in "A Portrait of Bascom Hawke."

+Also appears as Delia Hawke.

&Named for a brother named William, who died three months before the second William's birth.

176

Hawke Genealogy

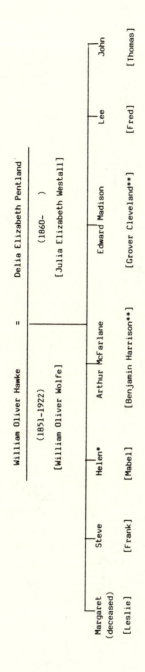

William Oliver Hawke   =   Delia Elizabeth Pentland
(1851-1922)   (1860-   )
[William Oliver Wolfe]   [Julia Elizabeth Westall]

Margaret (deceased)	Steve	Helen*	Arthur McFarlane	Edward Madison	Lee	John
[Leslie]	[Frank]	[Mabel]	[Benjamin Harrison**]	[Grover Cleveland**]	[Fred]	[Thomas]

*The Hawke family seems to have only one living daughter.

**Possibly the correspondence here is exactly opposite of the pairing suggested. Too little information is available to make incontestible pairings.

Joyner Genealogy

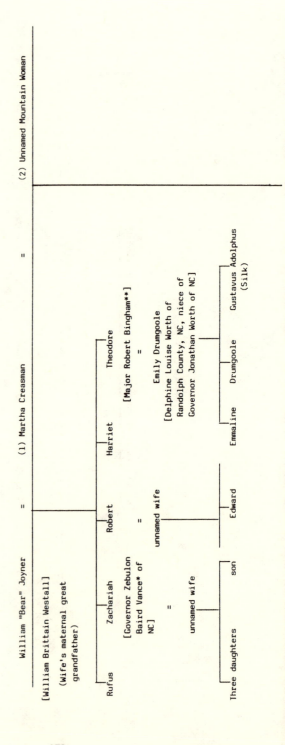

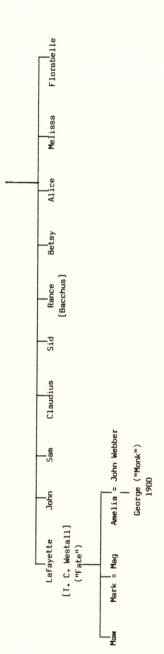

Lafayette   John   Sam   Claudius   Sid   Rance   Betsy   Alice   Melissa   Florabelle
[T. C. Westall]   [Bacchus]
("Fate")

Maw   Mark = Mag   Amelia = John Webber

George ("Monk")
1900

*Wolfe drew upon families other than his own in creating the Joyner lineage. Zachariah derives many of his traits from one of North Carolina's most celebrated governors, Zebulon Baird Vance, a mountain man who held office during the Civil War.

**Head of Bingham School, a military academy in Asheville, NC, who offered Wolfe a teaching position.

Webber Genealogy

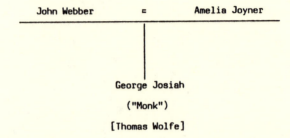

John Webber   =   Amelia Joyner

George Josiah

("Monk")

[Thomas Wolfe]

APPENDIX A

Information Sources

COLLECTIONS OF WOLFE MATERIALS

THE WILLIAM B. WISDOM COLLECTION
Houghton Library, Harvard University, Cambridge, MA

This is the central collection in more than fifty separate gifts of Wolfe materials to Harvard's Houghton Library. With few exceptions, it contains all of Wolfe's creative work from hurried notes on backs of envelopes or on margins of restaurant place-mats to page proofs of his published works. Included also are his famous ledgers, letters by and to Wolfe, his personal library, copies of contracts, termpapers, tests, course notebooks, and textbooks used at New York University during his time as a teacher. It contains material cut from Wolfe's novels and a great deal of other unpublished writing. The collection reportedly takes about 165 linear feet of shelf space.

The collection was catalogued by Patrick Miehe. The catalogue is available in the Houghton Library reading room.

Permission to use the collection must be obtained from the executor of Wolfe's literary estate, Paul Gitlin, whose address is 7 West 51st Street, New York, NY 10019.

THE THOMAS WOLFE COLLECTION
Wilson Library, Chapel Hill, NC

The second largest collection of Wolfeana includes only a few literary manuscripts but is rich in letters, especially those to and from members of his family and friends, photographs, scrapbooks, clippings, school compositions, and publications (newspapers, literary and humor magazines, and yearbooks) appearing during Wolfe's studies at the University of North Carolina, to many of which he contributed. Also in the collection are nearly 800 letters by Edward C. Aswell, most of them dealing with his role as the second executor of Wolfe's literary estate.

Copies of Wolfe's published works, including foreign editions, have been added to this catalogued collection, which is housed in Wilson Library as part of the North Carolina Collection. Persons wishing to use any of Wolfe's manuscripts or letters in the collection must have permission granted by the administrator of the estate of Thomas Wolfe, Paul Gitlin, 7 West 51st Street, New York, NY 10019.

The prime movers behind establishing this collection were Mabel Wolfe Wheaton and Fred Wolfe, who sought to honor their parents by arranging to place family-gathered Wolfeana in Chapel Hill.

THE BRADEN-HATCHETT THOMAS WOLFE COLLECTION
Memphis State University, Memphis, TN

Gathered by Professor William Hatchett and his wife, the poet Eve Braden, the Braden-Hatchett Collection includes letters by members of the Wolfe family, some of them on the subject of Wolfe's love affair with Aline Bernstein, photographs, clippings, articles, and other Wolfeana. This collection now ranks third in importance behind those of Harvard and the University of North Carolina. It has been catalogued, and copies of the catalogue are available. Copies of articles on Wolfe and his work are available upon request and, as of this time, are free of cost to scholars and critics.

The catalogue, compiled by the collectors, was published by Croissant Press, P.O. Box 282, Athens, OH 45701.

ST. MARY'S COLLEGE THOMAS WOLFE COLLECTION
Sarah Graham Kenan Library, 900 Hillsborough Street, Raleigh, NC

Friends and benefactors of St. Mary's College have donated personal Wolfe holdings or have pledged to give Wolfeana in coming years. The result is that a sizeable collection now exists. Of special interest in this collection are the George McCoy Papers, letters, articles, clippings, and memorabilia gathered by the Asheville journalist George McCoy; the Edgar E. (Jim) Wolf Papers, with materials about Wolfe's Pennsylvania roots; and the Richard Walser Papers, critical and biographical studies by a leading Wolfe scholar. The collection also has letters, pamphlets, photographs, audiovisual works, and secondary sources, many of them signed articles and books by Wolfe scholars.

The collection is housed in the Sarah Graham Kenan Library.

THE PACK MEMORIAL LIBRARY THOMAS WOLFE COLLECTION
Haywood Avenue, Asheville, NC

Legend has it that Wolfe's hometown library had no copies of his work, not because the city was too poor to buy his books but rather because Wolfe was in disgrace, owing to his treatment of Asheville and some of its citizens in LHA, until F. Scott Fitzgerald, upon learning that Wolfe's works were not in the city library, went out and bought copies to give to the Pack. Serious effort to build a collection of Wolfe materials began with the work of Myra Champion. Her collection of first editions, foreign translations, photographs of Wolfe and his family and of the Asheville of his era, adaptations of Wolfe's works, critical articles and reviews, and scholarly studies, is now one of Asheville's most cherished possessions. The collection also has clippings, some records of the founding of The Thomas Wolfe Memorial, and a few important letters.

THE SCRIBNER FILE
Firestone Library, Princeton University, Princeton, NJ

Letters by Maxwell Perkins and copies of contracts are among the several Wolfe-related items in the Scribner File. The chief use of the collection is by scholars interested in the publication history of Wolfe's works.

THE THOMAS WOLFE SOCIETY

Acting on the suggestion of Duane Schneider of Ohio University, interested scholars, librarians, collectors, and admirers of Wolfe joined together to form The Thomas Wolfe Society. The announcement of the founding of the organization was made in October, 1979, at St. Mary's College in Raleigh, NC, and the first slate of officers took office in Asheville, NC, in April, 1980, with Duane Schneider as the first president.

The purpose of the Society is to encourage scholarly study of, critical attention to, and general interest in the work and career of Thomas Wolfe, and to facilitate ways by which all who are interested in his writings—scholars, critics, teachers, students, and common readers—may learn from each other, meet together, and help one another in achieving a better understanding of his life and works.

The Society sponsors annual meetings, usually in mid-May, and has chosen to hold its conferences at places important in Wolfe's life and work: Asheville,

Chapel Hill, Cambridge, MA, and New York City. In honor of its place of birth, the Society held its fifth anniversary meeting at St. Mary's College.

Besides conducting yearly gatherings, the Society supports publication of writings by and about Wolfe (see the classified bibliography for a complete listing), administers the Zelda Gitlin Literary Prize (an annual award for the best article on Wolfe), and, from time to time, awards certificates of merit for excellent creative or scholarly work on Wolfe. The Society also placed a memorial plaque on one of Wolfe's Brooklyn dwellings. The Society maintains an archives, which is presently located in Richmond, Virginia. Information about the archives may be obtained from the Society president. Official correspondence, minutes, and personal letters by Wolfe collectors and scholars are among the items in the archives.

Any person, business, educational or corporate organization may join the Society. Dues for students are $5.00 a year; all other persons or institutions may join for $10.00. Applications for membership and dues should be sent to the treasurer of the Society. Members in good standing will have the right to attend meetings, participate in the Society's activities, run for office, and receive *The Thomas Wolfe Review*, the official organ of the Society. More than 500 persons now belong to the Society.

THE THOMAS WOLFE REVIEW

Launched in the spring of 1977 at The University of Akron under the editorship of John S. Phillipson and Aldo P. Magi as *The Thomas Wolfe Newsletter* (a designation it held until the spring of 1981 when "review" replaced "newsletter" in its title), the *Review* features critical essays on Wolfe's work, reminiscences by persons who knew him, articles on his family or persons important in his life, and pieces of interest to collectors and bibliographers. Its regular columns are: "Wolfe Trails," news and notes about Wolfe and Society members engaged in projects involving Wolfe; "The Wolfe Pack: Bibliography," an annotated listing of articles and books about Wolfe and his circle; and "Wolfe Calls," queries and answers.

As the official organ of The Thomas Wolfe Society, it carries reports of Society activities.

Subscriptions are $3.00 a year for the two issues. Checks should be made payable to The University of Akron, and mailed to *The Thomas Wolfe Review*, Department of English, The University of Akron, Akron, OH 44325.

The editors welcome news and articles about Wolfe. A length of 1,000 to 2,000 words is suggested for articles.

THE THOMAS WOLFE MEMORIAL

Through the efforts of Wolfe's family and friends in Asheville, the Dixieland of his fiction (his mother's boarding house, Old Kentucky Home at 48 Spruce Street in Asheville), became the Thomas Wolfe Memorial. Restored to the condition of an operating boarding house, the twenty-nine room structure contains items owned by Julia and W. O. Wolfe and members of their family, including

Tom, some of whose personal effects are on display there. Operated first as a civic project, the house has been a historical site of the State of North Carolina since 1976.

Conducted tours of the house are led by well-informed guides, and passages from LHA and OT have been extracted and posted to help visitors see the house as Wolfe described it. It is open all year, except holidays and Mondays. Operating hours are from 10:00 A.M. to 5 P.M. Tuesday through Saturday, and from 1 P.M. to 5 P.M. on Sunday. Admission is $1.00 for adults, 50 cents for children. Special programs are held from time to time, and there is an annual celebration of Wolfe's birthday.

A sales office stocks works by and about Wolfe, and a modest collection of Wolfe's works and family memorabilia is on display there.

RIVERSIDE CEMETERY, ASHEVILLE, NC

Thomas Wolfe's grave is in Riverside Cemetery in the Wolfe family plot. Signs in the cemetery direct visitors to the plot. O. Henry (William Sidney Porter) was buried in the same cemetery. Gates close at sundown.

THE THOMAS WOLFE MEMORIAL ANGEL

In tribute to Wolfe and his work, civic leaders and organizations in Asheville, led by the local chapter of the United Daughters of the Confederacy, erected a bronze copy of the marble angel, now in Hendersonville, NC, Municipal Cemetery, believed to have served as the model of the angel described in LHA. The work of sculptor Daniel Millspaugh, the bronze angel stands in Pack Square near the Zebulon Vance Memorial Monument and in front of the Old Pack Memorial Library. The statue was dedicated October 3, 1983.

APPENDIX B

Reference List: An Annotated Bibliography of Secondary Works

This annotated reference list can be used separately or with the analytic bibliography of Wolfe's work and the glossary, in which items listed here are cited by number.

1. Albrecht, W. P. "The Titles of *Look Homeward, Angel: A Story of the Buried Life*." *Modern Language Quarterly* 11, no. 1 (March 1950): 50–57. Surveys the working titles of LHA and explores the sources and meanings of each.
2. Aswell, Edward C. "A Note on Thomas Wolfe." In *The Hills Beyond*. New York: Harper Brothers, Inc., 1941. Argues that Wolfe's life gave form to his novels and comments on the state of Wolfe's manuscripts at the time of his death. Suggests that Wolfe's four novels are really just one big book.
3. Aswell, Edward C. "Thomas Wolfe Did Not Kill Maxwell Perkins." *The Saturday Review of Literature* (6 October 1951): 16+. Responds to charges by novelist Strothers Burt that Wolfe's break with Perkins and Scribner's hastened Perkins' demise.
4. Barber, Philip W. "Tom Wolfe Writes a Play." *Harper's Magazine* (May 1958): 71–76. Traces Wolfe's behavior when *Niggertown* (later called *Welcome to Our City*) was produced at Harvard.
5. Beja, Morris. "Why You Can't Go Home Again: Thomas Wolfe and 'The Escape of Time and Memory'." *Modern Fiction Studies* 11, no. 3 (Autumn 1965): 297–314. Like Joyce, Wolfe attempted to capture and fix the past. His dependence on time and memory led him away from selectivity and left him with too heavy a burden to transmute into truly illuminating fiction, except in retrospective epiphanies.
6. Berg, A. Scott. *Max Perkins: Editor of Genius*. New York: Thomas Congdon

Books/Dutton, 1978. Explores Wolfe's personal and professional relationship with Perkins, who considered his efforts to see OT to and through the press as one of his greatest achievements. Closely examines the friendship of Perkins and Wolfe and finds Wolfe assuming the role of a cherished but troubling son.

7. Bishop, John Peale. "The Sorrows of Thomas." *Kenyon Review* 1 (Winter 1939): 7–17. A lack of discipline and art hurt Wolfe's chance for greatness. His inability to win and hold love brought frustration and unhappiness.

8. Capek, Abe. "The Development of Thomas Wolfe in the Light of His Letters." *Zeitschrift fur Anglistik und Amerikanistik* 10 (Fourth Quarter 1962): 162–78. Wolfe's letters provide the best available means of tracing his concerns, hopes, plans, and frustrations as an American artist.

9. Church, Margaret. "Dark Time." *PMLA* 64 (September 1949): 249–62. Examines Wolfe's thoughts on time as viewed in three ways: time past, time present, and time immutable. Compares Wolfe's concepts on time with those of Bergson and Proust.

10. Collins, Thomas Lyle. "Thomas Wolfe." *Sewanee Review* 50 (October 1941): 487–504. Better than Dos Passos and Sandburg, Wolfe caught the essence of America, though he fell short of writing The Great American Novel. His aspirations were high but his artistic prowess was weak.

11. DeVoto, Bernard. "Genius Is Not Enough." *The Saturday Review of Literature* (25 April 1936): 3+. Charges Wolfe with artistic ineptitude while acknowledging his genius. Unable himself to give form to his work, Wolfe leaned too heavily on his editor, Maxwell Perkins. The result was fiction by production line.

12. Domnarski, William. "Thomas Wolfe's Success as Short Novelist: Structure and Theme in *A Portrait of Bascom Hawke*." *Southern Literary Journal* 13 no. 1 (Fall 1980): 32–41. Enlarging on C. Hugh Holman's thesis that Wolfe's forte was the *novella*, Domnarski shows how this prize-winning story reflects Wolfe at his artistic best.

13. Donald, David Herbert. *Look Homeward: A Life of Thomas Wolfe*. Boston: Little, Brown & Co., 1987. Written by a Pulitzer Prize winner in American studies, this biography will doubtless become the standard life of Wolfe. Unlike biographies of some of Wolfe's contemporaries, Donald's book stays within a readable length while offering fresh information.

14. Evans, Elizabeth. *Thomas Wolfe*. New York: Frederick Ungar Publishing Co., 1984. An introduction to Wolfe focussing on his fiction and giving informed attention to matters of style, narrative techniques, and imagery. Contains concise summaries of the novels and important short stories. Has a good bibliography.

15. Field, Leslie A. "Thomas Wolfe and the Kicking Season Again." *South Atlantic Quarterly* 69, no. 3 (Summer 1970): 364–72. In recounting critical responses to Wolfe and his work, Field offers one of the best surveys of Wolfe's thematic concerns and literary skills.

16. Field, Leslie A. *Thomas Wolfe: Three Decades of Criticism*. New York: New York University Press, 1968. Collects major pieces of Wolfe criticism, including essays by Holman, Rubin, Church, DeVoto, Warren, Perkins, Watkins, Reeves, and McElderry.

17. Foster, Ruel E. "Thomas Wolfe's Mountain Gloom and Glory." *American Literature* 44 (January 1973): 638–47. A survey of Wolfe's opinions about his native mountain region and its people, and the fictional use he made of those emotions, conditions, and characters. Wolfe's early desire to escape from the mountains gave way to his eagerness to use his mountain heritage for the Webber cycle.

18. Gatlin, Jesse C., Jr. "Thomas Wolfe: The Question of Value." *Thomas Wolfe Newsletter* 4, no. 1 (Spring 1980): 6–14. Turning from the aestheticism of his youthful days, Wolfe found cause to exalt the principles he found essential to a strong democracy: human dignity, equal rights, opportunity, dignity, and freedom. He vigorously opposed all greed and self-interest.

19. Geismar, Maxwell. *Writers in Crisis: The American Novel Between Two Wars.* Boston: Houghton Mifflin, 1942. From the first novel to his last, Wolfe grew as a man and artist, gaining objectivity as he developed, but his provincialism and defects of personality kept him from becoming a truly great writer.

20. Gray, Richard. "Signs of Kinship: Thomas Wolfe and His Appalachian Background." *Appalachian Journal* 1, no. 4 (Spring 1974): 309–19. Weighs Wolfe's ambivalent feelings about his southern Appalachia heritage; pays special attention to the Joyner material in HB.

21. Green, Charmian. "Wolfe, O'Neill, and the Mask of Illusion." *Papers on Language and Literature* 14, no. 1 (Winter 1978): 87–90. Suggests that Wolfe's expressionistic elements in MH and LHA are indebted to O'Neill.

22. Gurko, Leo. *Thomas Wolfe: Beyond the Romantic Ego.* New York: Crowell, 1975. Points out that Wolfe and his fiction make a big target, one unfriendly critics delight in hitting. Fewer darts would be thrown if readers returned to his work or came to him without prejudice. Wolfe is multifaceted as a man and artist but is seriously flawed, too. As he grew beyond his Romantic tendencies, his satiric talents became more evident.

23. Hagan, John. " 'The Whole Passionate Enigma of Life': Thomas Wolfe on Nature and the Youthful Quest." *The Thomas Wolfe Review* 7, no. 1 (Spring 1983): 32–42. Probes Wolfe's fiction and its relation to the ideas drawn from Romantic writers and the beliefs and techniques of naturalistic novelists. In Wolfe, pessimistic Naturalism often contends with optimistic Romanticism.

24. Hagan, John. "Structure, Theme, and Metaphor in Thomas Wolfe's *Look Homeward, Angel. American Literature* 53, no. 2 (May 1981): 266–85. A close, sensible, and sensitive reading of the only novel that Wolfe fully controlled. Shows that Wolfe's artistic abilities were considerable.

25. Hagan, John. "Thomas Wolfe's *Of Time and the River*: The Quest for Transcendence." In *Thomas Wolfe: A Harvard Perspective*, edited by Richard S. Kennedy. Athens, OH: Croissant and Company, 1983. Eugene Gant's quest for transcendence takes four overlapping routes: (1) a Faustian hunger for experience; (2) a search for knowledge; (3) a quest for security; (4) the pursuit of art or attainment of the role of the writer as artist.

26. Halberstadt, John. "The Making of Thomas Wolfe's Posthumous Novels." *Yale Review* 70, no. 1 (October 1980): 79–94. Charges Edward Aswell with unwarranted changes and additions to the Webber cycle, after exploring

how Aswell pieced together materials Wolfe left at his untimely death. See Richard S. Kennedy's rebuttal in *Harvard Magazine* (September-October 1981): 48–53, 62.

27. Holman, C. Hugh. "The Dwarf on Wolfe's Shoulders." *Southern Review* 13, no. 2 (April 1977): 240–49. Argues that as an inexperienced writer Wolfe leaned too heavily upon Perkins, who dropped the traditional role of editor and thrust himself in as a creative force, thereby instigating personal and professional problems for Wolfe.

28. Holman, C. Hugh. *The Loneliness at the Core: Studies in Thomas Wolfe*. Baton Rouge: Louisiana State University Press, 1975. Contains seven previously published essays, some of which helped to establish Wolfe's claim to a significant place among American writers. Comments insightfully on Wolfe's autobiographical methods, short novels, aspiration to write an American epic, feelings toward the South, and the rhetorical tradition within which Wolfe worked; an essential book by a major Wolfe critic.

29. Holman, C. Hugh. *Thomas Wolfe*. Minneapolis: University of Minnesota Press, 1960. The best brief introduction to Wolfe's achievements and failures as an artist.

30. Holman, C. Hugh. "Thomas Wolfe and America." *Southern Literary Journal* 10, no. 1 (Fall 1977): 56–74. Explains that Wolfe, like Whitman, worked to capture America, its landscapes, machines, dreams, and people. His medium was a blend of poetic prose and realistic description, and graphic characterization.

31. Holman, C. Hugh. "Thomas Wolfe and the Stigma of Autobiography." *Virginia Quarterly Review* 40, no. 4 (Autumn 1964): 614–25. Points out that Wolfe, like many authors, including Joyce and Hemingway, drew upon his own life for the substance of his fiction but ran into problems because, unlike more careful craftsmen, he failed to keep the reader's eye off the storyteller and on the story.

32. Holman, C. Hugh. *The World of Thomas Wolfe*. New York: Charles Scribner's Sons, 1962. A collection of essays and reviews arranged to give readers the basic materials for assessing Wolfe's place in American letters.

33. Idol, John L., Jr. "Angels and Demons: The Satire of *Look Homeward, Angel*," *Studies in Contemporary Satire* 1, nos. 1 and 2 (1976) : 39-46. Argues that the satiric element of LHA finds focus in Wolfe's attempt to reveal the foibles of Altamont's citizens, and to show the callousness of characters hindering Eugene Gant's development as a potential artist.

34. Idol, John L., Jr. "The Plays of Thomas Wolfe and Their Links with His Novels." *Mississippi Quarterly* 22, no. 2 (Spring 1969): 95–112. Shows that from his early attempts at drama through his decision to stop writing for the stage Wolfe was developing skills and discovering themes that would serve him well when he turned to fiction.

35. Idol, John L., Jr. "Responses of Contemporary Novelists to *Look Homeward, Angel*." *Thomas Wolfe Newsletter* 3, no. 2 (Fall 1979): 2–8. Contains extracts of letters from fifteen contemporary novelists on their opinion of LHA on the occasion of the fiftieth anniversary of its publication.

36. Idol, John L., Jr. "Thomas Wolfe and Jonathan Swift." *South Carolina Review* 8, no. 1 (November 1975): 43–54. Shows that Wolfe regarded Swift

as the greatest of satirists and looked to him whenever he dreamed of writing satire himself; suggests some possible sources of influence.

37. Johnson, Edgar. *A Treasury of Satire*. New York: Simon and Schuster, 1945. Contains one of the best estimates of Wolfe's satiric talents.

38. Johnson, Pamela Hansford. *Hungry Gulliver: An English Critical Appraisal of Thomas Wolfe*. New York: Scribner and Sons, 1948. Surveys Wolfe's work and claims that his output constitutes one great whole, and is more notable for its style and poetry than for its philosophy. Wolfe's major work depicts an energetic, passion-filled, and young American artist.

39. Kennedy, Richard S. "Thomas Wolfe and the American Experience." *Modern Fiction Studies* 11, no. 3 (Autumn 1965): 219–33. Explains that Wolfe used pocket notebooks to record his responses to men, books, and events in American life. Much of what Wolfe saw was through jaundiced eyes, but he consciously dedicated himself to the role of the chronicler of the American experience, to the role of an American epic writer.

40. Kennedy, Richard S. *The Window of Memory: The Literary Career of Thomas Wolfe*. Chapel Hill: University of North Carolina Press, 1962. Weighs each stage of Wolfe's development and follows the progress of each major work; offers critical analysis along with the biographical details; shows how Aswell functioned as an editor; contains an appendix showing the outline of Wolfe's Webber cycle. A major pillar in Wolfe studies.

41. Kennedy, Richard S. "Wolfe's *Look Homeward, Angel* as a Novel of Development." *South Atlantic Quarterly* 63 (Spring 1964): 218–26. Suggests that reading LHA as a *Bildungsroman* helps the reader understand and appreciate the character of Eugene Gant, who struggles to gain insight into life's mysteries and patterns as he moves toward maturity in Altamont and beyond.

42. Kazin, Alfred. *On Native Grounds*. New York: Harcourt, Brace, Inc., 1942. Explains that rhetorical excesses and undisciplined ways damaged Wolfe's standing; concedes that Wolfe nonetheless effectively treated many of the problems of growing up in America as well as the problems of a growing America.

43. Klein, Carole. *Aline*. New York: Harper & Row, 1979. A biography of Aline Bernstein containing the fullest treatment of Wolfe's love for and separation from his mistress; offers many views of Wolfe by Bernstein's friends and professional acquaintances.

44. Kussy, Bella. "The Vitalist Trend in Thomas Wolfe." *Sewanee Review* 50 (July-September 1942): 306–24. Asserts that Wolfe considered life an all-pervasive force and sought to celebrate it; suggests that Wolfe was sustained by a personalized form of vitalism and thus had little use for formal religion; points out that he rejected the doctrine of vitalism as practiced by Hitler.

45. Ledig-Rowohlt, H. M. "Thomas Wolfe in Berlin." *American Scholar* 22, no. 2 (Spring 1953): 185–201. Provides an account of Wolfe's visits to Berlin in 1935 and 1936, and traces his growing concern about Hitlerism.

46. McElderry, Bruce R., Jr. *Thomas Wolfe*. New York: Twayne Publishers. Twayne's United States Authors Series, 1964. A concise, informed, and judicious account of Wolfe's life, art, and critical reception. Finds Wolfe's

work in drama and his humor worthy of attention. A good book for beginning students.

47. MacLachlan, John M. "Folk Concepts in the Novels of Thomas Wolfe." *Southern Folklore Quarterly* 9, no. 4 (December 1945): 175–86. Shows that Wolfe made wide and ample use of his southern Appalachia heritage, but saw beyond his native hills to other parts of the nation and to Europe.

48. Miehe, Patrick, "The Outline of Thomas Wolfe's Last Book." *Harvard Library Bulletin* 21, no. 4 (October 1973): 400–401. Claims that Edward Aswell, not Wolfe, did the outline for WR and bases argument on typefaces. See Richard S Kennedy's response in the April 1973 issue of *Harvard Library Bulletin*.

49. Miller, Nolan. "Joyce and Wolfe." *Antioch Review* 16, no. 4 (December 1956): 511–17. Examines Wolfe's acknowledged indebtedness to Joyce by exploring what Wolfe found useful in Joyce's theory and practice of fiction. The study is not thoroughgoing, and should be redone by someone deeply versed in both authors.

50. Millichap, Joseph R. "Narrative Structure and Symbolic Imagery in *Look Homeward, Angel.*" *Southern Humanities Review* 7 (Summer 1973): 295–303. Stresses that as an apprenticeship novel LHA's structure is fitting and allows for a variety of thematic concerns. The recurring images of a stone, a leaf, and a door give the a novel a pattern and unity appropriate to Eugene Gant's self-discovery.

51. Muller, Herbert J. *Thomas Wolfe.* Norfolk, CT: New Directions, 1947. This is the earliest full-length appreciation of Wolfe, and is still one of the best. Muller sees Wolfe as a mythmaker, a writer in the Whitman-Melville tradition intent upon doing an American epic.

52. Natanson, Maurice. "The Privileged Moment: A Study of the Rhetoric of Thomas Wolfe." *Quarterly Journal of Speech* 43 (April 1957): 143–50. Turning from the deprecatory label pinned on Wolfe, a man given to excesses of southern rhetoric, Natanson attempts to account for the power, verve, and poetry of Wolfe's poetic prose. See also Floyd Watkins, "Rhetoric in Southern Writing: Wolfe." *Georgia Review* 12 (Spring 1958): 79–82.

53. Norwood, Hayden. *The Marble Man's Wife: Thomas Wolfe's Mother.* New York: Scribner and Sons, 1947. A "conversational biography" (Julia Wolfe talking) that sheds light on Wolfe, his family, and Asheville, and proves how much Wolfe's genius had left to do to turn a rambling storyteller into one of the greatest characters in American fiction.

54. Nowell, Elizabeth. *Thomas Wolfe: A Biography.* New York: Doubleday, 1960. The earliest major biography of Wolfe, stronger on his career in New York (where the biographer served as his literary agent) than on his childhood, college years, and foreign travels.

55. Owen, Guy. " 'An Angel on the Porch' and *Look Homeward, Angel.*" *Thomas Wolfe Newsletter* 4, no. 2 (Fall 1980): 21–24. Shows how Wolfe changed material written for LHA to fashion a self-contained short story for *Scribner's Magazine*.

56. Payne, Ladell. *Thomas Wolfe.* Austin, TX: Steck-Vaughn. Southern Writers Series, 1969. A helpful booklet treating Wolfe's themes, style and literary

pluses and minuses in a concise manner; gives a quick overview of Wolfe's failures and triumphs.

57. Perkins, Maxwell. "Scribner's and Thomas Wolfe." *Carolina Magazine* 68, no. 1 (October 1938): 15–17. Offers an assessment of Wolfe's personality and says that Wolfe wanted to reveal America to itself. Given space and time, Wolfe would have done so and, in the process, would have squashed the notion that his writing was largely formless.

58. Perkins, Maxwell. "Thomas Wolfe." *Harvard Library Bulletin* 1, no. 3 (Autumn 1947): 269–77. Sets forth Perkins' role in helping Wolfe shape LHA and OT; explains that not much of Wolfe's work was shunted aside, since what came out of one book might find a place in a later one; argues that Wolfe was wrong to abandon Eugene Gant; sees Wolfe as a symbolic American.

59. Pollock, Thomas C., and Oscar Gargill, eds. *Thomas Wolfe at Washington Square.* New York: New York University Press, 1954. Gives an account (not always free of resentment stemming from Wolfe's satiric use of his teaching career at the Washington Square campus) of Wolfe's years at New York University; draws upon students, colleagues, and others who knew him during his stay there.

60. Pusey, William W. III. "The German Vogue of Thomas Wolfe." *Germanic Review* 23, no. 2 (April 1948): 131–48. Germany's eager, warm reception of Wolfe's work was based not only on congenial themes but also on the excellent translations of Wolfe's stories and novels by Hans Scheibelhuth.

61. Reaver, J. Russell, and Robert I. Strozier. "Thomas Wolfe and Death." *Georgia Review* 16, no. 3. (Fall 1962): 330–50. Examines Wolfe's fictional treatment of death, with an especially close look at his handling of his brother Ben's death as transferred to the pages of LHA.

62. Reeves, Paschal. "The Humor of Thomas Wolfe." *Southern Folklore Quarterly* 24, no. 2 (June 1961): 109–20. Wolfe owes something to British and Irish humorists but much more to southwestern American humorists, especially in HB.

63. Reeves, Paschal. *Thomas Wolfe: The Critical Reception.* New York: D. Lewis, 1974. Reprints most of the important newspaper and magazine reviews of Wolfe's work; has good introductory matter.

64. Reeves, Paschal, ed. *Thomas Wolfe and the Glass of Time.* Athens, GA: University of Georgia Press, 1971. Contains papers and transcripts of discussions stemming from a graduate symposium on Wolfe, with essays and remarks by Richard S. Kennedy, C. Hugh Holman, Richard Walser, Ladell Payne, Fred Wolfe, and others.

65. Reeves, Paschal. *Thomas Wolfe's Albatross: Race and Nationality in America.* Athens, GA: University of Georgia Press, 1968. Standing between Wolfe and his goal of expressing the national consciousness was his racial prejudice. Time and experience taught him to accept a variety of ethnic types, but he never fully overcame the burden of his mountain-bred biases.

66. Rubin, Larry. "Thomas Wolfe: Halting the Flow of Time." *Americana-Austriaca* 4 (Spring 1978): 105–18. Discusses Wolfe's concept of time and explores the themes and images Wolfe used to present his notions concerning permanence and change.

67. Rubin, Louis D., Jr. "Thomas Wolfe and the Place He Came From." *Virginia Quarterly Review* 52, no. 2 (Spring 1976): 183–202. A thoughtful reconsideration of some of the points raised in his earlier book on Wolfe's relation to the South. See the following item.

68. Rubin, Louis D., Jr. *Thomas Wolfe: The Weather of His Youth*. Baton Rouge: Louisiana State University Press 1955. Examines Wolfe's four novels, identifying major themes and exploring the forces in Wolfe's early life that shaped the thought and art in his work; a vital critical appraisal of Wolfe's place as a southern writer, its weakest point being too little attention to Wolfe's southern Appalachia heritage.

69. Ryssel, Fritz Heinrich. *Thomas Wolfe*. New York: Frederick Ungar, 1972. A general introduction to Wolfe and an assessment of his work, with a good account of some of the ideas motivating his fiction.

70. Skipp, Francis E. "The Editing of *Look Homeward, Angel*." *Papers of the Bibliographical Society of America* 57 (First Quarter 1963): 1–13. Compares the typescript of the novel with the published version and shows cuts, additions, and corrections; finds only one significant transition and concludes that the novel emerged in the form in which Wolfe submitted it.

71. Skipp, Francis E. "*Of Time and the River*: The Final Editing." *Publications of the Bibliographical Society of America* 64, no. 3 (Third Quarter 1970): 313–22. Discusses cuts made by Perkins, especially passages of lyrical prose. Deletions were often the type that Wolfe should have made if he wanted the novel free of some of his usual faults: digressions, banalities, and disproportionate development.

72. Snyder, William U. *Thomas Wolfe: Ulysses and Narcissus*. Athens, OH: University of Ohio Press, 1971. A Psychological study drawing on Wolfe's fiction and letters in an effort to analyze his personal and creative life. The Freudian approach arrives at the unsurprising conclusion that Wolfe was narcissistic.

73. Stearns, Monroe M. "The Metaphysics of Thomas Wolfe." *College English* 6 (January 1945): 193–99. Traces Wolfe's ties to Romantic thought, especially to Coleridge. Wolfe was also indebted to Wordsworth, as shown in OT by a Wordsworthian theme and symbol.

74. Styron, William. "The Shade of Thomas Wolfe." *Harper's* (April 1968): 96 + . Reviews Andrew Turnbull's biography of Wolfe and weighs Wolfe's weaknesses and strengths. LHA, Wolfe's best work, validly depicts American provincial life in the early twentieth century.

75. Taylor, Walter F. "Thomas Wolfe and the Middle-Class Tradition." *South Atlantic Quarterly* 52 (October 1953): 543–54. Wolfe's values were largely fashioned by the attitudes and mode of life he experienced in an upper middle-class family in Asheville, a family choosing not to speak as truthfully of their wealth as their pocketbooks and bank accounts did.

76. Turnbull, Andrew. *Thomas Wolfe*. New York: Charles Scribner's Sons, 1965. A full-length biography of Wolfe, especially strong in its treatment of Wolfe's relationships with Maxwell Perkins and such fellow authors as Fitzgerald and Hemingway. Has a good collection of photographs and a dependable chronology.

77. Wade, John Donald. "Prodigal." *Southern* 1 (July 1935): 192–98. Forth-

rightly ticks off Wolfe's faults: verbosity, triteness, overblown rhetoric, and autobiographical approach, but sees a command of language and an appealing mysticism.

78. Walser, Richard. "The Angel and the Ghost." In *Thomas Wolfe and the Glass of Time*, edited by Paschal Reeves. Athens, GA: University of Georgia Press, 1971. Discusses Wolfe's ghost and angel in LHA as symbols of art and the creative inspiration of Eugene Gant as a developing artist.

79. Walser, Richard, ed. *The Enigma of Thomas Wolfe: Biographical and Critical Selections*. Cambridge: Harvard University Press, 1953. Contains a variety of critical views of Wolfe and his work, and publishes for the first time an episode by Wolfe on lawyers, entitled "Justice Is Blind."

80. Walser, Richard. "On Faulkner's Putting Wolfe First." *South Atlantic Quarterly* 78, no. 2 (Spring 1979): 172–81. Presents a thoroughgoing investigation of the much discussed remark of Faulkner about the relative place of Wolfe among the writers of his generation. Among the evidence given is a letter on the subject from Faulkner to the author. Faulkner ranked Wolfe highest because he tried hardest to do the most. The attempt was grand, but the achievement was not first rank.

81. Walser, Richard. "*Look Homeward, Angel*." In Paschal Reeves, comp., *Studies in Look Homeward, Angel*. Columbus, OH: Charles E. Merrill, 1970. A close reading of Wolfe's best work by one of Wolfe's best readers.

82. Walser, Richard. *Thomas Wolfe: An Introduction and Interpretation*. New York: Barnes & Noble, 1961. Offers a brief biographical sketch and informed, insightful, readable estimates of Wolfe's four novels.

83. Walser, Richard. *Thomas Wolfe: Undergraduate*. Durham, NC: Duke University Press, 1977. Covers Wolfe's years at the University of North Carolina and traces his rise from awkward, resentful freshman (Wolfe had wanted to attend the University of Virginia) to a confident, powerful senior. Examines the impact of such teachers as Frederick Koch, Edwin Greenlaw, and Horace Williams.

84. Walser, Richard. "The Transformation of Thomas Wolfe." In *The Thirties: Fiction, Poetry, Drama*, edited by Warren French. Deland, FL: Everett Edwards, 1967. Finds Wolfe moving from romanticism to realism, from autobiographical explorations of the self to issues concerning humanity at large.

85. Warren, Robert Penn. "A Note on the Hamlet of Thomas Wolfe." *American Review* 5 (May, 1935): 191–208. An extended review of OT faulting Wolfe for allowing his autobiographical impulses to control the form of the novel; recognizes Wolfe's knack for capturing and creating characters.

86. Watkins, Floyd C. "Thomas Wolfe and Asheville Again and Again and Again . . ." *Southern Literary Journal* 10, no. 1 (Fall 1977): 31–59. Looks at the Asheville Wolfe grew up in, the Asheville he used in LHA, and the Asheville that despised and then extolled his first novel.

87. Watkins, Floyd C. "Thomas Wolfe and the Southern Mountaineer." *South Atlantic Quarterly* 50, no. 1 (January 1952): 56–71. Although in revolt against much in southern Appalachian life, Wolfe cared deeply for mountain people and their traditions. His picture of southern mountain life is vividly realistic, but he did not present the mountaineer fully.

88. Watkins, Floyd C. *Thomas Wolfe Characters: Portraits from Life*. Norman: University of Oklahoma Press, 1957. Drawing upon newspaper and other sources in Asheville and surrounding areas, Watkins shows how Wolfe fictionally transmuted his hometown and many of its citizens.

89. Wheaton, Mabel Wolfe, and LeGette Blythe. *Thomas Wolfe and His Family*. Garden City, NY: Doubleday & Company, 1961. A lively, intimate narrative by Wolfe's younger sister (the Helen Gant of his fiction) of Wolfe's boyhood, the impact of LHA on Asheville, and the family's efforts to comfort him during his fatal illness. Based upon Mabel's written notes and recorded recollections.

Index

Harper and Brothers, 20, 59, 61, 62, 86, 186
Harvard University, 7, 29, 40, 54, 56, 64, 84, 86, 87, 92, 105, 181, 182, 186
Hatchett, William, 182
Hauser, Otto, 77
Hawke, Arthur McFarlane, 177
Hawke, Delia Elizabeth Pentland, 177
Hawke, Edward Madison, 177
Hawke, Helen, 177
Hawke, John, 50, 100, 136, 171, 177
Hawke, Lee, 177
Hawke, Margaret, 177
Hawke, William Oliver, 177
Hawthorne, Nathaniel, 35, 61
Hegelian thought, 7, 25, 26, 39, 65
Hemingway, Ernest, 12, 63, 67, 68, 71, 102, 189, 193
Hills Beyond, The, 2, 41, 42, 72, 81–82, 186, 188
"His Father's Earth," 3, 78
Hitler, Adolf, 18, 19, 30, 112, 190
Hogarth, William, 37, 71
Holding on for Heaven, 82–83
"Hollow Men, The," 4, 78
Holman, C. Hugh, 2, 4, 57, 65, 66, 68, 70, 73, 74, 86, 98, 99, 187, 189, 192
"Hollyhock Sewers, The," 4, 78
Hollywood, 16, 58
Hound of Darkness, The, 16–17, 82–85
"House at Malbourne, The," 84–85
"House of the Far and Lost, The," 3, 78, 98
Hudson River, 11, 89, 95

Idaho, 22
Idol, John L., Jr., 4, 83, 85, 89, 147, 148, 160, 174, 189–90
"I Have a Thing to Tell You," 3, 19, 49, 57, 78, 98
"In the Park," 2, 3, 78, 80

Jack, Esther, 10, 38, 43, 46, 49, 57, 71, 103–5, 110–11, 138–39, 172
James, Henry, 37, 67
James, William, 31
Jefferson, Thomas, 30

Johns Hopkins University Hospital, 23
Johnson, Edgar, 190
Johnson, Pamela Hansford, 34, 63, 190
Jones, James, 72
Jonson, Ben, 69, 87, 96, 114, 154, 171
Joyce, James, 28, 41, 43, 66, 69, 81, 87, 89, 94, 97, 112, 171, 186, 189
Joyner, Alice, 178
Joyner, Amelia, 178, 179
Joyner, Betsy, 178
Joyner, Claudius, 178
Joyner, Edward, 178
Joyner, Emmaline Drumgoole, 178
Joyner, Florabelle, 178
Joyner, Gustavus Adolphus, 178
Joyner, Harriet, 178
Joyner, John, 178
Joyner, Lafayette, 178
Joyner, Mag, 178
Joyner, Mark, 178
Joyner, Maw, 178
Joyner, Melissa, 178
Joyner, Rance, 178
Joyner, Robert, 178
Joyner, Rufus, 178
Joyner, Sam, 178
Joyner, Sid, 178
Joyner, Theodore, 178
Joyner, William "Bear," 178
Joyner, Zachariah, 178
"Justice Is Blind," 78, 194

"Katamoto," 3, 71, 78
Kaufman, George, 110
Kazin, Alfred, 73, 190
Keats, John, 27, 49, 87, 104
Kennedy, Richard S., 2, 4, 7, 34, 59, 60, 64, 72, 74, 76, 93, 100, 105, 106, 110, 146, 188, 189, 190, 191, 192
Kennedy, William F., 66
Kerouac, Jack, 72
Kesterson, David B., 148
"Kinsman of His Blood," 2, 78
Kittredge, G. L., 9
Klein, Carole, 190
K–19: Salvaged Pieces, 4, 11, 55, 56, 85

About the Author

JOHN L. IDOL, JR. is Professor of English at Clemson University in Clemson, South Carolina. He is the co-author (with Sterling Eisiminger) of *Why Can't They Write?* His articles have appeared in such publications as *The Mississippi Quarterly*, *The Southern Literary Journal*, and the *South Carolina Review*.